After the Demise of the Tradition

After the Demise of the Tradition

Rorty, Critical Theory, and the Fate of Philosophy

Kai Nielsen

Westview Press

BOULDER • SAN FRANCISCO • OXFORD

Copyright © 1991 by Westview Press, Inc.

Published in 1991 in the United States of America by Westview Press, Inc., 5500 Central Avenue, Boulder, Colorado 80301, and in the United Kingdom by Westview Press, 36 Lonsdale Road, Summertown, Oxford OX2 7EW

Library of Congress Cataloging-in-Publication Data
Nielsen, Kai, 1926–
  After the demise of the tradition : Rorty, critical theory, and
the fate of philosophy / by Kai Nielsen.
    p. cm.
  Includes index.
  ISBN 0-8133-8044-8
  1. Rorty, Richard. 2. Methodology. 3. Philosophy, Modern—20th
century. 4. Postmodernism. 5. Knowledge, Theory of. I. Title.
B945.R524N54 1991
191—dc20   90-23123
                                                                        CIP

Printed and bound in the United States of America

The paper used in this publication meets the requirements
of the American National Standard for Permanence of Paper
for Printed Library Materials Z39.48-1984.

10   9   8   7   6   5   4   3   2   1

191
N669a
1991

For Charlie,
who will snort.

Contents

Preface and Acknowledgements

This book emerged from a series of seminars given over the years at the University of Calgary and from papers and talks given at various universities in Europe and North America. I am indebted to more people than I can name who, by their queries and criticisms, helped me to make this book better than it would have otherwise been. In particular, I would like to thank my students in seminars and colleagues and friends from many universities whose probing of my views and, in some instances, alternative suggestions led me to revise my beliefs about philosophy and, indeed, to abandon not a few of those beliefs. This process of self-criticism and self-examination will go on as I think and think again about what philosophy has been, is, and might become. There is a cluster of perplexities that, in one form or another, has remained with me from my first rather chaotic contacts with philosophy.

I would like to thank the editors of *Philosophy*, *Inquiry*, *Grazer Philosophische Studien*, *Metaphilosophy*, *Philosophia*, *International Studies in Philosophy*, and *Free Inquiry* for allowing me to draw on previously published work. I would also like to thank Evan Simpson, editor of *Anti-Foundationalism and Practical Reasoning* (Edmonton: Academic Press, 1987), Douglas Odegaard, editor of *Ethics and Justification* (Edmonton: Academic Press, 1988), John Heil, editor of *Cause, Mind and Reality* (Dordrecht: Kluwer Academic Publishers, 1990), and their respective publishers for permission to reprint papers that were previously published in their volumes.

Last, but surely not least, I would like to thank Merlette Schnell for her rapid and accurate typing and retyping of various versions of the manuscript and for her meticulous and painstaking preparation of the final copy.

Kai Nielsen

About the Book and Author

This ambitious book addresses the "end-of-philosophy" debate and the challenge it presents to contemporary philosophy, both continental and analytic. It is a chain of argument as well as a conversation conducted in the presence of the major contributors to that debate: the critics (especially Richard Rorty) of the dominantly Platonic-Cartesian-Kantian tradition on the one hand and its defenders on the other. Nielsen's account draws on Wittgenstein, Quine, Davidson, Habermas, and Foucault, among others.

Nielsen takes Rorty's arguments seriously and insists that they demand a rethinking of the role of philosophy in a world in which the claims of relativism, nihilism, and historicism loom increasingly larger. But, unlike most who are impressed with the end-of-philosophy argument, he provides an original and constructive response: the development of a holistic, antifoundationalist account of philosophy that utilizes a form of critical theory and wide reflective equilibrium in carving out a positive role for a new kind of philosophy.

This is an important book not just for philosophers but for social theorists, for literary critics, and indeed for scholars in any field in which the status of knowledge has become problematic.

Kai Nielsen is professor of philosophy at the University of Calgary.

PART ONE

The Tradition

1

Subjecting the Tradition to Stress

I

Richard Rorty has had a not inconsiderable influence both within philosophy and in certain intellectual circles outside of philosophy. This influence is not without reason. His work—in a time of skepticism about philosophy—has been resolutely metaphilosophical and has deeply challenged the philosophical self-images of the reigning analytical tradition and the various species of "perennial philosophy." *Philosophy and the Mirror of Nature, The Consequences of Pragmatism,* and *Contingency, Irony, and Solidarity* are all attacks on systematic analytical philosophy in which epistemology and what is now called the "philosophy of logic" are taken to be the heart of philosophy.[1]

In *Philosophy and the Mirror of Nature,* Rorty sought to show that the core errors he finds in systematic analytical philosophy go back to what is common to the Cartesian, empiricist, and Kantian traditions—namely, a belief in the primacy of the epistemological, the belief that the philosopher is someone who knows "something about knowing which nobody else knows so well."[2] On such a model, what philosophy can and should do is ascertain how we can assess knowledge claims in any domain; determine, that is, what can count as knowledge and what cannot, or, alternatively, as in logical empiricism and movements growing out of it, set out a general

3

criterion of what makes sense. (It is an illusion to think that these two claims are very different.) Philosophy, on such a conception, is a cultural overseer that, in any domain, can adjudicate knowledge or intellectual claims and can at least generally ascertain what is rational and irrational to believe or do.

This is a pervasive philosophical self-image, and it is certainly understandable that philosophers should cherish it. That notwithstanding, Rorty claims that it rests on a series of mistaken beliefs and is presumptuous. Philosophers cannot provide such foundations. There is no coherent conceptualization of knowledge in which knowledge claims can be construed as correct representations of nature as if we at last found nature's own language. The philosophical illusion is that we can gain a firm foundational knowledge of what "the real" is, and, working from this, assess the soundness of various knowledge claims in art, science, morals, religion, and politics. The traditional conception of philosophy holds that philosophy can be a foundational arbiter of culture. Culture involves claims to knowledge very centrally, and philosophy adjudicates such claims. This has been the proud claim of philosophy, but, as Rorty would have it, the three great philosophical revolutionaries of the twentieth century—John Dewey, Ludwig Wittgenstein, and Martin Heidegger—have shown, in diverse ways and in very different idioms, such a claim to be without warrant. Philosophy cannot coherently go on in its traditional manner (including that of analytical philosophy). Is this a call for the demise not only of epistemology and metaphysics but of philosophy itself, or is it a call for its reconstruction and transformation?

We move too quickly and superficially, and indeed mistakenly, if we think Rorty is trying to deal a deathblow to philosophy. He is trying, rather, to transform philosophy, and the negative part of that transformation consists in trying to deal a deathblow to a self-image and a cluster of related practices that philosophers tend to have and indeed hold on to tenaciously. It is not surprising that first Wittgenstein and then Rorty upset philosophers so much. Rorty, in doing this, is attempting to extirpate certain associated conceits to which philosophers are prone. In doing this, he indeed seeks to undermine a certain conception of the philosophical enterprise, but it would be ethnocentric to think that this is tantamount to trying to undermine philosophy.

Rorty's own distinction between philosophy and Philosophy in his introduction to *The Consequences of Pragmatism* should make this evident enough. It is, he claims, only Philosophy that is problematic; philosophy, which is as old as the hills, is not problematic at all and will not wither away in an age of science or an age of analysis. It is not threatened either by modernity or postmodernity. When we speak of philosophy (as distinct from Philosophy), we are, in Wilfrid Sellars's well-known phrase, talking about "an attempt to see how things, in the broadest possible sense of the term, hang together, in the broadest possible sense of the term." Such a sense of philosophy is intimately linked with making sense of our lives, and although many philosophers—J. S. Mill, Spinoza, Plato, Bertrand Russell—have been philosophers in this sense, many people who are not in any technical sense Philosophers—Fyodor Dostoyevsky, Heinrich Heine, Thucydides, George Eliot—have also been philosophers. As Rorty puts it, Henry Adams is more of a philosopher than Gottlob Frege, and Christopher Lasch is more a philosopher than Saul Kripke. Where we take philosophy to be what Sellars is talking about—philosophy with a small *p*—it is plain enough that we get much more philosophy in Doris Lessing's *The Golden Notebook* than we do in R. M. Hare's *The Language of Morals*. Philosophy, as the steadfast attempt to see how things hang together, is not the property of professional philosophers and it is not at all evident that when they have turned to it they have typically done it better than other intellectuals—compare Doris Lessing and Robert Nozick. It is this enterprise—the attempt, in trying to make sense of our lives, to see how things hang together—that led many people innocently to philosophy in the first place. Rorty takes this enterprise (if that is the right word for it) to be utterly unproblematic. "No one," he remarks, "would be dubious about philosophy taken in this sense."[3]

On Rorty's account, then, philosophy is safe but Philosophy is not where the "word can also denote," as in Philosophy, "something more specialized, and very dubious indeed." He quite properly construes it as something that includes but is wider than the Descartes-Locke-Kant epistemologically based conception of Philosophy. Still, whether it be Platonic or Cartesian, Philosophy is something specialized and highly problematic. It not infrequently comes to "following Plato's and Kant's lead, asking questions about the nature of certain normative notions (e.g. 'truth', 'rationality', 'goodness') in the hope of better obeying such norms."[4] The idea is "to believe more truths or do more good or be more rational by knowing more about Truth or Goodness or Rationality."[5] These abstract accounts of the essence of Truth, Goodness, and Rationality, on such a specialized reading of "philosophy," form a set of "inter-locked Platonic notions," and these Platonic notions lead us, Rorty would have it, down the garden path.

Pragmatists, with whom Rorty identifies, believe that "the best hope for philosophy is not to practice Philosophy" and the best way of doing philosophy is to be anti-Philosophical in this Platonic-Kantian sense. This "Platonic-Kantian sense," it is important to note, Rorty construes very broadly. Pragmatists think, as Rorty puts it, that "it will not help to say something true to think about Truth, nor will it help to act well to think about Goodness, nor will it help to be rational to think about Rationality."[6]

There are number of pertinent questions to ask here, the most prominent of which is whether that pragmatist stance in favor of philosophy against Philosophy is sound; that is, whether the only alternatives are philosophy and Philosophy, construed on this essentially Platonic model. Is it really true that all such specialized endeavors in Philosophy are footnotes to Plato? Isn't there something more plausible that Philosophy can be without being simply philosophy? We should also ask—and I return to that in Chapter 6—whether even philosophy is as unproblematic as Rorty takes it to be.

Rorty is acutely aware of the issues about Philosophy and has a lot to say about them. What he wants to say—and we will consider this later—is that even a philosopher as distant from Plato as Hans Reichenbach suffers from the Platonic disease.[7] But there is also in Rorty's remarks (though seemingly unwittingly) a doctrine about the relation between *theory* and *practice* that is less than self-evident. If we do Philosophy, Rorty tells us, we are to ask questions about such normative notions as truth, rationality, and goodness in "the hope of better *obeying* such norms" (emphasis mine). If this were so, we would have good reason for caring about such concep-tual clarity. But that anything like this is so is, to put it minimally, quite problematic.

Suppose, however, someone says to Rorty, "We don't think about Goodness in order to be better, or attempt to get clear about

Rationality in order to achieve a more rational and humane social order or for that matter to be more rational ourselves. We are at least as skeptical as you about whether any such links between theory and practice can be forged, but we don't care about that; we are just curious about what can be understood about Goodness, Rationality, and Truth. That is our motivation, and our only motivation, for doing Philosophy." That would be a perfectly coherent thing to say *if* there really were anything to be understood here; but it would also be a remarkably superficial thing to say. Assuming for the nonce that conceptual analysis, if well done, can tell us something nontrivial about these concepts, what's the point of knowing about the concept of rationality or of having a clearer conceptualization of rationality if that will not in some way inform, directly or indirectly, our rational conduct? If it does not, then Philosophy surely becomes a little esoteric game of rather limited importance. And that is exactly what a lot of intellectuals who are not philosophers think of Philosophy; many, including some scientists and literary theorists, believe it to be by now a rather marginal discipline.

Whatever we want to say about the issues raised above, it is still evident, with Rorty's distinction between philosophy and Philosophy, and with his neopragmatist defense of philosophy, that he is not committed from his own premises, as Alasdair MacIntyre believes he is, to calling for the end of philosophy.[8] However, someone could agree that in this way Rorty has legitimately deflected MacIntyre's criticism, and she could reject as thoroughly as Rorty does such an essentially Platonic conception of Philosophy while still feeling ill at ease, and not unreasonably so. Rorty *is* arguing for the demise of something very fundamental and deep in our culture—something that will not be replaced by simply being committed to philosophy in his broad Sellarsian sense.

Some of this might be smoked out by attending to Rorty's remark that Philosophy as a specialized discipline, or as some attainable body of theory, does not "possess a secure matrix of heuristic concepts—categories which permit it to classify, comprehend, and criticize the rest of culture."[9] While positivism was still on the agenda, the attainment of something like this was still a hope, and Reichenbach's programmatic platform gave expression to that hope. But the developments of postpositivist analytic philosophy through Wittgenstein, Quine, Sellars, and Davidson have dashed that hope. If they are near to the mark, such a Philosophical Archimedean point—such an ahistorical Philosophical architectonic—is no longer a reasonable thing to hope for. It is a nonstarter as a research program. But if even in some fallibilistic sense, Philosophy (or for that matter philosophy) cannot hope to possess categories that permit it to classify, comprehend, and criticize society and the conditions of our lives, haven't we lost something very important? Haven't some of our central hopes been dashed? And wouldn't this be as true of Deweyan pragmatist hopes or Marxian hopes (to the extent they are philosophical) as Platonic and Cartesian ones? It is not, the argument goes, the quest for certainty or the nostalgia for the Absolute that is at issue, but the hope to somehow make sense of our lives and coherently take stock of what kind of world we live in, to have some kind of rational conception of how we might alter it to make it a more tolerable place.

I suspect that Rorty, like Jacques Derrida, would respond that someone with such impulses is still (though perhaps unwittingly) seeking metaphysical comfort where there is none to be had. Is it obvious that this is so? Are all people who ask such questions hungering, perhaps unconsciously, for the metaphysical? If so, isn't this the dark night of the soul? That is, if this were so, wouldn't philosophy, as well as Philosophy crumble and, if we were clear-headed, wouldn't we find some form of nihilism inescapable? I return to this question and a series of related questions from a number of angles throughout this book.

II

Part 1 shall be primarily devoted to an attack on what I call the Tradition. What I refer to here is a diverse set of philosophical conceptions and practices running from Plato and Aristotle, to the medieval and Renaissance philosophers, to the rationalist and empiricist traditions, Kant and the Hegelian reaction against Kant, logical empiricism, phenomenology and existentialism, through to systematic analytical philosophy. I try to give a rationale for setting aside those forms of philosophy that in various ways seek metaphysical comfort, whether it be forms of metaphysical realism,

Kantianism, absolute idealism, the metaphysical side of Peircean pragmatism, global conceptual relativism or foundationalist epistemology. I see Wittgenstein's *Tractatus* as being as metaphysical as the works of Aristotle, Scotus, or Leibniz.

Only with Dewey and the later Wittgenstein do we get a firm break with the metaphysical tradition. Even such holists as Sellars, Quine, and Davidson, philosophers who in effect (though hardly in intention) have shown us the way to set aside the Tradition, have a continued preoccupation with certain central problems of the Tradition, though in the tradition of rationalism or Kantianism and other conceptions of foundationalist epistemology we no longer have a philosophy conceived as an autonomous and in some sense foundational discipline. That just in itself, I argue, is a great leap forward. However, only with Wittgenstein and Rorty (much in Wittgenstein's debt) and the pragmatists—and then not thoroughly or always—do we get a firm break with the Tradition. Wittgenstein and Dewey make the cleanest break with the Tradition, but where they go from there is different indeed. Rorty, as I argue in Chapter 8, makes them seem more similar than they are by underplaying the Deweyan conception of philosophy as social critique.

I think in the demolition of the Tradition it is right to see Dewey and Wittgenstein as the decisive pathbreakers, though Quine and Davidson are also central figures here as were, though imperfectly and partially, the logical positivists.[10]

I operate out of that rejectionist tradition (though I am firmly formed by analytic philosophy) and, though less relevantly to the dismantling of the Tradition, from a Marxian and critical theory perspective: a kind of pragmatized analytical Marxian perspective, if you will. But in Part 1, where I am essentially concerned with the dismantling and setting aside of the Tradition, the influence of Dewey and Wittgenstein, most particularly of Wittgenstein, comes to the fore. In this, as the text makes evident, I am deeply and directly indebted to Rorty, who, as I read him, applies Wittgensteinian conceptions astutely and singlemindedly to the undermining of the Tradition. Without endorsing his "hermeneutical" positive turn (his learned and witty kibitzing), I elucidate and build on the core of his Wittgensteinian critique of Philosophy, though I argue in Chapter 6 that in an important sense it is not as through and through radical as Wittgenstein's own critique, though it has a far more adequate

historical sense: a narrative sense of where we have got in philosophy and where we can go from here. It also lacks Wittgenstein's
obsession with many of the philosophical problems that Wittgenstein
(and Rorty) would wish to set aside. Rorty really got out of the fly
bottle, not Wittgenstein. But Wittgenstein, though remaining
entrapped himself, showed us how to do it.

Rorty has come in for vigorous critique by some analytical
philosophers, perceptive defenders of the Tradition. In Chapters 2,
3, and 4, I am basically concerned to meet a variety of those
challenges from the most perceptive of his critics, namely Jonathan
Bennett, Jaegwon Kim, and Ian Hacking, as well as the more
sympathetic critique of another rebel from the analytic tradition,
Alasdair MacIntyre.

In Chapter 5 I set forth, and then critique, what I take to be
(for now, at least) the strongest defense of a modest foundationalism. (That account also contains a powerful defense of metaphysical realism.) Taken together, these two elements (given the
way they are argued) constitute a not inconsiderable defense of the
Tradition against Rortyan and Wittgensteinian deconstruction. I
refer here to the work of Alvin Goldman. It is impressively
conceived, systematic, thorough, and carefully argued.[11] In Chapter
5 I argue that in spite of these virtues and in spite of containing
many sound arguments that should just be incorporated into good
philosophy, it does not succeed in defending metaphysical realism or
even a modest foundationalism and has not given the Tradition a
new life.[12] In that chapter I also argue that Davidsonian holism and
arguments against the dichotomy between scheme and content
further aid in such a dismantling. Like Rorty, I would enlist
Davidson on the Tradition-battering side.[13]

Finally, in Chapter 6 I show the thoroughness of Wittgenstein's own critique of Philosophy and how, properly understood, it
even puts into question what Rorty and the pragmatists take to be
unproblematical, namely, philosophy. In spite of his own premodern
Kulturphilosophie in books such as *Culture and Value* (which I
critique in Chapter 6) and in his own obsessions with Philosophy,
Wittgenstein (particularly in *The Philosophical Investigations* and *On
Certainty*) shows us that a postphiiosophical culture is inescapable.
If we can be thoroughly tough-minded yet in a rather Nietzschean
spirit keep the urge to transvaluate values, that is the postphilo-

sophical culture in which we would be most at home. It is for such people the culture they would like to hurry along to ascendancy. Rorty assembles considerations that give us good reasons for believing that it is not only inescapable, barring some catastrophe like a sustained worldwide economic collapse (not just the collapse of capitalism) or a nuclear war, but that it is also nonthreatening. Where Wittgenstein remained ambivalent and alienated, Rorty is quite at home in this postphilosophical culture. We need not go around with a longing for certainty, a nostalgia for the Absolute or, what comes to much the same thing, a wish that God were in His heaven.

So Part 1 is essentially nay-saying whereas Part 2 is yea-saying, though I am also at pains to show that this yea-saying does not come to the dreary and frequent phenomenon noted by J. L. Austin of philosophers first saying it and then taking it all back.

With the Tradition firmly set aside, I argue for philosophy transforming itself into a form of critical theory. The fox in us should make us wary of potential hedgehoggish excesses and uncriticalness. Here we have what is in effect an Enlightenment project of modernity set against the cultural stances of post-modernity. But at least some postmodernist skepticism is not unreasonable, and the burden of proof is on me, I believe, to show that such a project is feasible and something of how it can be carried out.

Chapters 7 and 8 are devoted to that proof. There I articulate what I think a critical theory should look like and show how it grows out of something that is recognizably philosophical. In my transformed philosophy-as-critical-theory, I programmatically sketch and defend a holistic, uncompromisingly naturalistic theory, eschewing transcendental arguments and conceiving philosophy as continuous with the human sciences, literature, and literary studies. I do not treat philosophy as an autonomous discipline. Doing so was an error of late phases of the Tradition, e.g., Kantianism and logical positivism. But like Jürgen Habermas's account and unlike Rorty's piecemeal conversational account, critical theory is itself very much a part of the social sciences, for though its form is narrative, it seeks, while utilizing some standard bits of conceptual argument set in this narrative, to provide a descriptive-explanatory and interpretive account of our institutions, our social life, and our lives as social beings. But it is as well a normative account, and indeed one integrated into its descriptive-explanatory, interpretive structure. Moreover, like Deweyan pragmatists, critical theorists engage in normative critique (including a critique of ideology) and seek answers to what Dewey calls the problems of men, though in doing so they try to provide a more holistic account than do the pragmatists.

In Chapters 9, 10, and 11 I attempt to develop an underlying methodology for normative critique and for a critical moral theory that eschews foundationalism and becomes a proper part of a critical theory. I integrate that moral methodology—a distinctive development of methodological considerations central to the work of John Rawls and Norman Daniels—into the form of critical theory I adumbrate.[14] I also defend it against relativizing implications and critiques of it by Joseph Raz and David Copp that in reality turn back the clock to the traditional foundationalist concerns of moral philosophy. (If foundationalism will not work for epistemology there is little likelihood of its working in moral theory.)

I aspire to be a hedgehog (though I would like to have some foxlike qualities as well), but I certainly do not want to become a metaphysical animal. Free of metaphysics (and transcendental arguments or claims), I would like to articulate a coherent web of beliefs and make their acceptance plausible. In the domain of the human (including, of course, the social) I want to see how things hang together and to give an account of human life that makes it both plausible and attractive for things to hang together more adequately than they do now. It would be nice (if anything like this is at all feasible) to be able to see life as some kind of unity and not just as one damn thing after another. But surely there is room for postmodernist skepticism and irony here.

My account, however, is not so tightly woven that it is impossible to accept my critique of the Tradition (something congenial to postmodernism) and reject the very idea of a critical theory, or to accept that philosophy can, and indeed even should, be critical theory yet steadfastly remain a philosopher of the Tradition. I try to persuade you in the pages that follow to reject the Tradition *and* to adopt something like my program for a critical theory (or at least to take it seriously as a research program), but plainly the two theses (if that is what they should be called) are logically independent. They do not stand or fall together, though to me it seems plausible that they both stand. If, as I am confident will obtain for some, my setting aside of the Tradition—a very ambitious (perhaps even hubristic) project—does not persuade, do not, because of that, close out the possibility of there being a critical theory of society with the emancipatory potential I envision.[15] Whether or not you want, as I do, to call it critical theory matters very little. What matters is whether such a thing is a plausible activity perhaps capable of yielding a coherent cluster of beliefs and plans of action that are both important and warrantedly assertable.

2

Rorty and the Self-Image of Philosophy

I

In *Philosophy and the Mirror of Nature, The Consequences of Pragmatism*, and *Contingency, Irony, and Solidarity*, Richard Rorty has, as we have seen, forced us to reflect carefully on what we are doing or should be doing when we do philosophy and on the point of what we are doing.[1] Several decades ago, positivists made us wary of what metaphysics could come to, but Rorty cuts deeper by querying epistemologically based philosophy and even the ideals and the underlying rationale of conceptual analysis so dear to the heart of analytical philosophy.

This has understandably provoked reaction and resistance from philosophers. Rorty has cut to the bone with the questions he raises about the self-image and sense of vocation of philosophers. Some of the resistance has been irrational or at least knee-jerk which invariably happens when a well-entrenched way of doing or viewing things comes under powerful critical scrutiny or informed frontal attack. I shall not concern myself with that, but rather with some intelligent and reflective criticism—criticism so plausible and to the point that it should prod any fair-minded philosopher to think again about Rorty's "metacritique" of philosophy's central self-image. I refer to a defense of the Tradition emanating from Alasdair MacIntyre and Jonathan Bennett.[2] Their points are central, and, as

I have just remarked, extremely plausible.   Their plausibility notwithstanding, I argue that they do not deflect the underlying thrust of Rorty's critique of what has come to be the Tradition in philosophy and, apart from that tradition, philosophy's deepest self-image of its own vocation.

II

I begin with MacIntyre's response to Rorty's deconstruction of philosophy in *Philosophy and the Mirror of Nature*.[3] (It is echoed, with a slightly different twist, in Bernard Williams's later discussion of *The Consequences of Pragmatism*.)[4] Quentin Skinner has taken issue with it on Rorty's behalf.[5] And I discern in Rorty's "Philosophy in America Today" an implicit reply from Rorty himself.[6] In trying to show how MacIntyre's natural response does not undercut Rorty's "metacritique," I shall start with a little traditional sorting out.
MacIntyre begins as follows:

> Philosophers who do not wish relegation either to the salons of cultural conversation or to the lines of the unemployed will need to find an answer to Rorty, and I for one am anxious to stress how seriously we ought to take his challenge. Nonetheless, even my genuine admiration for one of the most interesting books in quite a number of years does not prevent my noticing one interesting feature of the cultural conversation of the West which Rorty invites us to rejoin. It is that if I am doomed to spending the rest of my life talking with literary critics and sociologists and historians and physicists, I am going to have to listen to a great deal of philosophy, much of it inept. And this will not only be because academic nonsense—structuralism and Althusserian fantasy and the wilder reaches of psychoanalysis—so often finds a home in some of these disciplines, but also because philosophical problems are not primarily generated from within academic philosophy at all. Indeed if, as Rorty does, we locate their origin and their nature so exclusively within philosophy, understood professionally and narrowly as it has for the most part been during the past two hundred and fifty years or so, we shall never understand the cultural power of these problems.[7]

We have here, on MacIntyre's part, but in a context in which it has a point, the familiar and seemingly modest *underlaborer* conception of philosophy. Philosophical problems emerge naturally and repeatedly out of the natural and social sciences, literature and art, and out of life itself. Whether we want to regard it as second-order commentary or not, it is plainly an attempt to reflect coherently on problems thrown up from these domains and not just from the self-contained reflections or controversies of philosophers.[8]

So far, MacIntyre's comments are on the mark. I think it is also fair enough, though slightly exaggerated on his part, to remark that much of the philosophy done in such contexts by scientists and literary critics will be inept. Indeed, it is often the case that metaphysical whoppers will come out of the natural sciences, the human sciences, and literary theory, *or at least from a certain treatment of those subjects*, in a way that will make an analytically trained philosopher want to scatter, unless he is rather aggressive or just likes clearing up conceptual confusions even if the theoretical import of such Augean stable cleaning is virtually nil. It is clear enough that bad conceptual analyses and confusions will not infrequently arise from these domains, though it may be that at least sometimes they principally arise when the engine in these domains is idling. When this is so, this talk about talk typically does not badly skew what substantively is at issue. A physicist can talk the worst sort of philosophical nonsense about physics and still do good physics. Be that as it may, MacIntyre sees the analytic philosopher coming in here modestly but usefully as an underlaborer to sort things out and to clear up conceptual confusions. Beyond that, MacIntyre also believes that in order to counter bad philosophy generated by the sciences and the arts, we need, Rorty to the contrary notwithstanding, "a synoptic and systematic discipline concerned with the overall problems of justification and representation."[9] This binds us to upholding some key elements of the Tradition, and doing this, in Rorty's view, takes us back into the swamp. This kind of perspective—or so Rorty claims—neither the philosopher nor anyone else can provide. Moreover, it is not needed. It is this challenge to the Tradition that we need to look at very seriously.

III

In this connection, it is worth taking into account Quentin Skinner's remarks about MacIntyre's critique of Rorty.[10] He says that MacIntyre's critique misses one of Rorty's most convincing claims: MacIntyre fails to recognize how Rorty's account shatters any confidence we might have in the powers of conceptual analysis to resolve or dissolve "conceptual confusions" emerging out of the sciences or everyday life.

To illustrate what he means, Skinner takes an example of conceptual analysis given by MacIntyre himself in one of his early books, *The Unconscious*. There he criticizes (in a way he would not today, judging from *After Virtue*) Freud's analysis of the unconscious by pointing out that it does not square with standard empiricist (roughly Hempelian) accounts of explanatory adequacy. Because of this insufficiency on Freud's part, which MacIntyre alleges makes his central concept of the unconscious dubious, we should recognize that Freud "cannot really be regarded as providing explanations at all, but ought instead to be classified among the imaginative describers of human behavior."[11] The philosophical underlaborer, with sharp conceptual analyses, has caught out—or so the usual view has it—the incoherence of a major theoretical conception in the human sciences. If it can be pulled off, this is worthwhile philosophical work. But MacIntyre's rigid commitment to his disciplinary matrix here prevents him, as well as his readers if they are similarly blinkered, from considering a possibility that obviously needs to be raised, namely, "that a new theory such as Freud's might force us to revise some of our most general beliefs—in this case, our beliefs about what constitutes a sound explanation."[12] Skinner goes on to remark:

> It is of course why MacIntyre is unable to countenance such a possibility. To do so he would have to give up one of the governing assumptions of his book (and indeed of his profession), the assumption that philosophers already know the answers to the basic "conceptual" questions (such as what counts as an explanation) and are thus in a position to criticize the exponents of the empirical sciences (such as Freud) for doing such a poor job. But, as Rorty points out, to insist that all the empirical disciplines must be made to fit a pre-existing conceptual grid is to incur a most ironic risk. While posing as the vigilant guardians of rationality, such philosophers expose themselves to the perpetual danger of elevating our local and fallible canons of argument into a set of imperishable truths. A more serious affront to rationality would be hard to imagine.[13]

I think it is misleading to say, as Skinner does, that (analytic) philosophers must believe that they "already know the answers to basic conceptual questions," though some of them surely act as if they do. But I think many do assume—and this is enough for

Skinner's point—that, in Rorty's words, they have not only their "well-known argumentative ability" but also "special, privileged knowledge about concepts" that gives them a privileged position in the assessment of culture.[14] Philosophers frequently suffer from the self-deception that they have a mastery of "conceptual questions" that others lack and that gives them a certain expertise in the articulation and critique of the forms of life. But that is an illusion. Philosophers have, as Rorty puts it, "no such higher standpoint." He remarks with his characteristic vividness, and even with a touch of passion:

> We have dismantled Reichenbach's heuristic scaffolding, and his list of "the problems of scientific philosophy" along with it. We have not substituted anything for it, and we should not try to do so. If there is one thing we have learned about concepts in recent decades it is that to have a concept is to be able to use a word, that to have a mastery of concepts is to be able to use a language, and that languages are created rather than discovered. We should renounce the idea that we have access to some superconcepts which are the concepts of no particular historical epoch, no particular profession, no particular portion of culture, but which somehow necessarily inhere in all subordinate concepts, and can be used to "analyze" the latter. We would thus give up the old dream, shared by Plato and Reichenbach, from which Wittgenstein woke us—the dream of philosophy as *scientia scientiarum*, as knowledge about the nature of scientific knowledge, as a result of successful inquiry into the nature of all possible inquiry.[15]

Rorty illustrates his point from the domain of "applied philosophy," where, as he puts it, "talk of 'conceptual issues' is unhappily common."[16] Suppose a physician is faced with the medical-moral dilemma of how to regard certain infants who are seriously disabled at or before birth. The dilemma is such that the physician worries about whether she should think of such severely damaged infants as persons or whether she should go on speaking about what is in their best interests. What is important to recognize in such a circumstance, Rorty claims, is that a philosopher with his "powerful analytic tools" is not going to be able to analyze and clarify these concepts for the physician in such a way that the physician will come to know what she meant all along or must have really meant in referring to them as persons or in speaking of their best interests. And she will not, armed with this knowledge, be able to resolve her original dilemma.

Rorty does not mean to deny that, by talking about the terms in question and in showing how other philosophers have used them, we may in some way add something useful to how the physician uses the terms and conceptualizes the situation. This may, but need not, be of some help to the doctor in coming to a decision about how to regard these newborns and even about what she should do. But the philosopher is not thereby doing anything other than what anyone operating out of the other humanities, or for that matter out of the human sciences, can do. The philosopher, by so proceeding, may enlarge "the physician's repertoire by giving her an enhanced sense of some new alternatives, new contexts, new languages."[17] But others can do that just as well. We must not be fooled here by nonphilosophers who use terms, often rather roughly and inexpertly, that originated with "one or another of the great dead philosophers."[18] We—that is we philosophers—who know the genealogy of those terms tend to assume that when nonphilosophers use them in such contexts, we know what is going on in a way those people do not. But that need not be true at all.

> If a physician is torn between respect of her patient and the need to minimize his pain, she is not confused on matters which the philosopher, able to discourse on the advantages and disadvantages of teleological and utilitarian ethics, is clear about. Being articulate is a virtue, but it is not the same as eliminating confusion, the attainment of clarity. One can become more articulate about one's alternatives by employing a web of words which are woven by a novelist, a literary historian, a social historian, or a theologian, as well. But in none of these cases, any more than in the case of a moral philosopher's web, is ability to say more a discovery of what one really meant all along, really presupposed all the time. One of the things Wittgenstein taught us, a lesson which helps us distance ourselves from Reichenbach, is that finding plausible premises from which an assertion can be inferred is not finding what the assertor "really had in mind." Another of the things he taught us was that learning to tell a story about what one is doing is not necessarily, or even usually, a discovery of one's original problem or motive or intention. Constructing an argument, in the scientific style, or a story, in the literary style, are both good things to do. But they are not discoveries of an antecedent reality which has been waiting to be unearthed by "analysis" or "reflection."[19]

Rorty's appropriation of Wittgenstein here is important. I think he is right to say that such an analysis will not tell us, when we are in such a live context as the physician's, what we really meant or what we must have meant—if anything clear was meant at all by such talk. However, and against this, the belief that we can do this is a deeply embedded assumption among a considerable number of philosophers. It is the belief of metaphysical realists and is central to much of the Tradition. Even those idealists who reject it take it seriously indeed. It should not be set aside lightly; moreover, I am not sure that this antirealist stance, *if* it should be so regarded, determines that any web of words, be it that of the novelist, theologian, criminologist, literary historian, or philosopher, is equally adequate to the task of helping the physician ascertain what is to be done. That is to say, I am not certain that all articulations and all achievements of articulateness are equally clarificatory or emancipatory. Be that as it may, it is important to recognize that we can nonetheless deny that any are canonical. It is a long way from recognizing that some ways of speaking and conceptualizing are better than others for certain rather standard purposes, to coming to believe that conceptual analysis has some special clarificatory and liberating role. But it was this traditional philosophical claim—that philosophers have such special expertise—that Rorty was questioning. MacIntyre just continues to assume that the philosopher, with his bag of analytical tricks, has some special expertise. The burden of proof is on MacIntyre.

IV

There is another turn in defense of the Tradition that we should examine. Philosophers, as Rorty readily acknowledges, do have considerable argumentative abilities that many of their colleagues, say, the average literature professor or historian, will lack. (I think this is more true of analytical philosophers than of other philosophers.) It could be argued that the expertise of the philosopher is in the sheer intelligence, the sheer problem-solving skill reflected in her argumentative ability. What this philosophical ability comes to is this:

> The able philosopher should be able to spot flaws in any argument he hears. Further, he should be able to do this on topics outside of those usually discussed in philosophy courses as well as on "specifically philosophical" issues. As a corollary, he should be able to construct as good an argument as *can* be constructed for *any* view, no matter how wrongheaded. The ideal of philosophical ability is to see the entire universe of possible assertions in all their inferential relationships to one another, and thus to be able to construct, or criticize, any argument.[20]

This is, of course, an idealization. Philosophers, particularly good analytical philosophers, have something approximating this to a considerable extent, and, as Rorty points out, it is a valuable asset in our culture.[21] There should be no knocking it. What unites philosophers, or at least what unites analytic philosophers with diverse techniques and interests, is neither a common set of problems nor a common genealogy but a common set of skills, skills—or so the self-image has it—that enable them to be the inspectors of finance of the academy.

With this stress on common skills goes a common style of writing and doing philosophy, namely, an argumentative style—a kind of "scientific style"—as distinct from the literary style characteristic of the humanist or the old-fashioned philosopher of the genteel tradition.[22] This argumentative "scientific style" asks that "premises be explicitly spelled out rather than guessed at, that terms be introduced by definition rather than by allusion," and the like.[23] Contemporary philosophy, with no well-defined subject matter or interuniversity paradigms of achievement, still has, at least among analytic philosophers, through its "scientific" argumentative style, a reasonably unified *stylistic* paradigm. (Even this is an exaggeration, for there is a world of difference between a Stanley Cavell and a Donald Davidson. Cavell, in his later work, neither has nor aspires to such an argumentative style.) But this is the *only* unity analytic philosophy has. It is the only nonpolitical, intellectual thing that unites Kuhn, Kripke, and Rawls.[24]

However, having an argumentative ability is hardly distinctive of philosophers. Lawyers typically have it, as do economists; some mathematicians have it, and so do some physicists. There is, with the fading of linguistic analysis, no specifically *philosophical* skill here, and the philosopher, we should remind ourselves, is not like the scientist in having some special domain of knowledge. He has neither a special skill nor something distinctive he can be skillful at. We have nothing definitive that could be called *philosophical* knowledge and we have no more definitive mastery of conceptual questions than do lawyers. At most, we are a little better at analyzing concepts because we think so intensely in determinate contexts about the uses of our language and have a penchant for drawing distinctions. Still, the ability that a philosopher has is, like that of a lawyer, the ability to "construct a good brief, or conduct a

devastating cross-examination, or find relevant precedents."[25] Rorty
puts it thus: "It is sufficient to be a good lawyer or a good analytic
philosopher that you be able to see at a glance the inferential
relationships between all the members of a bewilderingly large set of
propositions."[26] But having this ability, useful as it is, should not be
confused with having a set of firmly established concepts, perspicuously displayed, to classify, comprehend, and criticize the rest of
culture. This has been a traditional expectation of philosophy, a
grand hope of the Tradition, but that hope has been dashed.
Perhaps, to acquire such a set of critical categories or to be able to
understand their import, an argumentative ability is required, but it
is surely not sufficient. But such a set of critical categories does not
appear to be something that the philosopher or anyone else has.
We do not know what it would be like to have such a set of superconcepts.

Philosophers, Rorty claims, have no access to superconcepts
that enable them to perspicuously display "the ultimate nature of
reality" (whatever that means) or even just plain old reality, "plain,
unmasked, naked to our gaze."[27] The philosophical underlaborer has
nothing distinctive to contribute that would enable him to be an
overseer of culture or even an inspector of finance of culture.
All—or so Rorty claims—that his argumentative abilities will enable
him to do (that is, what is implicit in the stylistic unity of his work)
is what a sophist or a good lawyer is adept at doing, namely, to
"provide an argument for whatever our client has decided to do,
make the chosen cause appear the better."[28]

V

Jonathan Bennett, discussing Rorty's claims, makes an
important counter that deserves careful consideration. Bennett
remarks that beyond skill in argument and cleverness the vocation
of a philosopher is such that she or he has a "commitment to
thoroughness, consistency, and integrity—to following the argument
where it leads—to looking for the ways in which one's views on one
matter make trouble for one's views on another."[29] It isn't, of
course, only philosophers who have such a commitment. But others
do not emphasize it as much as philosophers do; it is not so central

to their vocation. It is part, Bennett claims, "of the reality of what is special to philosophy."[30] Max Weber, we should remember in this connection, spoke insightfully of the vocations of politics and science; he spoke, that is, of certain features internal in the very ideas (as different as they are) of what it is to be a scientist and of what it is to be a politician.[31] "Philosophy" does not seem to be a name for a natural kind—it does not seem to have an essence, and yet such a commitment to *intellectual thoroughness* is, in Weber's sense of "vocation," part of the vocation of philosophy, something the philosopher must strive for.

I think this is so and that it is important to acknowledge this in a way Rorty does not. (Perhaps Rorty just thought that was obvious?) It is not entirely clear, though, what this comes to beyond seeking (a) to see clearly the inferential relations of the various propositions one deems important to hold and (b) to order them in such a way that they will consistently and coherently hang together. This, assuming we can pull it off, is surely not nothing, and it is not at all to be scorned, nor does Rorty scorn it. But still, if this is all that Bennett's remarks come to, they do not give us what is so essential to the Tradition: namely, a set of concepts or categories that permit us to classify, comprehend, and criticize the rest of culture. The commitment to intellectual thoroughness and consistency is integral to or at least instrumental to such a search for an Archimedean point. But what this would come to beyond (a) and (b) above is unclear. We have some uncashed metaphors here, but that is all.

Without some such Archimedean point, there is little to Bennett's linking of philosophy to a love of wisdom by claiming that a man will be helped to be "wise" by his trying to make all the parts of this thoroughgoing inquiry fit together, trying, by this device, for unity and breadth, especially if "breadth is sought through depth."[32] But when all the rhetoric and metaphors are peered through, what does this actually come to beyond seeking a set of consistent propositions perspicuously arranged? We do not know what it would be like, Rorty argues, to have a set of critical concepts or categories that would in some nonarbitrary way serve to order and assess the reality of various practices, language games, and forms of life. It is right to want "intellectual wholeness," but with the pragmaticization of postpositivist analytical philosophy it is difficult

to understand what this could come to that would still be philosophically distinctive and keep philosophy as a kind of *Fach*. Bennett
rightly seeks to ascertain "the virtues of mind" that are associated
with contemporary analytical philosophy, but he no more than Rorty
thinks that philosophy can attain any "'higher standpoint' or mysterious special knowledge about 'concepts'."[33] But then it is unclear
what intellectual thoroughness can come to beyond a commitment
to attaining a consistent set of precisely stated beliefs that have
whatever empirical, moral, prudential, or aesthetic warrant that such
beliefs can be seen to have, where that warrant is what can be
established by the relevant procedures—empirical, moral, prudential,
aesthetic—that those people who have the proper understanding can
devise.   There is nothing distinctive that philosophy can give us
here. This is all that comes of talk about probing as deeply as we
can and seeing an issue through to its end. (Notice that we have
some rather well-used metaphors—metaphors that we have stopped
thinking about or have stopped referring to as metaphors. What
reading are we to give them if we want to be literal?)

I don't mean to mock this talk of probing deeply and seeing
things through to the end—it's for Derrida, not me, to be concerned
about sexual metaphors in philosophy. But I do mean to express
skepticism about what is of substance here, once Platonic-Cartesian-
Kantian-positivist beliefs about an Archimedean point are dropped.
What is it to probe deeply or see things through to the end? How
do we know when we have finally come to the end? To shift a bit:
it is not clear to me how, or even that, philosophy helps us to
understand ourselves. Bennett says it does, but how does it? I
know this is something we—or at least many of us—want if we are
at all reflective; indeed, we want it very much. We want to understand ourselves and make sense of our lives. That desire, if we are
not just people who like to solve puzzles, is very likely what drove
us to philosophy in the first place. Still, how is it that philosophy
helps us understand ourselves or make sense of our lives? It is part
of the proud self-image of philosophy to believe that philosophy, in
one way or another, has an important part to play here. Rorty, in
a way his critics have not even touched, makes us fundamentally
question that reassuring claim.

3

How to Be Skeptical About Philosophy

I

Alasdair MacIntyre and Richard Rorty agree (or at least seem to agree) on two fundamental matters, namely, to put it in Rorty's words, (1) "that philosophy as practiced professionally today lacks *any* systematic unity" and (2) that this very fact poses for us now, standing where we stand, "a central philosophical problem."[1] (I say "at least seem to agree" because MacIntyre puts the matter hypothetically, but I believe this is only a stylistic matter.)[2] It is also true that they both have a much more historicist view of philosophy than does traditional analytic philosophy; they regard (*pace* Quine and Reichenbach) the study of the history of philosophy as an integral element in the study of philosophy and think that philosophy is not to be sharply separated as a distinct discipline from other areas of learning. In this last belief they do not differ from Quine. And they both have worked themselves through the Tradition in analytical philosophy into a position of deep dissent within, or perhaps even from, that tradition. So the two are alike in what they are reacting against and in how they think we ought to proceed.

Yet MacIntyre also sees himself in fundamental disagreement with Rorty, though exactly what this comes to seems elusive. Indeed, I think many of MacIntyre's more perceptive remarks are actually complementary to Rorty's account rather than tending to undermine it. I also think—and I shall try to argue the point in this chapter—that MacIntyre's deconstruction of the Tradition appears to be more radical than it is, does not probe as deeply as does Rorty's, and often is too easily content with a sociological analysis when something more is required. MacIntyre is not critical enough about what can or cannot be done with conceptual analysis. He does not have Rorty's radical skepticism at all. But these remarks, left just like this, are dark sayings that need elucidation, explanation, and justification.

II

I shall do this indirectly by teasing out various elements of MacIntyre's critique of Rorty. MacIntyre rightly stresses what in reality is a Deweyan point, that philosophy flourishes when it is in active relationships with the other disciplines. In a remark that could well have been Rorty's, MacIntyre comments that the "destruction of any substantial version of the analytic-synthetic distinction also involves the destruction of the notion that there is some clear line of demarcation" between philosophy and something else—a line of demarcation that the philosopher must not cross if he wants to continue to do philosophy. A philosopher who works on issues raised by economics, politics, sociobiology, or social anthropology need not be doing philosophy *and* something else. Except in certain very specific contexts and for certain very specific purposes, there is no fruitful separating out of first-order and second-order considerations. By shifting to the formal mode from the material mode, one simply asks the same question again, though in a bombastic linguistic way. Nothing is gained by that linguistic turn or by semantic ascent. One only gets a pedantic redescription that makes the whole thing *sound* more scientific. We have scientism parading as scientific philosophy or exact philosophy. MacIntyre's point is that we should seek to break down such philosophical isolationism.

MacIntyre's claim that keeping philosophy and the "other" disciplines in such an integral relation is a good thing, and his further and related claim that, à la Kant and Thomas Reid, we should not take "philosophy" as a name for a distinct discipline, are claims that Rorty would heartily assent to.[3] What, then, is at issue between MacIntyre and Rorty?

III

Although MacIntyre does not make his fundamental arguments in "Philosophy and Its History" turn on what I shall now quote, he still remarks,

> At perhaps its most fundamental level I can state the disagreement between Rorty and myself in the following way. His dismissal of "objective" or "rational" standards emerges from the writing of genealogical history, as do all the most compelling of such dismissals—Nietzsche's for example. But at once the question arises of whether he has written a history that is in fact true; and to investigate that question, so I should want to argue, is to discover that the practice of writing true history requires implicit or explicit references to standards of objectivity and rationality of just the kind that the initial genealogical history was designed to discredit. Indeed when Rorty invites us to assent to the version of the history of philosophy which he has presented both in his book and in his paper he is surely not merely trying to elicit our agreement in the light of presently socially accepted standards of work, within philosophy and history. For he is—as philosophers characteristically are—himself engaged in advancing a philosophical theory about the nature of such standards. And this theory he presumably takes to be true, in the same sense as that in which realists understand that predicate.[4]

MacIntyre's claim in this passage is mistaken, indeed deeply mistaken, in several ways. First, Rorty's dismissal of a certain *reading* of what "objective" and "rational" standards come to, though it emerges out of a genealogical history, is also in certain key parts established to be true by standards for assessing the truth of assertions generally accepted in the discipline. (Remember that people can have agreed-on standards for assessing the truth of particular claims while not agreeing about the correct *analysis* of the meaning of "truth." They might agree about those standards for determining which statements are true without agreeing that truth is correspondence or even having any agreed-on theory or any theory at all about what "truth" or "true" means.) In this genealogical history with a philosophical point, it is important that there was one chap, Quine, and another chap, Sellars, both working out an essentially positivist background, and that one said the analytic/synthetic distinction wasn't what it was said to be and the other said that belief in the given was a myth. In addition, it is significant that their views were influential. But it is *vital* for Rorty's genealogical history (and Rorty recognizes this) that Quine's and Sellars's arguments are actually sound, or by minor modifications can be made sound, and that, for example, the Paul Grice and Peter Strawson counter to Quine does not carry the day. A genealogical history is essential to *place* all this and to see what its overall *import* is, but it is equally essential that the key claims of this history be warranted so that it is not a "just-so story," that its key claims be true or at least approximately true. Second, to raise questions about the truth of an historical account is one thing; to insist that talk of truth must be in terms of a correspondence theory of truth—the account of truth of the realist program—is something else. MacIntyre is assuming that anyone who believes that there are true and false propositions and that there is a distinction between history and pure legend must accept a certain very unclear and challengeable account of what "truth" means. We might, to play it safe, stick with Alfred Tarski or F. P. Ramsey. In writing a history, we employ standards of rationality and objectivity that, in part at least, are internal to the discipline. Rorty, in making his claims about Quine and Sellars, for example, does not take his standards of rationality and objectivity from out of the blue. Using arguments that Reichenbach would surely have recognized as being to the point, he shows how Quine's and Sellars's critiques of positivism reveal that Reichenbach's powerful "analytical techniques" are not such. And then, without changing the rules of the game at all, he draws out the consequences for philosophy of the pragmatization of positivism. In Wittgenstein's terminology, working with a language game, he shows that *some* of the conceptions of that language game, that the standards of rationality and objectivity utilized in that context, need correction. But that correction is not in terms of some alien language game. Even Wittgensteinian fideists have not denied that such critique from *within* was possible and sometimes desirable.

Rorty's genealogical account of the history of philosophy does not require, for its acceptance, "standards of objectivity and rationality of just the kind that the initial genealogical history was designed to discredit."[5] When Rorty argues his case as he does, there is no reason to believe—at least MacIntyre has given us no reason—that he must, in using the word "truth," be committed to giving, or assuming, a realist *analysis* of "truth" in the technical philosophical sense of "realist" intended. (Here his discussion of realism in his introduction to *The Consequences of Pragmatism* is important, as are his arguments, in various places, to the effect that pragmatists are not idealists in disguise.)

Starting with those accepted standards of rationality and objectivity presently operative in our intellectual life (including, of course, philosophy and history), Rorty tries to show that, employing them carefully and concretely in the light of his narrative, one would end up with a considerable deconstruction of the conception of philosophy accepted in systematic analytical philosophy and earlier in the Kantian and Cartesian traditions. He has not hoisted himself by his own petard.

IV

I turn now to some of MacIntyre's specific criticisms of Rorty. MacIntyre, as we have seen, is as concerned as Rorty to link up our philosophizing with a sense of our own history of the subject. He will not accept Quine's bifurcation into those who are interested in philosophy and those who are interested in something quite different, namely, the history of philosophy. But MacIntyre, like Ian Hacking, thinks Rorty has got his history wrong and that his mistakes about history distort his understanding of the present possibilities of philosophy.[6] Rorty's history, MacIntyre claims, starts too soon, is too internally fixed on the development of philosophy as a separate discipline, and mistakenly tries to explain the malaise of contemporary systematic analytical philosophy in terms of the "disintegration of the neopositivist program of the Vienna Circle and its allies."

Even if we accept MacIntyre's "correction" of Rorty's conception of philosophical genealogy, how would this touch Rorty's arguments about the present status of philosophy?[7] Rorty is asking: "Given that this is how philosophy has been, what, if anything, can philosophy now be?"[8] This does indeed link up philosophy with its history, but how would accepting MacIntyre's history, rather than Rorty's, alter or tend to undermine Rorty's claim that there is a disintegration of philosophy as a distinct discipline, with a distinct subject matter, methodology, and an underlying critical role vis-à-vis culture?   This is the heart of the matter and plainly the core of Rorty's metaphilosophical claims.   Perhaps we should say, if we accept MacIntyre's history that it is not *philosophy* that has ended its own history, but that the principal causal agent is the modern bureaucratization and professionalization of the world resulting from our present corporate capitalist and state socialist division of labor. This latter phenomenon and not the internal development of the discipline itself is the primary cause of philosophy's disintegration and delegitimization.   This—though MacIntyre might not like that way of putting it—is a fragment of a historical materialist explanation, but if this did give a partial or even a complete causal explanation of the disintegration of philosophy as a distinct discipline that serves as a cultural overseer, such a critique still would not cut deep enough.   Suppose we were in a future communist society where the state with its bureaucratic structures had withered away and a capitalist or capitalistlike division of labor with rigid bureaucratically controlled professionalism was a thing of the past.   Would not Rorty's questions about the future of philosophy still remain perfectly intact?   We would have, if such a thing really obtained, a truly human society.   But how would this enable us to discover how to make philosophy "whole again" or whether to reconstitute or reconstruct philosophy?   All of Rorty's questions would remain intact.   This suggests that looking to the *internal* history is, to understate it, also important in explaining the demise of philosophy as a distinct discipline.   We should further ask, given the culture of modernity and postmodernity, what rationale, if any, it could have.

MacIntyre might try to resist this by saying that we could reconstitute philosophy if (perhaps *per impossible*) culture were to become whole, or perhaps he would say "whole again."   It isn't, MacIntyre might very well argue, that intellectually speaking some of us do not know our way about in philosophy or have no sense of how to proceed in philosophy.   Rather, the professionalization, bifurcation, and bureaucratization of our lives makes the flourishing of philosophy impossible—cripples its institutional life.   As Wittgenstein was aware (and Rorty, too), we philosophers may know the subject well and sometimes even have the freedom and leisure to pursue the subject as we wish but still (sometimes at least) feel that we are at a dead end. Even when we are somehow captivated by philosophy, we can be deeply perplexed by, and indeed suspicious about, whether it has a rational point.[9]

MacIntyre's stress on the institutional impediments to philosophy, however, does not get to the heart of the matter. I will try to explain why, while elucidating and commenting on MacIntyre's own rationale for his claim.

MacIntyre, despite his radical-sounding rhetoric, sees philosophical questions in a traditional, analytical way as conceptual questions arising from the sciences and humanities and sometimes at the boundaries of these disciplines. MacIntyre thinks it is important to recognize that all the disciplines, including the hard sciences, have their philosophical, i.e., *conceptual* sides, and that we should not try to detach these philosophical inquiries from the actual scientific or humanistic work going on and the path of inquiry being followed in the discipline. Where such a separation is made, these conceptual inquiries, MacIntyre claims, will be without content and will be, even when the discipline of philosophy tries to unify them, "a set of fragments lacking any fundamental unity."[10]   What MacIntyre believes has happened with the "professional separation of philosophy from the other disciplines" is that people working in those other disciplines have failed to see "the extent to which their own inquiries necessarily involved philosophy."[11] MacIntyre stresses that "their inquiries are...in part, but in key and essential part, philosophical."[12] What needs to be done, MacIntyre maintains, is to bring to the philosophical side of those disciplines the strict and distinctive standards of argumentation and relevance developed by philosophy. (Here he plainly means developed by philosophy as a discipline.)

I do not think this gets to the heart of the matter because I do not believe that it faces Rorty's radical challenge (characterized in the previous chapter) that there is no distinctive mode of argumentatation that philosophers have that others (say, economists or lawyers) do not.[13] It does not face this nor his related challenge that philosophy brings no distinct methodology or methodological understanding to these disciplines that will give us some valuable purchase on certain central questions of those disciplines. Neither does it face the related hard question whether philosophers really do have special expertise with concepts or have any superconcepts that will enable them, in some expert way, to come to grips with the conceptual problems that arise in science. MacIntyre also does not, in spite of his acknowledgment of the points take to heart that if Quine is close to the mark, there is no sharp demarcation between conceptual and empirical questions, second-order and first-order questions.   There is nothing distinctive here—some conceptual something or other—that a philosopher qua philosopher, even when deeply acquainted with whatever other discipline is in question, can rush in and get his hands on to deftly perform conceptual analysis with his "powerful analytical tools." There are no such tools. Such talk is all useless metaphor.

MacIntyre differs from standard analytical philosophers, at lease those of a pre-Quinean vintage, in believing that philosophical inquiry must not be carried out in separation from the other disciplines.   He is also distinct from them (including Quine) in stressing the necessity that philosophers have a thorough understanding of the history of their subject, a reflective understanding of their relation to it, and the ability to read and interpret texts, particularly texts that are culturally at a distance from where they stand.   But he is like the traditional analytic philosopher in assuming that philosophical questions are conceptual questions and that philosophers have some special expertise such that they can command a clear or clearer view of the conceptual terrain—a view that is rather special and not open to others unless they themselves become philosophers.   MacIntyre does not face Rorty's complex challenge that this is a piece of philosophical mythology.   This challenge from Rorty would remain even if we were in a classless society free of bureaucratic control.   Even if MacIntyre's sociology is exactly right, he has not disposed of these questions.   And these questions pose a deep challenge for philosophy.

V

MacIntyre holds that in order to escape deformation "philosophy" would "have to become the name for the whole intellectual enterprise."[14] He rightly remarks, with a good sociological eye, that that is impossible.

The bureaucratic organization of academic work which the modern university requires and the type of division of labor which it entails are quite incompatible with any state of affairs in which "philosophy" is not treated as the name of one discipline among others. Professionalization with all its drawing of boundary lines and its invocation of sanctions against those who cross them, its conceptions of what is central to "the" discipline and what is marginal, is the inevitable accompaniment of bureaucratization. Hence there is at least a tension between the professionalization of philosophy and its flourishing, except of course as technique and idiom. For professionalization is always favourable to the flourishing of technique and to making narrowly technical proficiencies the badge of the fully licensed professional; and it is equally favorable to the development of idiosyncratic idiom, an idiom by which professionals recognize one another and for the lack of which they stigmatize outsiders.[15]

This is a sound and important sociological observation—one typically ignored by the philosophical profession, e.g., members of the Canadian Philosophical Association or American Philosophical Association, as well as by other professions, unless, perchance, their profession is to study professions. But I do not see why Rorty should do anything other than welcome it as complementing his own diagnosis.

But even if we could with some magic wand escape the memories of such a bureaucratically organized professional world, we would still face the problems that Rorty, through Wittgenstein, Heidegger, and Dewey, places before us. What does it *mean* to say that "philosophy" is the "name for the whole intellectual enterprise?" Presumably, it means, if anything at all, that intellectuals working in those disciplines should try to see things in a holistic way. They should, in Sellars's phrase, try to see how things hang together. But that is to use "philosophy" in the utterly untechnical and at least putatively unproblematic sense in which "a philosopher" is just another name for "an intellectual" or, if that is too broad, for "an intellectual who thinks rather holistically." So here "science" or "humanities and science" in their generic senses could just as well be substituted for "philosophy."

However, MacIntyre still seems to want—indeed he seems to assume and hanker after—some intellectually unproblematic logical space for philosophy in a more technical or formal sense. In that way he still wants it to be autonomous. According to him, we just don't have the sort of society that makes room for it. MacIntyre's sociologizing of the issue is important, but it does not face the deep problem posed by Rorty about what, if anything, philosophy can be now, given what we know and even if we could radically change our institutional arrangements.

VI

MacIntyre has *assumed* that philosophy has its own standards of argumentation and relevance. But he has not *shown* us how philosophy has, or can come to have, even in ideal conditions, its own standards of argumentation and relevance; standards that will enable us to criticize our culture, critique the institutions of our society, or be arbiters of legitimacy claims in society. Whether philosophy can in any coherent way have an overseer role is what is at issue.

Even with such a critical incapacity (if such is the case), philosophy may be an issue vis-à-vis other disciplines in still another way. MacIntyre criticizes the positivists—and he thinks that Rorty makes the same false assumptions as they do—for "supposing that there is indeed such a thing as science innocent of philosophical preconceptions."[16] MacIntyre asserts that demarcating astronomy from astrology (thus distinguishing good science from bad science) or settling the issues between energeticists and atomicists in late nineteenth-century physics requires that we take a position on the philosophical issue of realism.[17] But he offers no evidence or argument for these claims. And in view of what Rorty has said about such issues, the burden of proof rests with MacIntyre. Is it not by an appeal to a cluster of interdependent practices—observational, theoretical, and conceptual—*within those disciplines themselves* that we are able, if we are able at all, to resolve these issues? Isn't that what we in fact do, and isn't it the only thing that we can do? Both pragmatists and realists think that "there is a world out there"—what else could they think if they were not insane?—but they interpret differently how that should be conceptualized. Physicists or geologists and the like need not and should not bother about such arcane issues that may well be pseudo-issues. They have more important things to do.

MacIntyre thinks that what makes analytic philosophers *philosophers* is their historical continuity with certain problems; what makes them *analytic* philosophers is "their common preoccupation with meanings."[18] But how common is this "common preoccupation"? A. J. Ayer, Austin, C. I. Lewis, O. K. Bouwsma, Wittgenstein, Rudolph Carnap, Roderick Firth, Cavell, and Quine are all analytic philosophers, and they are all in some way preoccupied with meanings or the rejection of meanings but in such different ways that it is rather misleading to call it a common preoccupation. MacIntyre goes on to remark that what makes them all philosophers, as distinct from other folks concerned with meanings, is the way that this preoccupation with meanings is embedded in certain traditional philosophical concerns, namely, questions about "cause, personal identity, the nature of belief, what goodness is."[19] In contemporary analytical philosophical culture these perennial concerns frequently get talked about in the context of speech-acts, logical form, extensionality, and the like. But what gives those latter discussions philosophical life, and what gives discussions about meaning life, is their relation to the perennial questions of philosophy.

MacIntyre puzzles me here. For much of his essay he seems as historicist as Rorty, denying that there is a list of historical questions that demarcate what philosophy is. But in the above remark—which he repeats twice in his essay—he seems to be invoking a somewhat scaled-down version of the tradition of perennial philosophy. (Recall that he goes on to claim that contemporary French philosophy has those same underlying concerns.) It is in this antihistoricist claim that he conflicts with Rorty.

I think Rorty's response to MacIntyre would be the Wittgensteinian one that such talk has point only in determinate language games and against certain preoccupations. Thus we can wonder what belief comes to in the salvation religions or among the Azande when they practice witchcraft or among people when they say they believe or do not believe in the programs of various political parties. But we can hardly usefully talk about belief in this contextualist way ripped from some determinate language game. At best we will come up with a few dressed-up platitudes, at worst with more or less disguised falsehoods or incoherencies. Similar things should be said for the other topics MacIntyre mentions. Perhaps, if we bring to it enough background, we can say what good coffee is, what a good teacher is, what a good film is, what, in some determinate culture at some determinate time, good relationships between women and men are, and, at the outer limits, what, under conditions of productive plenty, a good society would look like or at least what a decent political order would look like. But it is a pointless and perhaps hopeless enterprise, shorn of any such determinate language game, to say what goodness is. (I have in mind something like Paul Ziff's saying, even if correctly, that to say "x is good" is to say "x answers to y's interests.") Moreover, in this context, MacIntyre seems completely oblivious to the pragmatist claim, championed by Rorty, that "it will not help to say something true to think about truth, nor will it help to act well to think about goodness, nor will it help to be rational to think about rationality."[20]

4

The Tradition in Retreat

In two important books, *Philosophy and the Mirror of Nature* and *The Consequences of Pragmatism*, Rorty has developed an iconoclastic metaphilosophy (philosophy of philosophy, if you will) that, as we have seen, has struck at the heart of the traditional self-image of philosophy, including "scientific analytical philosophy." Several distinguished analytical philosophers, among them Jaegwon Kim, Ian Hacking, and Alvin Goldman, have tried to defend the Tradition. I will turn a critical eye on that defense and, in doing so, show how far the Tradition is in retreat.

Kim, in his critique of Rorty, notes that "three central themes emerge as fundamental components" of the philosophical tradition Rorty rejects and sets out to transcend.[1] Kim thinks it is important that we isolate these three components and inspect them separately. The thing to look for, he believes, is whether they are equally vulnerable. Rorty may give us good grounds for rejecting one of them but not another, and one may be more fundamental to sustain in defending the Tradition than the others. The three components are: (1) the Platonic doctrine concerning *truth* and *knowledge*, (2) the Cartesian doctrine of mind, and (3) the Kantian concept of philosophy as foundational for the rest of culture.

Kim characterizes them as follows:

1.   The Platonic doctrine is a doctrine concerning *truth*
        and *knowledge*, according to which truth is *correspond-*
        ence with nature, and knowledge is a matter of
        possessing accurate representations. (589)

2.   The Cartesian doctrine is the doctrine of the mind as
        the *private inner* stage, "the Inner Mirror," in which
        cognitive action takes place. The Platonic doctrine
        of knowledge as representation was transformed into
        the idea of knowledge as *inner representation* of outer
        reality. The Cartesian contribution was to *mentalize*
        the Platonic doctrine. (589)

3.   The Kantian doctrine is a conception of philosophy
        according to which it is the business of philosophy to
        investigate the "foundations" of the sciences, the arts,
        culture, and morality and adjudicate the cognitive
        claims of these areas. Philosophy, as epistemology,
        must set *universal standards of rationality and*
        objectivity for all actual and possible claims to
        knowledge. (590)

Kim agrees, as does Hacking, that Rorty's attack is well directed
against both the Cartesian and the Kantian components.[2] Philosophers trying to defend or save something from the Tradition
would, Kim believes, do well to abandon these two components as
well as the "queen of the sciences" conception that goes with them
and to concentrate on (a) a defense of a more modest conception
of philosophy as the *handmaiden* of science and (b) a defense of
Platonic doctrine concerning truth and knowledge.

        Before I proceed with a characterization of Kim's theses, I
think three preliminary comments are in order. First, Kim's remarks
would be echoed by a large number of philosophers who are
defenders of the Tradition in its contemporary analytic forms.
Second, Kim's theses about the handmaiden conception should be
distinguished from his defense of Platonic realism. Someone could
be an antirealist or wish to diffuse the whole realism/antirealism
controversy and still accept the handmaiden conception; someone
could be a realist and reject the handmaiden conception. Finally, it
is crucial to see at the outset how sticking to Kim's handmaiden

conception would fetter philosophy—standard systematic analytical philosophy—and how it suggests, but does not quite entail, a *scientistic* image. It reins in philosophy in striking ways because it rules out not only the overseer of culture function but also rules out the philosophy of politics, social philosophy, aesthetics, philosophy of law, moral philosophy, and philosophy of religion. It would as well make impossible what MacIntyre takes to be so vital to philosophy, namely, its critical role where there are flashpoints at the borders of the various disciplines.[3] Much that the Tradition has coveted would also be lost to philosophy. Reichenbach and Carnap might welcome this, but most contemporary analytic philosophers would not. Many would think that, if really taken to heart, it would incredibly and unnecessarily cut down the scope of philosophy; more specifically, it would narrow the scope of systematic analytic philosophy. (A good bit of the curriculum in most philosophy departments would have to be junked.)

I also spoke of Kim's conception as probably being scientistic. The word "scientistic" is for me a term of abuse, though it is not *merely* a term of abuse, for it has a descriptive meaning as well as an illocutionary force. Typically, when philosophers use the term "scientistic" they use it much as Habermas does to mean the doctrine that says that what science—and most particularly the natural sciences—cannot tell us humankind cannot know. It is the belief that the sole mode for knowledge and understanding is science, nothing else has or can have any genuine cognitive status. Physicists and chemists and the like know something first-order, and philosophers of science, with their second-order talk about the talk of the natural sciences, know something very modest comparable to what grammarians know about how language works, but all the rest is emotive flim-flam. Logic is a discipline of its own akin to mathematics. Only as applied logic does it have a handmaiden function. There are the logicians (including analytical philosophers of science) and the lotus-eaters and nothing else in between. I doubt that Kim would, if pushed on this, really want to say anything quite so extreme. But the cluster of things mentioned above is what his essay, sometimes more tightly and sometimes less, commits him to. And this, whether rightly or wrongly, does severely limit the scope of systematic analytical philosophy.

Without going far from the spirit of Kim, one could extend his handmaiden conception and do so entirely in line with current orthodoxy in the Tradition. In so proceeding the image would go from a handmaiden of science, to a handmaiden of the law, of the humanities, and the like. Still, *pace* the Kantian overseer conception, such a notion of philosophy does not seek to change science or the law, or to criticize it or rationally appraise it. There is no place anymore for saying, "I know the legal system has characteristics *x, y,* and *z,* but that is an irrational or, in important ways, an inadequate legal system." At most the philosopher could point out that *x, y,* and *z* form an inconsistent triad. And this, to give the handmaiden conception its due, might only be apparent when we look closely at the legal system. Still, it could not tell us where to go from there. Do we drop *x, y,* or *z,* or which do we alter and how? What are we to do? What would a more reasonable or more humane legal system look like? There is no room for any of these questions, given the abandonment of the Kantian component of the Tradition with its cultural overseer conception, for with such an abandonment we can have no such independent standards of rationality or coherence to which we can appeal. The handmaiden conception, no matter how much it is broadened, will not give us that. Perhaps the Kantian conception Kim articulates, knowing what we know now, is unreasonable to expect. Yet it is also important to recognize that its loss is a considerable loss; a fundamental promise that the Tradition has held out will be seen to be a promise that cannot be kept.

When we give up the Cartesian "mental turn" we give up the *quest for certainty.* Most of us, touched by the fallibilistic tenor of modernity, do not have any trouble with the abandonment of the mental turn. We have long ago, at least consciously, put aside a nostalgia for the Absolute. How a rational person could expect anything other than a fallibilistic view of the world seems quite mystifying to us. Even some religious people—since Søren Kierkegaard and Karl Barth—have also learned to live with fallibilism, though where people continue to quest or thirst for certainty we should expect some irrational hang-up with religion somewhere in the background. But for most of us, the Cartesian mentalistic turn designed to give us certainty no longer grips us but only seems to be historically interesting or to generate some quaint puzzles.

However, as I have already suggested, the Kantian component cuts closer to the bone. It is a deeply engrained, flattering self-image of philosophers and it is understandable that many people—and not only philosophers—would want such an Archimedean point for assessing and criticizing culture. It is surely understandable that reflective and intelligent human beings would want some standards of rationality and adequacy to assess the condition of our social life and to make judgments about social evolution (if such there be). But Rorty's narrative places the very possibility of such a critical perspective under a cloud, and Kim and Hacking—and indeed most of Rorty's analytical critics—make no attempt to defend the Tradition at this key juncture. Where they do draw their defense lines, and where many other analytical philosophers would as well, is around what Kim calls the Platonic doctrine of *truth and knowledge*: where truth, crudely put, is correspondence with nature, and knowledge is a matter of possessing accurate representations.

II

We have now seen how much is given up by drawing the defense lines there. Still, something of importance remains. So let us see how Kim defends that part of the Tradition. He sees clearly that rejecting the Cartesian component—the mental turn—"is wholly consistent with continued allegiance to the Platonic doctrine of realism" (591). And it is also his conviction—one I do not share for reasons given above—"that rejection of Platonic realism is a much more radical departure than a rejection of...the Kantian conception of philosophy" (591). It is true, of course, that Platonic realism need not carry in its train *epistemological* foundationalism, privileged representations, or analyticity and necessity. But as the discussion in the previous section should have made clear that is not the point. Only a myopic view of philosophy could make it seem so.

Kim claims that what is at rock bottom in Rorty's critique of Platonic realism is Rorty's claim that the notion of correspondence in the correspondence theory of truth is hopelessly metaphysical and without content (592).[4] Kim believes, however, that Rorty, in his deconstruction of realism, is caught in a self-referential paradox.

Rorty, in a way reminiscent of Kierkegaard, wants to keep edifying philosophy from being a view itself about having views and thus being the kind of system—the very having of a view—that it decries. He does not want to get trapped into offering another system whose aim is to show the untenability of all systems.

Rorty's attempted way out of that paradox is to deny, as he does in *Philosophy and the Mirror of Nature*, that "when we say something we must necessarily be expressing a view about something."[5]   But for this to be possible, we must come to understand that speech is "not only...not externalizing inner representations...it is *not a representation at all*.   We have to drop the notion of correspondence for sentences as well as for thoughts, and see sentences as connected with other sentences rather than with the world."[6]

Kim takes this to be a reductio—a ridiculously high price to pay for "the possibility of edifying philosophy, or the impossibility of systematic philosophy" (596).   To make language, and with it edifying philosophy, free from all representation and to make his "keeping the conversation going" not itself one view among others, Rorty has to try to deprive language, Kim claims, of any *cognitive content*. No assertions can be made in that language and thus nothing can be denied in it.   And, it is also the case that no questions can be framed, wishes or hopes expressed, or exclamations conveyed.   All these speech-acts presuppose the *assertorial function*.   Without it, language, communication, conversation, and thought itself is not possible.   It is evident that the assertorial function is rock bottom. But Kim claims the assertorial function is not possible unless language has representational functions in some ways.   Without representational functions, and thus without an assertorial function, we would have no language at all. Rorty, however, takes the very idea of nuanced conversation to be at the heart of his hermeneutical or edifying way of doing philosophy and this, of course, requires language.   But a "language" incapable of making any representations at all is not and cannot be a language, for it would not have what is at the basis of all speech, namely an assertorial function (596). So Rorty's conception, Kim claims, self-destructs.

Kim goes on to add, rather redundantly, that if the assertorial function of language goes, it is not just all kinds of philosophical talk that goes, but all discourse:

> The rejection of Platonic realism has wider implications. It makes not only philosophical discourse but all discourses, including scientific discourse, nonassertoric and nonrepresentational. Language in general, not just philosophical language, becomes nonrepresentative. Truth and knowledge in science, too, are matters of social practice and approval, not representation. Science, too, must cease to be inquiry and become conversation. (597)

If Rorty's rejection of Platonic realism and his conception of language as nonrepresentational actually committed him to denying that science is inquiry or investigation, that any cognitive activity can be carried out by the use of language, and that language has any assertorial function at all, then I would readily agree that the account is both absurd and self-refuting. If that were so, it would indeed self-destruct. I am unconvinced that Rorty's views entail these absurdities.

I suppose the core of Kim's claim is that if you take, as Rorty does, speech as not being representational at all, then you must deny that it has any assertorial function and that we can make any assertions or denials. Rorty plainly doesn't want to accept such a conclusion, and he does not for a moment deny what is plainly true, namely, that we make assertions and denials all the time. Communication would be impossible if we could not do so, and it is plain that we sometimes do successfully communicate. Any philosophical account that tried to deny that would be absurd and itself self-refuting. Kim's claim is that this absurdity is what Rorty's account of speech as nonrepresentational in fact commits him to. Does it?

It does not. In the very passage Kim quotes, Rorty, immediately after saying that speech is not representational at all, goes on to gloss that remark as the denial that sentences correspond to some state of affairs free from linguistic encoding; rather, it is the case that sentences are linked with other sentences. (But sentences, of course, are in the world. Where else could they be?) What we do not and cannot do is to break out of the web of language and have some *brute state of affairs, some fact, that is nonlinguistically specifiable* for the sentence to correspond to. Rorty is making the familiar point—the point we have seen in Quine, Davidson, Nelson Goodman, Peter Winch, and Norwood Hanson (if not Kant)—"that scientists do not bring a naked eye to nature, that the propositions of science are not simple transcriptions of what is present to the senses."[7]

To the response that this claim is far weaker than the claim that speech is not representational at all, we need, if an adequate response can be made to that, a further reading of the claim that speech is not representational. Rorty, in saying that speech is not representational at all, is making the undeniable linguistic point that any specification of a referent is going to be in some vocabulary, and thus one can only be comparing two descriptions of a thing rather than a description with the thing itself. There is no possible comparison of the description of the thing with the thing itself, for any specification of the thing is going to be in some vocabulary. There are many descriptions that we can and sometimes do give of "the same state of affairs," but there is no privileged description that can "just give us the state of affairs as it is in itself." We cannot get, as Rorty puts it, to nature's own language.

When Rorty says that speech is not representational at all, I take him to be denying that a word-world relation can take place that relates the world to the word in any other way than that portrayed above. But this does not even suggest that we cannot make assertions. Language games are complex social practices with many different kinds of speech-acts. There are, quite uncontroversially, the speech-acts of asserting, exclaiming, questioning, proclaiming, expressing one's hopes and fears, and the like. There is no need to invoke Platonic realism to explain the assertorial function of language or to trot out some mysterious conception of representation about how words match up with the world. Words are not pictures or anything like pictures. When I assert, "It's getting dark," I surely think, in normal circumstances, that it is getting dark. But I either specify getting dark in terms of the linguistic expression "getting dark" or I specify it in some other English terms or the terms of some other language. Nature does not have its own language; we can never escape a set of conventions here. Language never functions so that something in it points as an arrow or points (if that is the right word here) as a picture to something there before us, unconceptualized, naked to our gaze. (Indeed, as Wittgenstein has shown, even "−" does not function in such a simple, unconventionalized way.) When I make an assertion, say, that it is getting dark, I get further word-world relations, all of which are embedded in social practices that in turn are linguistically encoded. And where else would these practices be but in the world? Nothing else is even intelligible. Still, there is no word-world relationship in my assertion (or present to my assertion) in which there is a getting dark that is just there requiring a certain lingustic representation determined by the state of affairs itself. Commonsense realism is one thing; Platonic realism or metaphysical realism is another. The latter doctrines, if not just pedantic ways of stating commonsense realism, are very contentious doctrines of unsure coherence. The denial of the former, if not unintelligible, is insane.

III

I turn now to another fundamental defense of the Tradition against Rorty's metaphilosophical moves. In reflecting on Kim's and Hacking's responses to Rorty, we must not lose sight of the depth of their agreement with Rorty on two basic issues. Both Kim and Hacking agree with Rorty that foundationalism is dead and that it is an impossible dream to try to carry out the Kantian project or, if you will, the research program of attaining a rational Archimedean point for assessing belief systems, i.e., whole domains such as science or ethics as well as social practices and institutions. No one, they agree with Rorty, can attain such an Archimedean point. They continue predictably, however, to dislike and reject hermeneutical conceptions of a philosopher's task and Rorty's conception of philosophy as dialogue and conversation. Philosophy, Hacking would have it, involves not initiation but apprenticeship, not conversation but investigation. It is a discipline that can give us knowledge and provide us with crucial clarification of knowledge claims in certain domains, and perhaps it can justify certain determinate beliefs. However, that this is not as straightforward as it may appear can be seen from Rorty's response.[8]

Rorty responds that such inquiries into conceptual foundations have not been helpful. It is a research program that has not panned out. At best it has been the owl of Minerva; usually it has been a block to creative thought. (This is a point also stressed by Paul Feyerabend.) In a verbal exchange during an APA symposium on his *Philosophy and the Mirror of Nature*, Rorty pressed Hacking and Kim to give an example where some philosophical inquiry into the conceptual foundations of *x* provided any furtherance of our understanding of *x* or anything else. Hacking didn't take up the challenge, but Kim gave as an example the work done in the conceptual foundations of mathematics by Frege and Georg Cantor. Even if we take this response at face value, it is interesting that the only example that was given was from mathematics and from work by mathematicians—something very conceptual from the start. But to get anything that would look like a convincing example we would need to break out of the charmed circle of purely conceptual investigations and get examples from philosophy, history, politics, the natural sciences, or the social sciences. No such example was proffered. I think that is revealing. Even if we stick with Kim's example, however, we have what in effect is John Rawls's worry about it.[9] We need to recognize that it is only after fundamental work in mathematics was actually carried out that we progressed in metamathematics. Again, we see the truth of the claim that the owl of Minerva flies only at dusk.

It has been said in response that Rorty's point about philosophical inquiries into conceptual foundations being unhelpful is overblown, the paucity of examples from Kim and Hacking notwithstanding.[10] There are in reality, it has been contended, plenty of examples. Galileo on motion is one and Einstein on simultaneity is another. Bohm, Bohr, and Schrodinger on the conceptual foundations of quantum theory is a third. Moreover, Hobbes and Locke did similar things in politics.

I do not want even to suggest a denial of what is evident, namely, that there is a conceptual side to inquiries such as science and activities such as politics. Of course there is, but it is, as Quine has also stressed, hardly autonomous with respect to the structured empirical side of these inquiries. Moreover, it is not such that we could just sit back and examine the conceptual foundations of quantum theory or capitalism without examining them empirically and in detail. It is also striking that in the natural science cases it is scientists fully engaged in science itself who, *in the course of doing science*, sometimes make remarks that have a conceptual side. But these remarks were made in the process of constructing a theory—an empirical scientific theory—and not just in giving the "conceptual foundations" (whatever that is) of an already worked-out theory. The philosopher does not rush in as the overseer here or even as the underlaborer who, by conceptual analysis, clarifies what was unclear to the scientists. There is nothing extra, distinctive, or autonomous that philosophers do that is of great help, or indeed any help, here. Where conceptual clarifications are of value, scientists make them in the course of constructing or advancing their scientific theories.

In politics, looking at the examples of Hobbes and Locke, it is important to remember that they wrote before philosophy had been partitioned off from science or politics as an autonomous discipline. Their work concerning politics is no different in kind from Weber's or Durkheim's. It would qualify today as social science, but, like Weber's and Durkheim's work, it also has a conceptual side, though there is nothing isolable there to be called "conceptual foundations." In that way the natural science and the social science cases run parallel. And Rorty's challenge remains unmet.

Someone might respond that philosophical investigations into the conceptual foundations of morality have been valuable in clarifying the moral life and helping us to come to grips with genuine moral problems that are, without doubt, deeply a part of our lives. But it seems to me, as it seems to Rorty as well, that precisely in moral issues is the least likelihood that "examining or setting out conceptual foundations" is going to be of much use. First, in the domain of morality, it is far from clear that there is anything very useful or perhaps even intelligible that counts as its "conceptual foundations." We can make second-order remarks about the use of "moral" and the logical status of moral utterances. We may even be able to give a characterization of something called the structure of practical reasoning. But it is not at all evident that such talk, such elucidations, even if well done, will yield anything like "the conceptual foundations of morality." Moreover, if epistemological foundationalism is broken-backed, it is doubtful that moral foundationalism will be successful. Certainly the history of such endeavors has not been encouraging. There is, of course, something called metaethics (an activity that flourished in Anglo-American philosophical circles during the first half of this century), but the interminable and inconclusive discussions of and disputes between

ethical naturalism, intuitionism, and noncognitivism during that
period and the largely useless and again inconclusive discussions of
the is/ought problem give us little reason to think that philosophical
work in the foundations of ethics clarifies the moral life or gives us
rational guidance in the solving of moral problems. Rawls, Dworkin,
Cohen, Daniels, and Walzer, among others, have said some very
perceptive and important things about morality and have provided
abstract accounts of morality that help guide moral practice. But
these accounts do not rely on or make any claims about the
conceptual foundations of morality or of philosophy, and they do not
deploy distinctively philosophical conceptual tools that reveal or
presuppose a distinctive philosophical expertise. Rather, they are
persons who, knowing the history of moral and social philosophy
very well indeed, have reflected carefully on it and think clearly and
probingly about moral matters. But there is no appeal to a distinctive philosophical expertise or a philosophical *Fach* in their work.
They could just as well be, and indeed two actually are, lawyers,
political scientists, economists, sociologists, or historians as they
could philosophers.

　　　Hacking and Kim have not, in defending the Tradition
against Rorty, succeeded in showing how a philosophical examination
of any "conceptual foundations" can give us anything of worth.
"Scientific analytical philosophy," if it is to come to much, must make
good the claim that philosophy yields some determinate expertise,
that it possesses some analytical tools to provide us a knowledge of
the conceptual foundations of science, morality, law, and the like
that will in turn enlighten those practices. Rorty, following Wittgenstein, maintains that these claims of the Tradition are hollow.

                                    IV

　　　Let me come at Rorty's challenge to systematic analytic
philosophy from another direction. From Descartes through Kant,
philosophy took an epistemological turn and, in a change more
apparent than real, theories of meaning and reference have replaced
theories of knowledge as the *ground* of philosophy or the alleged
central core of philosophy with both the founding fathers of
analytical philosophy (figures such as Russell and Carnap) and third-

generation anti-Quinean, anti-Wittgensteinian philosophers (such as Kripke), returning to something like the atomism of the founding fathers. But, through all these traditionalist shifts, the underlying intent remained much the same: It is the intent to do foundational work, to treat philosophy (*pace* Kim and Hacking) as foundational to or for the rest of culture. Put in the older epistemological idiom, the heart of philosophy—the principal task of philosophy—is to ascertain how we can assess knowledge claims: determine what genuine knowledge is. On that conception the very core of philosophy is epistemology. The underlying rationale for this is evident enough. A sound epistemology—meeting an underlying foundational rationale of philosophy—would enable philosophy to set itself up as an arbiter of culture. On that self-image, philosophy is to determine where genuine knowledge claims in art, morality, religion, the sciences (both natural and social), and politics are made and what they are worth. On this Cartesian-Kantian view, implicitly shared by positivists with their claims to having a criterion of cognitive significance, philosophy is "foundational in respect to the rest of culture because culture is the assemblage of claims to knowledge, and philosophy adjudicates such claims."[11]

This "presumptuous self-image," as Charles Taylor calls it, has been repudiated by most of the analytical philosophers who have examined with any care Richard Rorty's claims.[12] They, as we have seen Kim and Hacking do, agree with Rorty that such a self-conception can no longer be sustained, though some of them qualify this and hedge their bets by saying "at least for now."[13] And some add, forgetting a lot of the public relations rhetoric in which analytical philosophers engage, that it was never part of the analytic philosophy to make such a claim. Others say that what is needed is a more modest foundationalism.[14] Rorty shows, such critics say, that *strong* foundationalism rests on a mistake. There is no way of providing an *indubitable* foundation for knowledge. Indeed, they agree that there can be no such foundations. The work of the second generation of analytical philosophers, particularly Quine, Sellars, Goodman, and Davidson, has established that. But why must epistemology, they ask, take such a strong form? Why must it ask for *indubitable* foundations? They counter (a) that there can be modest forms of foundationalism that do not claim certainty—there are no basic propositions that are self-certifying or in any way certain; and (b) that the basic propositions are about physical objects rather than inner states or sense data. We need not, the claim goes, be Cartesian or Kantian foundationalists to be foundationalists. I will return to this modest foundationalism in a moment. (I also return to it in examining Alvin Goldman's views in Chapter 5.)

Other critics of Rorty, among them Hacking, are not even modest foundationalists.[15] They agree with Rorty "that a project of finding foundations for knowledge-in-general is not appropriate right now."[16] But that, Hacking adds, should not signal the end of epistemology. Philosophers, at least in the Western tradition and right back to the Ionians, have had a fascination with knowledge: "thinking about knowledge has been integral to philosophy."[17] We should give up the will-o'-the-wisp of finding foundations for knowledge-in-general and let "epistemology" denote "an attempt to understand the possibility and nature of various kinds of knowledge and styles of reasoning."[18] Noam Chomsky's investigation of the knowledge of grammar possessed by every human being is an example of the direction in which epistemology should go.

It seems to me, even if all this is accepted, that it is a very weak response to Rorty's argued rejection that philosophy, through its epistemological turn, can provide foundations for knowledge claims for the whole of culture so that philosophy could show (for example) that there is no moral knowledge or, alternatively, that there is or that philosophy could show that social anthropology, as distinct from chemistry, can make no genuine knowledge claims, that it is ideological through and through. Philosophy—the illusion goes—can so sit in judgment because philosophy knows what genuine knowledge claims look like and anthropological claims, to continue with my last example, no matter how central to that discipline, do not fit the bill.

With the Hacking turn, or even the modest foundationalist turn, no such cultural overseer role can be maintained or even coherently attempted. Philosophy cannot be the arbiter of culture. It cannot tell us which of the various claims extant in the culture are really genuine bits of knowledge. With the Hacking turn we instead take various activities—not only science, but art, morality, literature, law, politics, religion—and investigate what knowledge in those domains comes to and the styles of reasoning involved in those practices. This means we can no longer ask, "Is there religious knowledge? Is there knowledge of God? Is such a thing even possible?" Nor can we ask, "Is there moral knowledge?" or "Do moral claims make genuine truth claims?" On such a dispensation, after the question about whether there is religious or moral knowledge has been settled somehow—but not by philosophers—all we can do is characterize, hopefully perspicuously, what that knowledge looks like. We may, given the Hacking turn, not even be able to speak of its being settled in any way that there is moral knowledge or religious knowledge, for because there are moral and religious language games, there must be moral and religious knowledge. We cannot say what is or is not knowledge, or what it makes sense to say. All we can do, if we are skillful and lucky, is give a lucid representation of what has already been certified as knowledge or as being coherent in some particular domain.

Epistemology set out to be normative, but this activity is purely descriptive. We can, if we are good at that sort of thing, clearly display what mathematical knowledge and styles of reasoning look like, what archaeological knowledge and styles of reasoning look like, and what moral knowledge and styles of reasoning look like and how they are alike and different. But we can never justifiably make a reductionist or critical move to assert that in some of these domains there are no genuine or justified knowledge claims or, for that matter, warranted beliefs. We will, if we are interested, try to command a clear view of *how* knowledge of God is possible, but we will turn aside all questions concerning whether or not it is possible. There is no room on such a dispensation to ask, "Is there actually such knowledge?" let alone to ask, "Is it even possible that there could be such knowledge?" This is an eviscerated epistemology or, better still, it is no epistemology at all.

If we try to so naturalize epistemology and take as paradigmatic of what epistemology should be certain work in cognitive psychology or Chomsky's complicated investigations into the kind of knowledge that native speakers have of their own grammar, we have drastically changed the subject matter of epistemology. More importantly, we have given naturalized epistemology the kudos that properly belongs to empirical science. We have taken some complicated, highly theoretical, empirical investigations into knowledge—investigations giving us some new knowledge—and we have called that epistemology. The philosopher has, like an uninvited guest, crashed the party and associated himself, quite gratuitously, with the genuine investigations of science that show us that we have a certain kind of knowledge we were unaware of and of what that knowledge is like. But it doesn't give us, or even try to give us, criteria for knowledge, in a particular domain, much less criteria for knowledge in general, so that we could have a modest foundational discipline that could still be the arbiter of culture.

If, alternatively, we espouse a modest foundationalism without certainty in which the basic propositions are about physical objects, we still need to know how to decide which propositions are basic. (If no propositions are basic, we do not have a foundationalist account.) To take a certain cluster of propositions as basic cannot be done without being reductionistic, and it is just this that in various ways the second generation of analytic philosophers (Quine, Sellars, Goodman) have shown, against the first generation, to be a very fundamental mistake. To avoid the reductionist turn, we must say, "We can only speak, if we want to speak that way at all, of certain propositions as being basic to a certain domain." But this returns us to most of the difficulties I discussed in criticizing the Hacking turn. We can also ask about how the philosopher gets off telling the physicist, geologist, or social anthropologist which propositions are basic to her discipline, and how the philosopher, or for that matter the scientist in question, decides which propositions are basic. Even if they can do this, is there any point in doing so? Even if all these questions can be answered and the difficulties I found in the Hacking turn answered or shown to be inapplicable here, it is still the case—and this is the most crucial point in this context—that, if our modest foundationalism is domain-relative, such a modest foundationalism cannot be an overseer of culture. In this context, Goldman accurately sees what is going on in Rorty's account when he remarks:

> On Rorty's view, Kantianism led philosophy to set itself up as the arbiter of all culture, as the underwriter or debunker of all claims to knowledge by science morality, art or religion. It can be "foundational" with respect to all of culture because it studies man-as-knower, or the "activity of representation" that makes knowledge possible. Rorty sees analytic philosophy as a variant of Kantianism, in which analysis of language rather than transcendental critique provides the foundations for judgment. Part of his animus is against this broader conception of philosophical foundationalism.[19]

Yet Goldman, as a defender of modest foundationalism scaling down such Kantian claims—like Hacking and Kim, and many (perhaps most) analytic philosophers—does not seem to have the slightest sense of what has been given up when this Kantian-positivist dream is abandoned and of how little is left if we take the more modest foundationist, coherentist, or the domain-relative epistemological turns. By contrast, Charles Taylor, who like Rorty is a renegade from the analytic tradition, sees the hubris here of the Kantian and the positivist (Reichenbach is paradigmatic), but he also is keenly aware of how much is lost when we give up the Kantian-positivist dream.[20] Such a hope was a deep hope for philosophy, one that gave philosophy a clear reason for being. For it to be dashed is no trivial matter allowing us, once we acknowledge it, to go on with business as usual. This retreat is so considerable that it is better thought of as a demise. If philosophy or its successor subject is going to come to anything it must take a different turn.

5

On Being Ontologically Unserious

I

Even now, there are philosophers who want to be ontologically serious. They tell us we need to see the world rightly, and to do this we must work out a fundamental ontology that will display the most basic features the world must have. This is not a matter of careful, experimental investigation linked with adroit and imaginative theory design, but rather in some way essentially a matter of pure, rigorous thought. Disciplined philosophical reflection—the engagement in careful, purely conceptual exercises—will yield the basic categories of the world.

It seems to me that people who think this way have learned nothing from history. It is far too late in the day to think something like this. If we want to know what the basic features of the world are, beyond truisms (e.g., things tend to persist through time), many of which may be true but hardly require philosophy for their rational acceptance, we should go to physics and its allied sciences. That, of course, will not quench the philosophical thirst for certainty. Indeed nothing nonillusory will. What physics tells us now and what it will tell us (if it is still around) two hundred years from now are likely to be significantly different from each other.

The whole thrust of our intellectual history since the Enlightenment (including the empiricist and Kantian revolutions in philosophy with what in effect are their continuation in logical positivism and linguistic philosophy), together with the importantly different turnings by the pragmatists and by Quine, Davidson, Wittgenstein, and Habermas, has added up to teach us the inescapability of fallibilism and the impossibility, or at least nonnecessity, of foundationalism. It has also made apparent to us why the steady demystification of the world is not an arbitrary shift in the *Weltgeist* and has made it second nature, in those touched by the Enlightenment, to accept, as Peirce put it, the authority of science rather than that of religion or philosophy in fixing belief concerning what is and might become the case. It is far too late to be ontologically serious. Such activities invite (depending on temperament) either a yawn or Kierkegaardian, Derridian, or Rortyan irony.

II

It is incorrect to say that the above reveals the scientistic attitude that what science cannot tell us humankind cannot know. It does not commit us to scientism, for it says nothing about how we come to know the way we ought to respond to other people, what sort of life plans to form for ourselves, or anything like that. It is not even necessarily so about the human sciences (studies) where it is at least arguable that we should go in a much more Habermasian or hermeneutical way. Rather, it is about how we determine what is the fundamental stuff—the furniture, if you will—of the universe and how we make reasonable judgments about how the world (the nonhuman world) works.

For all I know scientific cosmology may be shot through with scientific mythology and may have (if that is not pleonastic) all sorts of bad metaphysical residues in it. Philosophical analysis should, in the standard debunking ways, clean that Augean stable (if such it be), thereby helping science, in a modest underlaborer way, to gain a more adequate cosmology. But philosophy can never replace, provide a foundationalist underpinning for, or go beyond scientific cosmology to show us, at long last, what the world truly, and perhaps must, be like.

This is indeed skepticism about certain traditional claims of philosophy—a rejection of going on about ontology—but not general or global skepticism, for it is cheerfully confident about the capacities of a developing science to give us a reasonable fallibilistic account of what there is. Fallibilism—an eschewing of the quest for certainty, an unrepentant nonnostalgia for the Absolute—is not skepticism. Ontological commitments, where they are not held in a fallibilistic way, tend to be religiose. The old link between philosophy and religion dies hard even for those contemporary atheists who also have a philosophical itch.

III

     Some have said that this setting aside of ontology is rooted in taking the curse of Kant too seriously. It is rooted, that is, in what some take to be an unfortunate modern tendency to give priority to epistemology over ontology. Don't ask, some have said, how we can know or warrantedly believe ontological claims about what there is. Instead, just speculate carefully about what there is, trot out your possible worlds, and worry about validation and epistemological foundations later. What is warrantedly assertable, even ideally so, and what is the case or true, need not come to the same thing. The world is determinate—the world is what it is and not another thing—even though we may never be able to know or even make a terribly educated guess as to what this determinate structure is. Even global epistemological skepticism does not touch that. That is, or at least should be, commonplace.

     The natural response to this is not to deny the determinateness of the world (after all, what else could it be but determinate?). The response, rather, should say that an investigation into what there is will give us, if we do not have some sense of when we are going right or wrong in our inquiries, nothing but the dreams of a spirit seer. We need, in making responsible claims about what the world is like, at least some rough conception of how to validate our claims. There is very good reason, some believe, to put something like the Kantian project first, even after concerns about a contextually sensitive method of belief acquisition have replaced foundationalist, epistemological concerns.

     Someone might, in assenting to this, go on to remark that although classical foundationalism is out, partly for the reasons given in earlier chapters, there is still the possibility of and need for a modest foundationalist epistemology working fully in the spirit of fallibilism and capable of providing us with the epistemological foundations for constructing an ontology. I am thoroughly skeptical of that, but it is clear enough that such an enterprise has its appeal. So I turn now to an examination of what is perhaps the most distinguished effort currently available to articulate an epistemology with an appropriate normative force. What is most fundamentally at issue is whether we can gain a set of basic, systematically related propositions (sentences) that will provide us with the grounding and test for all else we can know or reliably believe and that itself is more certain than any of these derivative knowledge claims or warranted beliefs and would give us the philosophical basis for claims in fundamental ontology about the structure of the world. It is dubious whether anything like this is even remotely possible. But my aim here is to see whether what is perhaps the best effort at a systematic epistemology going can yield anything like that. (It might, I should add, do the former things without doing the latter.)

IV

The work I have in mind is that of Alvin Goldman as articulated in his *Epistemology and Cognition* as well as in a series of articles.[1] Goldman's work is systematic and thorough, and it has a masterful grasp of the literature. It is extensive in scope, original, and contains a considerable array of careful arguments. In an area where lack of judiciousness and common sense often prevails, Goldman's work is remarkably judicious and level-headed, avoiding philosophical excesses while still containing a distinctive philosophical thrust.

While operating within an overall naturalistic framework, Goldman defends, in contrast with W. V. Quine and Fred Dretske, both a traditional, normative conception of epistemology and a modest foundationalism. But unlike many traditional conceptions of epistemology, Goldman's holds that psychology and the social sciences have, in the nonfoundational parts of epistemology, an important role to play in conjunction with philosophy. In opposition to Hilary Putnam, Charles Taylor, Rorty, and their Continental counterparts Theodor Adorno, Max Horkheimer, and Jürgen Habermas, Goldman thinks that there are and ought to be such things as theories of epistemology and that among them are epistemological theories that articulate the foundations of knowledge. Indeed, on his view, there is something that can rightly be characterized as "the foundations of knowledge."

Goldman is, however, a modest foundationalist. In discussing Rorty's views he makes it clear that he is with Rorty in rejecting the claims of a Cartesian epistemology—a species of classical foundationalism—that would claim a sphere of privileged knowledge that forms the basis of all genuine knowledge about the world, man, and society.[2] The task of epistemology, so construed, is to give us the foundations of knowledge and justified belief. Goldman, as firmly as Rorty, rejects any such claim to *privileged* knowledge or *certain* knowledge. (Like Rudolf Carnap and a host of others since Carnap, he clearly sees that "certain knowledge" is not pleonastic, though knowledge does require truth, i.e., you cannot have knowledge of what is not true.)[3]

Rorty, as we have seen, would have it that when we drop such a quest for certainty we in effect drop epistemology and even philosophy as the dominant modern tradition has come to know it.[4] It is here that Goldman starts to demur. He is plainly unhappy with coherentist epistemologies and naturalized epistemologies, à la Quine, that reduce epistemology to psychology and deprive it of any critical normative function. He wants (reasonably enough) a foundationalist, normative, and critical epistemology that is still fallibilistic. In line with this, he thinks we can and should be foundationalists without being classical foundationalists, Cartesian or otherwise. This means that we will not claim certainty for basic propositions that in turn form the ground for all other legitimate claims to knowledge. He defends, rather, a modest version of a foundationalism where the basic propositions on which the rest of knowledge is established are about physical objects, not inner states, and are not thought to be certain, though as basic propositions they are epistemically prior to all other propositions. (What this latter claim means is not translucent.)

Part 1 of his *Epistemology and Cognition* is about foundations and constitutes a nuanced defense of a modest foundationalism. But here Goldman (unlike Quine, who rejects any "First Philosophy") does not appeal to cognitive psychology or any science, cognitive or otherwise, in trying to set out the foundations, fallibilist though they be, of knowledge. (In his later book he does call upon cognitive psychology in attempting to identify belief-forming and problem-solving processes.) That is for him, as is classical foundationalism, a purely philosophical activity. He is traditionalist here, as if the Quinean revolution had had no effect on him. At least there seems to be implicit in Goldman's view, in a way that would not obtain for a naturalistic coherentist like Quine or Putnam or for a pragmatist, a claim that there is something distinctive that is *philosophical knowledge* that gives him a touchstone to truth and to the proper limning of the structure of reality (whatever that phrase means, if anything).[5]   On such a traditionalist view we would have an epistemology that would give us a neutral, ahistorical basis or matrix for inquiry and that in turn would yield the rational basis for an ontologically serious metaphysics. This metaphysics would, in the tradition of First Philosophy, tell us what "ultimate reality" (as if we understood that) is like. Thus, even with this modest foundation-alism, we have a thoroughly traditionalist conception of First Philosophy as a metaphysical realism distant from the iconoclasm of Wittgenstein or Rorty.

Goldman believes, like traditional epistemologists and like a resolute metaphysician such as C. B. Martin, that even global skepticism should be taken seriously. Indeed, he sets out to refute it with his modest foundationalism. So for him, the problem of epistemic justification ("global justification") looms large, and he carefully articulates and defends a reliabilist conception of justifica-tion. We want to know what "has to be true of a belief for it to qualify as justified. What factual standard determines justifiedness?" (23)   Beliefs formed by a reliable process, Goldman argues, are justified beliefs. A reliable process is one that tends to produce a high truth ratio of beliefs (26).

The distinctive philosophical task is to articulate and perspicuously display this reliabilist account of justification and compare it with alternative accounts, assessing which accounts have the best claim to being sound. There is here a division of labor between science and philosophy. The task of cognitive psychology, by contrast to philosophy, will be to identify basic belief-forming processes and show how they work. With this information clearly arranged and empirically validated, it will be a purely philosophical task, Goldman would have it, to articulate an adequate conception of reliability, state criteria of reliability, and evaluate different processes of belief formation for their reliability. (For Goldman, *pace* Quine, it is here that epistemology, unlike psychology, has a normative or directive function.)[6]

As part of his reliabilist account, Goldman, following in a broadly Lockean tradition, runs a causal theory of knowledge. Knowledge, to state such an account crudely, is a distinctive relation between a person and an object. It arises when an object makes an appropriate impression on a person's mind. Foundational propositions are those propositions, because of the reliability of their causal connections between persons and objects, in which we are justified in being most confident. They are propositions we believe because of the strong impression an object has upon us.

Sellars and Rorty have rejected such an account because, they claim, it confuses causes and reasons. Goldman responds that there are causes that are not reasons, and there may be reasons that are not causes. But there are reasons that are also causes. The causes appealed to in the causal theory of knowledge are such causes that are also reasons. It is crucial in gaining knowledge to ascertain the appropriate causal links. A reliabilist account shows us how this is to be done.

It is also a nonstarter against such an account to point out, as Sellars and Rorty do, what is still plainly true, namely, that we cannot analyze epistemic facts into nonepistemic facts, say, causal facts. Such a crude reductionism cannot be carried out. "Knowledge" or "justified" cannot be *defined* in nonepistemic terms. To think we can so define them is to commit something akin to the naturalistic fallacy. But this truth is still a nonstarter because, in a response analogous to the one contemporary ethical naturalists (e.g., J. L. Mackie or Gilbert Harman) have given to nonnaturalists, Goldman and other modest foundationalists can reply that what we should seek is not a definition of "justified" but "a specification of the nonepistemic conditions that make a belief justified—the nonepistemic facts on which epistemic status 'supervenes.'"[7] These nonepistemic facts can and indeed should include some causal facts. A belief constitutes knowledge at least partly because of how it is caused and how it is causally sustained.

Goldman, though not without a keen sense of the difficulties facing him and a half-belief that such a project cannot be achieved, seeks to give what he calls an objectivist account of epistemic justification. Here he faces head on what are no doubt the deepest challenges to the whole epistemological tradition from antirealists such as Putnam and Goodman, from the pragmatists, and from Wittgensteinians.[8] These philosophers, as different as they are, all argue that justification is irreducibly social. It is within our heterogeneous, though not unconnected, social practices that we find whatever epistemic authority there is. Justification consists in giving reasons in accordance with certain norms embedded in social practices within historically determinate communities. (Sometimes these norms are explicit, sometimes they are not.) Epistemic authority is most fundamentally grounded in what society lets us say. Causal interaction with objects cannot by itself confer epistemic authority. That can only be conferred by society. We cannot, the Tradition's expectations to the contrary notwithstanding, appeal to any society-independent conception of the accuracy of representation of how the mind or language represents reality.

Goldman believes that this pragmatist-Wittgensteinian turn presents us with a *false dichotomy*. It says in effect "either knowledge (or justification) is a matter of accuracy of representation, or causal interaction, or it is a matter of social or linguistic practice."[9] But, Goldman comments, "these theories aren't really mutually exclusive; both can have elements of truth. It is true, for example, that standards for judging beliefs to be justified or for judging them to pieces of 'knowledge' are socially evolved. But what these social standards or linguistic conventions *require* often involves accuracy of representation, or belief-causation."[10] A belief will count as knowledge only if true. According to Goldman, this entails that knowledge is partly a matter of accurate representation, though he concedes to the Wittgensteinians that "its being so is a matter of their being a certain socially evolved concept."[11]

He also maintains, against the claim that justification is irreducibly social, that, socially evolved or not, "our standards of justifiedness specify that a belief is justified only if it is caused by appropriate psychological processes."[12] *Pace* Wittgenstein and Rorty, justifiedness is "partly a matter of mental causes."[13] Suppose, for example, I claim to know that my copy of the *Investigations* is in my office. I know (know a priori?) that *if* the *Investigations* is in fact in my office and I am justified in believing that it is in my office, I know that it is in my office. And, more to the point here, whether I am so justified is, Goldman claims, independent of what any social authority may think. It is not like my belief that I have just struck out while playing in a baseball game. Whether that is true plainly does depend on what some social authority, namely, the umpire, thinks and says. But my belief that the *Investigations* is in my office is not like that. If that belief is true and I have an appropriately formed belief that it is true, then no matter what my peers think or what society allows, I know that the *Investigations* is in my office. No social authority can gainsay that. Knowledge is not, as we can see from that example, in a whole range of important cases, a matter of what society lets us say. Moreover, Goldman tells us we can most certainly "imagine a possible world in which knowledge exists without society."[14] There could be a lone Robinson Crusoe without his man Friday who, even as a solitary cognizer, has some perceptual knowledge about his environment.

Goldman's response to the Wittgensteinian at first blush looks like the most sound and unexceptionable bit of sturdy common sense, brushing aside philosophical fantasies and excesses. It is something that the plainest of plain persons, unsullied by philosophy, could not deny—or so it seems.

Let us see if appearances here are deceiving. Goldman *seems* to come down on the Ayer side of the old debate with Wittgenstein about the possibility of a private language. And, if he does, there is the problem as to how our solitary cognizer could possibly cognize—could have any *developed* understanding at all—unless he is socially formed (say, like Crusoe) so that he has in his repertoire a whole battery of speech-acts and conventions. In short, he is a person with "a public language." Without some "public language," there would be no possibility for him to invent a "private language" for his own purposes, though, of course, once a public language is in place and we understand it, you or I (if we were clever enough) could invent a secret code, a private language parasitical on the public language. But that never was at issue. What is at issue is whether an individual without a public language could invent a private language that only she could understand. Even our perceptual knowledge—which, as Putnam shows, is never without some interpretation—is embedded in bits of other things. (Typically it is embedded in a whole linguistic framework.)

However, Goldman's case (his example) is underdescribed. Given what he said about "being socially evolved" and knowledge, Goldman's solitary cognizer could be socially formed with a "public language" and then come to be in a world without society. That case so understood is quite unproblematic, but it also provides no case at all of a human being's having an understanding and beliefs that are not socially grounded. It would be like one of us being dropped on some uninhabited island without means of communication with anyone else. The conceptual trouble comes if we try to imagine someone recognizably human who is not a social animal, has never been part of society, has no public language but has a (putative) language that is only logically possible for him to understand. Wittgenstein's case about the impossibility of a private language hinges on whether such a "possible world" is consistently thinkable and thus really a possible world. It is not, to put it conservatively, so evident that this is a possible world.

Goldman could, however, drop any reference to language and comment that whatever we should say about amoebas and protozoa, it would be arbitrarily parti pris (both Wittgenstein and Davidson to the contrary notwithstanding) to deny that dogs and cats and deer and tigers have perceptual knowledge. Yet they certainly do not have a language and are socialized only in a tenuous sense. Moreover, a dog at birth could be taken from its mother and fed without any "socialization" and that dog (still recognizably a dog) could come to have perceptual knowledge like any other dog. (At least this is not a wild hypothesis.) The Wittgensteinian reply that if we speak of a dog's knowing here we must be using "knowing" in a different sense than when we speak of humans' knowing, is at best begging the question. As far as perceptual knowledge is concerned, it is not unreasonable to think that what is involved here with dogs and what is involved with humans is quite similar (though surely not identical).

Another response might be that the kind of knowledge or justified beliefs that could be shared by dogs and humans is very limited. Most human knowing is a socialized affair, thoroughly embedded in social practices that in turn are rooted in natural languages with their various conventions and constitutive rules and norms.[15] Social epistemic authority is inescapable here. We need, even for such mundane claims I list below, a complicated and distinctive socialization to merely understand them, let alone be able to assess whether they are true or justified. Consider, to take examples more or less at random, claims about how much stress a bridge can safely take, whether a carburetor is malfunctioning, whether Jack is sad, whether Jane is intelligent, whether inflation is damaging the economy, whether Hondas are fuel efficient, whether religion is socially integrating, or whether family bonds are disintegrating in modern societies. Just consider what we would have to understand even to understand any of these claims, much less to justify or come to know that they are true. There is no having such knowledge or even such understanding without society and without social epistemic authority. The traditional epistemologist's penchant for fastening on rather brute perceptual knowledge obscures this from us and makes us prone to a solitary cognizer model: the subject and objects that impinge on the subject. This classical empiricist, Cartesian, and Kantian model, as the pragmatists stressed, has had an unfortunate effect on our picture and understanding of what knowing and belief acquisition are.

It should also be said that if we limit ourselves to the types of knowledge that (at least putatively) do not require social authority, we would have very thin porridge indeed. We could not have what the epistemologist needs to make his work interesting or significant. It is clear that on a Cartesian or Kantian epistemological foundationalism the point, or at least the central point, is to put philosophers in a position where they could be the "arbiters of all culture, as the underwriter or debunker of all claims to knowledge by science, morality, art, or religion."[16] But to do this epistemology cannot limit itself to what perceptual knowledge or a "proto-language" (if such there be) might yield. Such pieces of knowledge would not give us the grounds for such a critique and assessment of culture. We would instead need something like a set of more robust basic propositions whose truth was more secure than that of any other propositions and from which all propositions in science, morality, art, or religion, if they are genuine propositions or at least warranted propositions, can be derived. (Perhaps "derived" is too strong, but then they must in some relatively straightforward sense be based on them.) But such empiricist and rationalist programs have failed, and a modest foundationalism of the Goldman sort does not even attempt to revive them.[17]   Moreover, much of the knowledge that would have to be part of those basic propositions, if we were to have them, would have to rest on social epistemic authority. Epistemology is only significant when it holds out the possibility of providing the rational basis for the Cartesian-Lockean-Kantian task of being an arbiter of culture and of being able to challenge any social authority, epistemic or otherwise. If not, it just becomes another specialist's trivial inquiry with little interest beyond that domain. But that Archimedean point is just what foundationalist epistemology, modest or classical, cannot yield. (Nonfoundationalist epistemology, if that is really epistemology, will not yield it either, but for different reasons.) For the requisite reaches of knowledge, epistemic authority is irreducibly social and with a clear recognition of this we can say good-bye to epistemology.

It might appear that this misses Goldman's essential point about a false dichotomy and in effect addresses itself to his last point only.   Goldman could concede the Wittgensteinian point that standards for judging beliefs to be justified must be socially evolved. There is not and cannot be any place to stand outside some society or other—there is no God's-eye view or view from nowhere—nor any way, except as a social animal socialized into some culture or other with its distinctive language and ways of conceptualizing things, to have much in the way of an understanding, knowledge, or any justified beliefs of the requisite range to make a distinctively human understanding possible.   Goldman occasionally seems prepared to grant something like this; indeed, at least for the reasons adumbrated above, it should be granted.   However, even if this is accepted, we need now to consider further the important point, essential for his false dichotomy claim, that "what these social standards or linguistic conventions require often involves accuracy of representation or appropriate processes or belief-causation."[18] Epistemic authority is inescapably social, but for a belief to be justified that authority itself requires that it be caused by appropriate psychological processes (indeed mental causes). And to have knowledge, and thus truth, we must, as that social authority insists, have accuracy of representation.

The part about accuracy of representation (*pace* Rorty and Davidson) sounds like the sturdiest of common sense that only someone suffering from a philosophical malaise could deny.

Although I am at least as anxious as Goldman to stick to the stable ground of common sense and to avoid philosophical extravagance, I think that things are not at all that easy and we cannot so vindicate a modest foundationalist epistemology. To best argue for this, meeting Goldman on his own ground, I need to turn from his suggestive but dark sayings in his critique of Rorty to his important discussion of "truth and realism" in chapter 7 of *Epistemology and Cognition*. What are dark sayings in his discussion of Rorty receive a carefully reasoned articulation in *Epistemology and Cognition* in the course of his rejection of the antirealism of Goodman, Michael Dummett, and Putnam and of his own articulation and defense of metaphysical realism, along with a defense of a demythologized version of the correspondence theory of truth that goes beyond what he takes (tendentiously, I believe) to be the inadequacies of a disquotational or Tarskian understanding of truth.[19] (For Goldman there can be no successful defense of metaphysical realism that does not involve a successful defense of a correspondence theory of truth.)

V

I begin by setting out the core of his contentions in chapter 7. Truth is important for Goldman's conception of epistemic justification. Moreover, the truth that is in question must be a nonepistemic, nonpragmatist, nondisquotational, realist conception of truth. Sophistications on Ramsey, Goldman has it, will not do. "Realism" is, of course, (though not only) a philosophical term of art that gets many readings, so Goldman seeks to specify what he means to claim in defending metaphysical realism. (That is his term, not mine.) He takes his departure, appropriately enough, from Dummett's characterization of realism. Goldman rightly rejects *bivalence* as a necessary condition for realism, but accepts what Dummett calls *verification-transcendence* as essential for realism. What is critical for realism, Goldman contends, is the belief, and the correctness of this belief, that when statements of putative fact are true, including statements about the future and subjunctive conditional statements, what makes them true (or false) is independent of our knowledge or of verification (143). This is what is meant by the claim that truth is verification-transcendent. It is essential for, and indeed definitive of, metaphysical realism. The realist is claiming that "a statement is true or false independently of our knowledge, or verification, of it (or even our *ability* to verify it)" (143). Truth so understood is not an epistemic matter about what is warrantedly assertable or rationally acceptable. Goldman's central concern with realism is, as he puts it, "a concern with truth; with what makes a statement, or belief, true, if it is true" (143). This concern, he believes, requires that he develop a realist theory of truth (143). He then immediately points out that his theory of truth, like Tarski's, is interested in "the 'meaning' of truth, not in procedures or marks for telling which propositions are true" (144). Classical coherence theories of truth have conflated these quite different enterprises: "They run together coherence as a *test* of truth and coherence as a definition of truth" (144). Coherence, suitably understood, has a certain plausibility as a test, or partial test, for truth but no plausibility at all as a definition of truth. Goldman's theory of truth is concerned exclusively with the definition and elucidation of its meaning and does not concern itself with tests for truth that Goldman treats under the central epistemic topic of a theory of justified belief (144).

In articulating a proper theory of truth, we face, in his estimate and in a way disquotational truth theory does not, the substantial questions that divide realists from antirealists.[20] And these issues must, Goldman believes, be resolved in favor of the realist if his own defense of epistemology against the Wittgensteinian attack (discussed in the previous section) is to be sustained. The realist conception of truth that Goldman defends asserts (put in modal terms) that the very idea of a proposition's being true is the idea of a state of affairs such that it could happen (or could have happened) that it be true, even though we are not in a position to verify it (148).

Goldman offers a cogent if not a strikingly original critique of epistemic theories of truth (144-51). His criticisms are fairly standard and unexceptional and, given that its two major contemporary exponents (Rorty and Putnam) have abandoned it, I shall not discuss it.[21] But it is important to keep firmly in mind that Goldman's alternative realist conception insists on a sharp distinction between a proposition's being true and a proposition's being verified, and it stresses that it is the "latter, but not the former" that "involves processes by which the truth is detected or apprehended" (149). Indeed, it is by maintaining just this distinction—the distinction between what truth is and how it is known—that we "can make good sense of certain of our verifying procedures" (149). Realists' conception of reality is of something robust, something that has objects or properties invariant under "multiple modes of detection. The use of multiple procedures, methods, or assumptions to get at the same putative object, trait, or regularity is commonplace in ordinary cognition and in science" (149). In this way, in careful inquiry we seek to triangulate the objects or relationships under study. We can best make sense of this "on the assumption that truths, or facts about the object or system under study are sharply distinguished from the processes of verification or detection of them" (149). The point is to use different techniques or methods "to get at the verification-independent properties of the target object" (150). The underlying realist and commonsense assumption is that there are truths about the world to be discovered by verification processes. Is there any good reason at all to think something is mistaken or even problematic in this pretheoretical, prephilosophical assumption? The assumptions seems, at least, to be very difficult to sensibly deny. (We might, in a way that exhibits some skepticism concerning Goldman's problematic, also ask whether it requires a theory of truth, an epistemology, or an ontology for its defense and whether the claims made in any such putative defense would not be less certain than that very claim itself.)

One reason that has led what Goldman regards as the antirealist camp (Wittgenstein, Goodman, Rorty, and Putnam) to reject both metaphysical realism and the taking of an epistemological turn is a belief that the correspondence theory of truth is incoherent. Goldman brings out their central criticisms of what he takes to be the strong classical conception of the correspondence theory of truth. He shows how these arguments are well taken such that this correspondence theory must be abandoned, and he shows, too, the implications of this for foundationalist epistemology. Taking these criticisms to heart, he then seeks to articulate a demythologized and weakened correspondence theory that would be immune to these criticisms and still provide the basis for a foundationalist epistemology. This takes us to the core of his account and of his defense

of a modest foundationalism. If this account, or some modification
of it, stands, it is at least plausible to believe that the case against
epistemology collapses. So it is of considerable importance that we
carefully inspect Goldman's ideas here.

The Tractarian version of a correspondence theory of truth,
Goldman argues, is a nonstarter for the usual reasons. It claims that
the world is a totality of facts. A proposition is true just in case it
corresponds with a fact. But the world does not consist of factlike
entities of the sort that would correspond exactly to propositions or
sentences. It is at best false to portray the world "as being prestructured into truthlike entities" (151). (This, of course, in the face
of William James's derision, assumes that we understand what
"correspondence" could come to here.)

Antirealists and antifoundationalists alike (*sometimes* they are
the same persons) also argue that the world is not prefabricated in
terms of kinds or categories. The claim Goodman and Putnam make
is the familiar Kantian one that objects and kinds do not exist
independently of conceptual schemes. As Putnam puts it, "We cut
up the world into objects when we introduce one or another scheme
of description."[22]   There are no self-identifying objects. It is we
conceptualizers, conceptualizing in our various ways, who sort the
world into kinds. The world does not sort itself into kinds.
Goldman expresses this familiar, seemingly vital point in arguing
about the case against foundationalism and against epistemology:

> The point here is essentially a Kantian point, and one also stressed by
> Nelson Goodman. The creation of categories, kinds, or "versions" is an
> activity of the mind or of language. The world itself does not come
> precategorized, presorted, or presliced. Rather, it is the mind's "noetic"
> activity, or the establishment of linguistic convention, that produces
> categories and categorial systems. When truth is portrayed as correspon-
> dence, as thought or language *mirroring* the world, it is implied that the
> world comes precategorized. But that, says the antirealist, is a fiction.
> (152)

One might expect Goldman to take a Davidsonian turn here
and reject the whole Kantian schema/content dichotomy, but he does
not, and he seems to accept that critique of a strong form of the
correspondence theory that relies on the belief "that the world is
prestructured into truthlike entities (facts) and that truth consists in
language or thought mirroring a precategorized world" (152).

Goldman seems to think that *such* a realism with *such* a strong correspondence theory of truth is indefensible, and he turns instead to what he calls "weaker variants of correspondence" that he thinks are defensible and are sufficient to yield a realist theory of truth without making a mystery of "correspondence." Traditional correspondence theories used the metaphor of mirroring; Goldman provides a new governing metaphor, namely, that of being fitting, or fittingness. He believes it gives us, with the use of an analogy, the key to a demythologized correspondence theory of truth. Goldman introduces his conception as follows:

> The mirror metaphor is only one possible metaphor for correspondence. A different and preferable metaphor for correspondence is *fittingness*: the sense in which clothes fit a body. The chief advantage of this metaphor is its possession of an ingredient analogous to the categorizing and statement-creating activity of the cognizer-speaker. At the same time, it captures the basic realist intuition that what makes a proposition, or statement, true is the way the world is. (152)

To bring out the force of his case, Goldman works with his analogy of the sense in which clothes fit a body. Just as there are "indefinitely many sorts of apparel that might be designed for the human body," so there are "indefinitely many categories, principles of classification, and propositional forms that might be used to describe the world" (152). The human body indeed has parts, but it is not "presorted into units that must each be covered by a distinct garment" (152). Custom and sartorial ingenuity decide what parts to cover, what types of garment should cover which parts, whether the garments should be loose-fitting or snug, and the like. Moreover, for many parts of the body, there is a considerable array of different garment types used to clothe them. It is people with their interests, preferences, and inventiveness who devise standards for proper fittingness. We have a wide variation with shifts in style and fashion. "Styles specify which portions of selected bodily parts should be covered or uncovered and whether the clothing should hug snugly or hang loosely. This is all a matter of style, or convention, which determines the *conditions of fittingness* for a given type of garment" (153). Conditions of fittingness for a given type of garment are determined by the creators and designers, not by the world, and reflect human choice and devising and the interests people have. However, whether a given garment (a token of a type) for a given person fits that person's body is determined by the world (by what the garment is like and the way that person's body is). Custom or human devising or both determine *how* it shall fit or what counts as fitting in such cases. But whether in that particular case that fit obtains is a matter of what a part of the world is actually like, namely, what that person's body is like and what that garment is like. Convention determines the *conditions of fittingness* for a given type of garment. As Goldman well puts it, "Once such fittingness conditions are specified...there remains a question of whether a given garment token of that type satisfies these conditions with respect to a particular wearer's body. Whether it fits or does not does *not* depend solely on the fittingness conditions; it depends on the contours of the prospective wearer as well" (153).

The analogy vis-à-vis a realist theory of truth and Kantian critique is apt. Though forms of mental and linguistic representation are human artifacts and constructions and not products of the world per se, it remains the case that "whether any given sentence, thought sign, or proposition is true depends on something extra-human, namely the actual world itself" (153). But which "things a cognizer-speaker chooses to think or say about the world is not determined by the world itself. That is a matter of noetic activity, lexical resources in the speaker's language and the like" (153). For a sentence or proposition to have any truth-value it must have associated conditions of truth. But the conditions of truth are no more read off the world or pried off the world than are conditions of fittingness. These are determined by the resources of a given language, the interests, devising, and choices of agents in a particular culture and often at a particular time or at least epoch. These conditions of truth are set by human convention and devising: a devising that in many cases answers to various human interests. But, Goldman continues (bringing out firmly his realist commitments and reflecting back on his earlier discussion of Rorty), whether or not these conditions of truth, socially *derived* though they are, *are satisfied* is determined by how the world is, and not by any human "world-making." "Truth and falsity, then, consists in the world's 'answering' or 'not answering' to whatever truth-conditions are in question" (153). This specifies without miracle, mystery, or authority, a demythologized sense of "correspondence" for a chastened correspondence theory of truth in a way that squares with realist intuitions. Moreover, this account does something that good philosophical accounts frequently do: It meets intuitions that realists properly insist on while at the same time finding a place for the valid points made by antirealists. In doing this, we get a much better picture of what should be said and believed than with more tunnel-visioned approaches.

In deftly proceeding so, Goldman points out that *which* truth-conditions must be satisfied is not determined by the world. (I would prefer to call it the nonhuman world because there is nothing else but the world.) Conditions of truth are laid down not by the nonhuman world but only by thinkers or speakers: agents acting in the world with certain purposes, interests, and conceptions. "This is the sense in which the world is not precategorized, and in which truth does not consist in mirroring of a precategorized world" (153). With such a display of the conceptual terrain, we have a way of doing justice to the realist claim that truth and falsity, at least for matters of fact, are determined by how the world is, while still doing justice to "the constructionist themes of Kant, Goodman, and Putnam" (153). That is a pleasant and perfectly coherent way to have your cake and eat it, too.

A considerable part of the motivation for the Goodman-Putnam type constructivism is epistemological or, more precisely, to make a case for an antifoundationalist, antiepistemology. We can never, they argue, compare a thought or statement or a network of such thoughts or statements giving us a "version of the world" with an unconceptualized reality, so as to tell whether the world answers to that thought or statement or network of thoughts or statements (154). Moreover, "comparison of a theory with perceptual experience is not comparison with unconceptualized reality because perceptual experience is itself the product of a sorting, structuring, or categorizing process of the brain. So all we can ever do cognitively is compare versions to versions" (154).

Relying on his account of fittingness as a replacement for mirroring, Goldman remarks that he can concede that point to the constructivists without undermining his weakened correspondence account of truth or his metaphysical realism, for on his own correspondence account no utilization is made of mirroring or of the strange idea that "true thoughts must resemble the world" (154). An "epistemology of getting or determining the truth need not involve comparison" (154).

Perhaps this will do, and with it we will have laid the foundations for a realist modest foundationalism. However, there is at least this kind of worry: Suppose someone sloganizes, "There can be no fittingness without at least a 'mirroring' that unavoidably involves comparison. We cannot give sense to whether something is fitting or not without making comparisons." In trying to see if there is anything in that, let us go back to the garment analogy. Suppose I am buying a certain sort of hat and I am told (reflecting a sartorial convention) that one of the fitting conditions for that sort of hat is that it not rest on the ears but fit snugly one quarter of an inch above the ears. Perhaps I see a model of a hat so fitting (a wax head with a hat of the requisite type on it) or have a mental image of a hat on my head one quarter of an inch above my ears. I try on a hat and walk to a mirror and see that it fits a quarter of an inch above my ears, or if I have no mirror, I feel it with my fingers and ascertain that it does fit just a quarter of an inch above my ears. Or perhaps I just feel the pressure of the hat on my head at the requisite place. Perhaps (if I am a pedantic sort) I will even measure it, carrying out certain elementary operations. The point is that fitting here does involve comparisons. Now take the thought or the sentence, "There is a tree before me." I cannot, as the constructivists show, compare a thought or sentence with an unconceptualized reality. It is not like looking at the hat on the wax head and then looking in the mirror at the hat on my head. But how, then, can we determine fit without comparison? Goldman poses something like this difficulty (if that is what it is) himself when he says: Suppose it is asked if the realist's world is unconceptualized (as he agrees it is). How can it be grasped or encountered in a manner that determines fittingness? How can we determine fittingness here? Or can we? Is it not, after all, the case that on Goldman's account we can never grasp or encounter the world so as to determine whether some thought or sentence of ours fits it? His realist theory, the claim goes, so understands the world that it turns it into a noumenal object that cannot be known or correctly described, a vast something, I know not what.

Goldman, of course, resists this. Because his response is vital for his defense of a realist foundationalism, let me quote it in full.

> Perception is a causal transaction from the world to the perceiver, so perception does involve an encounter with the world (at least in nonhallucinatory cases). To be sure, the event at the terminus of the transaction does not *resemble* the event at the starting point. The terminus of perception is a perceptual representation, which involves figure-ground organization and other sorts of grouping and structuring. The initiating event does not have these properties. Still, the transaction as a whole does constitute an encounter with something unconceptualized. We are not cut off from the world as long as this sort of encounter takes place.
>
> But is this sort of encounter sufficient for knowledge or other forms of epistemic access? As far as I can see, realism about truth does not preclude such knowledge. Suppose that the (unconceptualized) world is such that the proposition "There is a tree before me" fits it, that is, is true. And suppose that the perceptual process is a reliable one, both locally and globally. Then, according to my account of knowledge, I may indeed *know* that there is a tree before me. The world that I learn *about* is an unconceptualized world. But *what* I learn about this world is that some conceptualization (of mine) fits it. *How* I learn this is by a process that begins with the unconceptualized world but terminates in a conceptualization.
>
> Does this (realist) theory make the world into a noumenal object, an object that cannot be known or correctly described? Not at all. On the proposed version of realism we can know of the world that particular representations fit it. So the world is not a noumenal object. (154)

VI

Goldman's account is impressive. Does it stand at least in essentials, and if it does, does the case against epistemology collapse? I think much of Goldman's account stands and should simply be incorporated into good, clean, intellectual work. But I also think central elements of his thought, even elements crucial for his case against those who would reject epistemology and with it foundationalism, need careful querying. Indeed, I believe that in certain essential respects, his case, impressive as it is, does not stand. It is to this I now turn.

At the very end of his discussion of metaphysical realism, Goldman, almost as if it were an aside, brings up a criticism of metaphysical realism by Hilary Putnam that turns on indeterminacy of reference. Putnam's critique here cuts to the heart of the matter and Goldman must, I believe, deflect it if he is to make his case for metaphysical realism (155). I argue that Goldman has not adequately responded to it, and that Putnam's arguments both undermine metaphysical realism and fundamentally scuttle epistemological foundationalism.

   In criticizing the correspondence theory of truth, Putnam points out that there are too many correspondences. He claims that correspondence is, if it comes to anything, a word-world relationship. But, given indeterminacy of reference, there are just too many word-world relationships. In situation after situation there are too many candidates for the reference relation. Although there may be one satisfaction relation under which a given sentence turns out true, there will be other equally plausible satisfaction relations under which it turns out not to be true. Interpretation is inescapable here, for "for any word-world relation purporting to be the 'intended' truth relation, there are other, equally good candidates. Since no unique word-world relation can be identified with truth, the correspondence notion of truth is untenable" (155). Reference relations are always indeterminate and this, according to Putnam, has key implications for truth.

   Goldman strangely denies that this is so. Putnam's problem, he tells us, if it really is serious, is a problem about interpretation or the establishment of truth-conditions and not about truth (155). Goldman rightly points out:

> Questions of truth cannot arise until there is a suitable bearer of truth-value with an established set of truth-conditions about which it can be queried which truth-value it has. Sentences or thought events construed as meaningless marks or nerve impulses are not bearers of truth-values. Only when a sentence or thought event is interpreted—when it has suitable semantic properties (including reference of singular terms and sense or reference of general terms)—is it even a candidate for being true or false (155).

Putnam presses us to ask how words and thought signs get their meaning and reference. How, that is, do truth-conditions get attached to thought signs? Goldman throws up his hands at this problem (155) but claims that regardless of how it is resolved, it is not a problem for him "for unless and until sentences and thought signs are conceded to have interpretations, or truth-conditions, the question of truth cannot arise" (156). Although I do not deny the truth of what he has just said, I continue to have trouble with its relevance to the problem at hand. As we have seen Goldman cogently argue, when such an assignment is made, when such an interpretation is given, we can have (under that interpretation) definiteness of reference and (under that interpretation) accuracy of representation, and we can determinately ascertain in many circumstances what (under a certain interpretation) truth-value a particular employment of a given sentence has. We can ascertain, that is, whether it is true that there is a poisonous snake in my berry patch. "Given truth-conditions for a sentence, or thought, what makes it true or false is surely the way the world is, or whether it fits the world" (156).

It seems to me that this response to Putnam will not do at all and that, when we think it through, it is a great letdown to realist hopes. Such an account cannot meet the realist's pretheoretical intuitions, and giving up those intuitions would be tantamount to abandoning realism. What the metaphysical realist wants is for the world *quite unequivocally* to determine what is true and what is false. As Goldman puts it himself, it is the realist's expectations that objects and properties in the world determine whether propositions are true, quite independently of what cognizers or interpreters (if any there are) think or what conceptual schemes (if any) are extant and accepted. This being so, the realist's intuition goes, it is just true or false that at a given time and place there is a poisonous snake in Nielsen's berry patch quite apart from whether Nielsen or anyone else is around to assert or deny it or to place a certain interpretation on the sentence "There is a poisonous snake in Nielsen's berry patch." The realist expectation is that if the proposition that there is a poisonous snake in Nielsen's berry patch fits with a certain segment of the world, then it is true and we need not be concerned how some cognizers interpret it or what conceptual schemes are accepted.

Putnam's analysis of indeterminacy of reference shows this realist belief to be a myth. What counts as "poisonous," "snake," "poisonous snake," "berry patch," "being in the berry patch" all admit of different readings. There is no determining what is the correct reading independently of societal conventions or determinate uses of terms in certain language games built into the linguistic practices of a given society or a family of societies. In that way, society determines what we can say, think, and believe and what has the most fundamental epistemic authority.

We cannot say *sans phrase*, and make it stick, that there is a poisonous snake in Nielsen's berry patch. What we can say, given a certain interpretation of the sentence expressing that proposition, a certain specification of truth-conditions, *and* a certain condition of a part of the world, is that (if all these conditions hold) it is true. But under other interpretations it is false and under still other interpretations it is indeterminate. It can never just be the case that there is a poisonous snake in Nielsen's berry patch. There is no truth to be had here that is independent of conceptualizing things in accordance with some conceptual framework. And as this is perfectly generalizable, the commonsense sounding claim of metaphysical realism has been undermined. (It also *seems pace* Rorty and the general thrust of my own arguments in this book, that we have been pushed over into the antirealists' camp.)

Perhaps a richer set of examples will help drive this point home. Consider the standard South African racial classification system. As South African road and city maps (at least of the 1976 vintage) will tell you, there are whites ("Europeans"), blacks, coloreds, and Asians making up the major racial groupings of South Africa, and there are supposedly a determinate number of such peoples in the various townships. Let me concoct the following not utterly unrealistic dialogue. Suppose while I am walking down the main street of Stellenbosch with an Afrikaner, we pass two chaps chatting in front of the drugstore. I say to the Afrikaner after we have passed, "They were blacks, weren't they?" He replies, "No, they were coloreds." I respond, "They looked like blacks to me. They were very dark." He says, "No, they were coloreds. They were speaking Afrikaans and they had straight noses." I ask, "Can't some blacks speak Afrikaans like native speakers?" He allows that a few can and that some blacks have straight noses. I then allege there is no racial difference between blacks and coloreds but only an ethnic one connected with certain cultural traits and certain distinctive historical circumstances. He says, "No, there are distinct racial groupings, answered to by whites, blacks, coloreds, and Asians." We both agree that there are borderline cases where nothing would settle, except the vicious arbitrariness of the racial reclassification board, what race a given person was. But the Afrikaner also alleges that over populations, and with respect to clear paradigmatic cases, there are in the world such different races and that the two chaps we passed in front of the drugstore were plainly coloreds. (He, of course, could be right about the first while being wrong about the second.) He can associate certain conditions with "being colored" that will vindicate his claim that they are coloreds but nothing in the world will force on me an acceptance of that reading or, alternatively, force on him an acceptance of my denial that there are (culture and convention apart) coloreds. All we can say is that, given the acceptance of a certain conceptual framework and when certain conditions obtain, the sentence "Those chaps were coloreds" is true. But the conditions by themselves are not enough to settle the truth claim here. The conceptual framework must also be accepted, but there is nothing in the world that forces on us that or any other conceptual framework. (That is not to say, however, that decisionism is king and that there are no considerations of a pragmatic sort that may reasonably incline us to one framework rather than another. There is a further twist here counting against anything like incommensurability that will be brought out in my discussion of Davidson in the next section. But acceptance of that will force us to be much more holistic than Goldman or any foundationalism can allow.)

VII

Such views about the indeterminacy of reference as expressed in the previous section, seem at least to undermine Goldman's metaphysical realism and with it his modest foundationalism. If nothing in the world independent of choice of conceptual framework makes sentences or thoughts true, then there can be no basic propositions whose truth is just there to be discovered independently of whatever conceptual framework we adopt. However, such views about indeterminacy of reference have sometimes given rise to forms of relativism or idealism that should be looked at with a not inconsiderable amount of skepticism. Given Putnam-type arguments about word-world connections, some have thought, though not

Putnam himself, that we should conclude that truth is relative to a scheme of thought. People, and particularly different peoples, have various visions and versions of the world. Indeed, the world, on these accounts, is such a noumenal object that perhaps we have (if that makes sense) just versions *sans phrase*. But this is plainly an implicit reductio. That there are sticks, stones, and bits of earth around is not something that is mind-dependent or depends for its being the case on the adoption of a conceptual scheme or framework or the like. These realities are not a matter of our devising, though how we classify them is. Perhaps, as Putnam believes, it is even a matter of consent, or at least human conceptual devising, how we individuate and count objects. That there are, will be, or could be cognizers capable of conceptualizing and cognizing such phenomena has no bearing on its being true that there are sticks, stones, and bits of earth around. (They are just there to be discovered.) It is plainly more reasonable to believe this than to believe *any* philosophical claim that would deny it. If a philosophical claim (to adapt G. E. Moore) is incompatible with its truth, then the philosophical claim should be rejected or at least revised until it is compatible with its truth. Whatever we may want to say about metaphysical realism, this commonsense realism is perfectly firm and quite unproblematic.[23]

While these Moore-like moves may rid us of idealism and global skepticism, they will not suffice to rid us of more local skepticisms or of all forms of relativism. (It may very well *not* be desirable to be rid of all such skepticisms or relativisms. Religious skepticism is only the most obvious case.) If we do not accept something like Goldman's modest foundationalism, are we caught in a form of relativism? I do not think it is obvious that we are. Here we can perhaps take a page or two from Donald Davidson.[24] Perhaps we can soundly reject relativism (at least in its nonbenign forms) without being foundationalists. Davidson has famously denied that it even makes sense to speak of alternative realities, each with its own truths untranslatable into another way of thinking. The literal meaning of sentences is given by their truth-conditions. To know the truth-conditions of a sentence, an utterance, thought, or thought-event is to know the conditions under which it would be true or false. The sentence "The eraser is on the table" is true if and only if the eraser is on the table. But in doing this we do not compare the sentence with the eraser's being on the table. Rather Davidson, like Quine, is much more holistic. Our sentences are part of a web of sentences whose truth-conditions depend on one another.

How does this bear on the rejection of the claim that truth is relative to a scheme of thought and to the related claim that there are some others (perhaps in a different culture) who have a different version of the world with alien concepts that can have no place in our lives but that, being untranslatable into our scheme of things, are incommensurable with our views? Davidson responds that there is no good reason for accepting claims of incommensurability. We come to understand the languages of others, including people from very different cultures with very different languages, in basically the same way we come to understand our own language, namely, by systematically coming to understand the truth-conditions of the sentences in the language in question. To understand the language of another is to follow a systematic method for generating the truth-conditions of her declarative sentences. If I am a field linguist and I profess to understand the language of another society in gaining such an understanding, I match its sentences with our truth-conditions. I understand the German sentence "Schnee ist weiss" if I know it is true if and only if snow is white. What I am doing here, acting as a field linguist, is to propose in our language a theory of truth for their language by proposing a systematic set of hypotheses, of which this hypothesis is simply one, concerning what the truth-conditions of various sentences in their language are.

That sounds commonsensical and straightforward enough, but how can we be confident, say, if the people we are studying are Azande or Doubuans, that they do not have a *wholly* alien scheme of thought from our own? Davidson asserts, again famously and at least initially surprisingly, that we cannot attribute a *wholly* alien scheme of thought to an articulate people. (Part of the problem is over what the logical status of "cannot" is here. C. B. Martin— hardly using a principle of charity—gives it a reading that makes Davidson's claim implausible. I give it one that makes it plausible.)[25]

Davidson's claim is remarkable in any event and, if true, a very important one. Is it just a sophisticated form of foot stamping on Davidson's part? And, if not, what are his arguments here, and are they sound? Or can sound arguments be teased out of the core of what he says? For starters, as different as people are in various culturally specific ways, it is perfectly evident (Michel Foucault to the contrary notwithstanding) that there is at a certain level of abstraction a common human nature.[26] All peoples have beliefs and desires and a language they use. Moreover, some of these beliefs and desires are very much alike, and the languages that we use all find ways of expressing them. Given all this—things that are as evident as can be—we are perfectly justified in attributing to other people in other tribes a massive number of mundane beliefs and concerns that run together with ours. They (that is, all statistically normal people in all societies), like us, see the clouds and hear the wind and feel the rain. They, too, believe they need water to drink and food to eat, that they require upon occasion rest and need to defecate, that they will have young, and that the young for a time need to be cared for to survive (even the IK believed that), that there is such a thing as its getting dark and its getting light, and on and on. We can so list commonplace beliefs in massive numbers and in an indefinitely extended number of ways. That these beliefs are true is as plain as anything can be. If we know anything at all, we know these things; and that we do not know anything at all is vastly less evident than that we know these things. (Here we have Moore again.) Moreover, we not only know that all people have these beliefs, we know these beliefs are true, or (if that is too strong) at least we know it is more reasonable to believe that they are true than to believe any philosophical theory or account or any other kind of theory that would deny that we can know these things to be true or (if that is also too strong) that would deny that we are justified in believing them. (Here G. E. Moore—though some say he was only copying Locke—made, or at least should have made, a permanent difference to philosophy. If we take Moore seriously— think carefully through what he says and then take it to heart—we cannot go on doing things in the old way.[27] We will either stop doing philosophy altogether, something Wittgenstein would approve of, or philosophy will be radically transformed. There can be no taking global skepticism seriously.)

      If we do not assume such Davidsonian things about other tribes with radically different languages (as well as tribes nearer to home, including our own), we could not even understand what it is for them to have a language for us to try to interpret or understand, because if we did not make such assumptions we could not match their utterances with our truth-conditions. For the literal meaning of an utterance—at least for a reasonably simple utterance—is given by its truth-conditions. Thus, if I walk up to a high mountain stream with a person from an alien culture whose language I do not understand, and I see him put his foot in the stream and then, as he quickly pulls it out, I hear him utter a set of sounds, I can reasonably conclude (though surely not with any great confidence) that he is saying in making those noises something like, "The water is cold." He may, of course, not be; he might have been saying instead, "I don't like its feel," "It feels funny," "It tingles," "Shit!" or any of a rather limited range of things. In the light of other things he utters and other things he does, I could correct my original hypothesis (if I am systematic and persistent enough) until I can be reasonably confident that I have a correct translation. (Remember fallibilism is the name of the game.) Our sentences, as I have remarked, following Davidson and Quine, are part of a web of sentences whose truth-conditions depend on one another. The identifying of truth-conditions doesn't simply go one by one. But my initial hypothesis about what he would be saying in such a circumstance is very likely right, and we can correct or refine it by utilizing the coherentist method of wide reflective equilibrium. (This could very well include abandoning my original hypothesis for another one.)

It is, of course, *logically* possible that his utterance could have meant "God speaks to me" or even something more plainly nonsensical such as "Water speaks harshly" or any of a considerable number of odd things (sensible or otherwise). (We see here, once again, of what little interest *mere* logical possibilities are. This should chasten us about the demand for proofs.)

However, if the field linguist gives such an exotic reading to all or even most of his informant's utterances, given our common situation in the world, common human nature (having beliefs, desires, intentions, needs, and interests), we have the best of reasons for thinking the field linguist has mistranslated most of the utterances. (Natives *sometimes* say exotic things but then sometimes so do we as well, e.g., talk of God, but these are very much the exception.) It makes no sense to attribute a *wholly alien* scheme of thought to an *articulate* people. If we tried to we could not even identify it as "a scheme of thought" or as "a language"; we can have no understanding of it (if such it be) such that we could say coherently that it is alien if all or even the great mass of the utterances were "translated" in ways that made no sense to us or did not run together with a considerable portion of our common-place beliefs. (*Perhaps* that is overstated, but then a more moderate replacement will do. We should not look for an algorithm here.)

To have an understanding between different cultures we must have such bridgehead beliefs and they must be reasonably extensive.[28] And (their theories to the contrary notwithstanding) as a matter of fact, as even Edward Sapir and Benjamin Lee Whorf believed, there is cross-cultural understanding. Moreover, as they also recognized, there are no untranslatable languages. (These points are, of course, linked.)

What makes us go wrong here and fly in the face of common sense and our actual human and anthropological practices of cross-cultural understanding is adherence to a deeply beguiling and culturally embedded (at least in intellectual circles), basically Kantian conception that has its hold on both Goldman and Putnam as well as on Goodman, namely, what Davidson calls the dogma of scheme and reality.[29] As part of an ancient philosophical tradition, it sets mind, thoughts, thought-events, words, utterances, cognizers, and reactors (somehow, magically) apart from the world—as if they were not part of the world—and then worries about how to get them with their conceptual schemes back together with the world. Again, the tides of metaphysics are running high. The picture beguiling us, a picture Davidson thinks is incoherent, is basically that there is a given reality and then there are various human schemes for perspicuously presenting (displaying) this reality by carving it up or categorizing it in different ways. What tempts us to think it makes sense to go in this way—that indeed we must go in this way—is a comparison with literal (actual) maps and their different ways of depicting the earth. We have stereographic maps, mercator maps, and so on. These projections do give us contrasting ways of mapping the earth. This is not untoward, however, for we simply have different methods for mapping an *independently identifiable earth*. But in the wide-ranging Kantian picture of scheme and reality (scheme and content) there is, as the account stresses, no way of identifying independently (even rather obscurely) "the reality."

There is no possibility of standing outside one or another of these conceptual schemes and identifying the reality we are talking about. Unlike maps, these conceptual schemes are utterly ubiquitous. We are, the narrative has it, in a kind of linguacentric predicament. This is not at all the case with the literal mapping of the earth. We have independent access to both the map and earth, but this is not and cannot be the case with scheme and reality. Once we see this and firmly take it to heart, we should recognize that there is nothing to the scheme and reality conception, and the picture should no longer entrap us. (Here we need Wittgensteinian therapy, not a new metaphysics.)

Freed from this beguiling picture, we simply work, in the way I have described with our own language, with the languages of other cultures by systematically ascertaining as best we can the truth-conditions of their sentences, taking those sentences as a part of a web of sentences whose truth-conditions depend on one another. We make hypotheses in our language about sentences in the alien language. We do not try to get below the level of truth-conditions for sentences to how individual words refer. Reference *may* be inscrutable. The problem Putnam poses about the relativity or at least the indeterminateness of reference that troubled Goldman's foundationalism is not a difficulty here. For with such a Davidsonian approach we do not have a building-block method by which we are trying to show how individual sentences, some of which are supposed to express basic propositions, correspond to the world, the world just containing factlike entities there to be discovered like trees. The kind of objectivity we achieve is not in this foundationalist way or of a foundationalist sort, but as a way of seeing how the sentences of a natural language hang together as part of a web of belief and whose truth-conditions are in a parallel way mutually dependent. In understanding someone from an alien culture or another person from our own culture or even in understanding ourselves, we arrange, by our own lights—the only lights, as Hacking well puts it, that we can have—the beliefs, desires, and utterances of ourselves or others (from our own tribe or from another) into as coherent a bundle as we can.[30] (We see here the ineptness of saying that Davidson—or for that matter Quine—is really a foundationalist in spite of himself. Such holism is the exact opposite of foundationalism. Nothing is taken as being basic, as foundational.)

When another language of an alien belief system is in
question, we have good reason to say we have correctly interpreted
it when we have got the sentences, desires, and beliefs into a
coherent set, coherent by our lights, of course. When it is our own
belief or belief system, we are justified in thinking it to be true to
the extent that we have shown it is maximally coherent. (Justification is clearly something that admits of degrees.) We are *not* in so
speaking saying truth is coherence or is what is maximally coherent.
"The eraser is on the table" is true if and only if the eraser is on
the table; "The pencil is yellow" is true if and only if the pencil is
yellow; and so on. (This is one of the virtues of the disquotational
theory.) But to so regard things need not come to believing that
truth is a property of any kind and it need not assume *any analysis
of truth at all.* It could very well take, as Davidson does, "truth" as
a primitive. We *are* saying that it is coherence and perhaps something else *as well*, say, experience embedded in a web of belief, that
justifies an ascription of truth to a belief, utterance, thought, or
sentence. But we need not try to state or search for any set of
foundational beliefs or basic propositions that must be true in a
correspondence sense (weak or otherwise) and on which all other
beliefs must be based if they are to be justified.[31]

VIII

Such Davidsonian moves may very well block *global* skepticism without appealing to foundationalist epistemology or perhaps
to any epistemology at all. However, it will not block, or so
evidently block, more *local* skepticisms or *local* relativisms. Let me
explain. Someone might say that over such mundane, utterly
commonplace, bridgehead beliefs it is true that we must assume, if
cross-cultural communication is to be possible, such cross-cultural
general agreement. But we cannot reasonably assume such consensus over scientific beliefs, political beliefs, some moral beliefs, beliefs
about religion, and a host of really crucial beliefs. (This would
apply as well to the random sample of beliefs I listed in Section
VII.) It is even true of beliefs in mathematics or logic. Think here
of problems generated for a truth-conditional analysis by intuitionism
in logic and mathematics.

It is certainly no difficulty for Davidson's account if there is divergence, intraculturally or interculturally, in the more exotic beliefs or if there is nontranslatability of some of the theoretical concepts of some societies (such as the concepts of mass or fields of force in the scientific community of our society). Davidson does not say all beliefs are unproblematic. Only the great mass of common-place beliefs are, and then not all of them. Azande belief in witchcraft and North American belief in God are, to understate it, pretty strange and problematic, and they are only some of the more obvious examples of a plethora of strange beliefs that circulate in the various tribes of the world (including, of course, our own). We should beware of principles of charity here that seek an interpreta-tion of "matter is infinite evil and mind is infinite goodness" (to paraphrase Mary Baker Eddy) or even of "God created the heavens and the earth" or "history has an end" (to use something presently in wider currency) that makes such sentences come out true. We may rightly assume that in commonplace matters foreign beliefs and our own come out pretty much the same or are so close to being the same as to make no difference, and that these beliefs are generally true. But there is "difference aplenty," as Hacking puts it, about a host of speculative and ideological matters.[32]

As we have seen, it was the hope of traditional epistemology that once we come to have a good foundationalist epistemology we would then have a rational way of sorting out such claims using the foundational epistemological measure as a yardstick to decide which are justified claims and which are not. Goldman's modest founda-tionalism, as we have seen, will not help us out, and it is not so evident that the coherentism Davidson gives us will either, though I am anything but confident that it was ever meant to do that. It may be, as Davidson believes, that in every natural language we can find structures of first-order logic that we can use in the proofs of Tarskian T-sentences so that every language (everything that is to be counted as a language?) will have an underlying logic identical to our own.[33] But even so, do we have a translation manual that will get us and others to the more recherché beliefs in our language or any language so that we could assess whether they are sensible or nonsensical, or (once that is settled) true or false? We can perhaps develop a theory here as a *horizontal* extension of a first-order theory of truth. This extended theory will perhaps have sufficient structure to give us rulings on the more recherché beliefs or at least some of them. A Davidsonian hope (though I do not know if it is Davidson's) is that, given the immense agreement about mundane matters (that is, agreement about what is true and false here), once there is translatability of simple sentences in which this agreement obtains, "then the recursive generation of truth-conditions for more complex sentences will enforce such a uniform method of translation that the spectres of incommensurability and indeterminacy will vanish in the dawn of a thoroughly worked out theory of truth."[34] This is an interesting and not implausible speculative (though empirically disciplined) possibility, but it is hardly Luddite to be skeptical of such a grand holism given the multiplicity and complexity of social practices and their related language games and the seemingly different styles of reasoning that go with them.[35] Even the strength of intuitionism in logic should give us pause here. In such situations, it appears to be the case that we have rather more localized social epistemic authorities, though appearances here *may* be deceiving. I think the burden of proof (something *sometimes* very difficult to establish) is on the Davidsonian to carry out such a program at least in a rather more filled-in outline if nothing else. However, it would not, even if successfully articulated, show that epistemology is a viable enterprise or that there is any point in engaging in metaphysical inquiry unless one wants to (rather eccentrically) count such a holistic, but still empirically grounded, account of what can be said as an epistemology or a metaphysics. But then we have used these terms so broadly that they come to lack utility and a tie with the Tradition. When Carnap, Schlick, Neurath, Hägerström, and Ayer set out to eliminate metaphysics, they did not set out to eliminate that or anything like that.[36] That instead could be, and to my mind should be, a theoretical part of a systematic, empirically constrained critical theory of society.[37]

6

Wittgenstein, Wittgensteinians, and the End of Philosophy

A philosopher is a man who has to cure many intellectual diseases in himself before he can arrive at the notions of commonsense.... Philosophy hasn't made any progress? If someone scratches a spot where he has an itch, do we have to see some progress? Isn't it genuine scratching otherwise or genuine itching? And can't this reaction to an irritation continue in the same way for a long time before a cure for itching is discovered?

— *Ludwig Wittgenstein*

I

The very doing of philosophy became problematic with Wittgenstein. His critique of the enterprise—something keenly brought to our attention when his *Philosophical Investigations* first appeared and then quickly forgotten—runs very deep. Richard Rorty has given a distinctive reading of Wittgenstein's turn here and has built on it a critique of philosophy as a kind of *Fach*, any kind of disciplinary matrix or science.[1] He has also argued, as we have seen, that there is a rudimentary sense of "philosophy" (a kind of Ur-philosophy, if you will) that is as old as the hills and is not part of any disciplinary matrix and is, Rorty would have it, utterly unproblematic. That conception is construed in the broadest possible sense in the attempt to see how things hang together. Rorty contrasts a "foundationalist" sense of "philosophy"—a conception he takes to be thoroughly problematic—in which we seek to determine "the foundations" of knowledge and morality (we attempt to determine what knowledge, truth, belief, rationality, and value really and essentially are) with what he takes to be the unproblematic though surely taxing enterprise of attempting to see how things—in the broadest sense of "things"—can be fitted together into a coherent whole.

It has in turn been argued that Wittgenstein's later work, if taken to heart, makes *both* conceptions—the foundational and the synthetic—thoroughly problematic.[2]   In that way, it is claimed, Wittgenstein cuts deeper than Rorty. Wittgenstein seeks to show with his emphasis on the extensive diversity of our practices and language games that we must, if we are to have anything like a perspicuous understanding of things, do without synthesis as well as foundations. We are never in any significant sense going to come to understand how things hang together. This ancient and compulsively persistent philosophical wish cannot be met. There is in Wittgenstein a passive and almost religious acceptance and acknowledgment of the vast diversity and contingency of things. "My life," as he puts it, "consists in my being content to accept many things." Although Wittgenstein is as deflationary about philosophy as any of the positivists, he, like Rorty but unlike Russell, Carnap, and Ayer, is also a resolute opponent of scientism: the belief that what science cannot tell us humankind cannot know. Moreover, again unlike the positivists (Neurath perhaps aside), Wittgenstein, after the *Tractatus*, is not a metaphysician in spite of himself. There are—or so the claim goes—on his view of things neither foundations to be uncovered nor the possibility of an Arnold-like seeing of things together and seeing them whole.

I will explicate and explore Wittgenstein's underlying rationale and, against his profound probing, argue that Enlightenment conceptualizations, chastened from superficiality by the Counter-Enlightenment and freed from scientistic and foundational fetters, are not undermined by Wittgenstein's critique. The power of Wittgenstein's obsessive but all the same powerful philosophical critique of philosophy—in that sense there can be no metaphilosophy—should be uncoupled from his cultural pessimism, quietism, and what in effect are his religious attitudes to life.[3] It is crucial to ask how sweeping an Arnold-like seeing of things together and seeing them whole is supposed to be. Wittgenstein plainly would have no sympathy with "grand metanarratives," with attempts to see how the whole of reality hangs together. With his stress on the plurality and diversity of language games, practices, and forms of life and how they set the very conditions of intelligibility, Wittgenstein could have no truck with anything like that. There is no room for a broad synthesis in Wittgenstein's thought. Grand Weltanschauungen are anathema to him. But Wittgenstein also, starting with the diversity of our language games and practices, sees how in their limited ways they hang together, albeit loosely, so that, grand synthesizing metaphysical claims aside, there is at least no conceptual roadblock to a modest Arnold-like seeing how things hang together so that we can make some coherent sense of our lives. Synthetic pictures of how the whole of reality hangs together are one thing; making sense of our lives is another. Our practices could very well make coherent sense without its being the case that we can have a synthetic picture of how the whole of reality (as if we understood what that means) fits together.

II

I come at these matters indirectly by first noting and explicating some central elements in *On Certainty* that, if their underlying claims are within the ballpark, will undermine the very doing of philosophy, at least as standardly understood. Foundationalism will be out as well as a synthesizing coherentism à la Hegel or Engels.

In battling the Cartesian skeptic, Wittgenstein tries to show the incoherence of the skeptic's position. Whereas G. E. Moore tried to show its falsity, Wittgenstein tries to show that the skeptic's position does *not* make sense. Doubts, to be intelligible, need grounds, must be specific, and presuppose certainty and a mastery of a language game; doubt about a whole language game, form of life, world-picture, or system of principles or deeply embedded convictions is impossible. Understandably, this claim will provoke resistance, and not only from people who would in some form like to rekindle a Cartesian or classical empiricist foundationalist quest.

One could hardly read *On Certainty* with any attention at all without coming away with the realization that Wittgenstein insightfully raises questions about what it could mean to doubt or affirm those fundamental but often unarticulated beliefs that compose the framework within which doubting and affirming occur. Georg von Wright, in explicating Wittgenstein's account, makes an important point when he remarks that Wittgenstein thought that "most of the 'commonsense' things Moore said he knew are things which nobody can, in fact, be correctly said to know."[4] That is, we could not correctly say we know these things in the context in which Moore said he knew that he had a hand, that he was a human being, that the earth had existed for many years past, and the like. Moore could not, Wittgenstein claims, know these things, and, "moreover, Moore was mistaken in thinking that there was evidence for the truth of the propositions in question."[5]

Wittgenstein's remarks may very well seem to many an excessively paradoxical cluster of claims. They should seem less so, though still perhaps not fully satisfactory, if we remember that at least in normal circumstances in order to vindicate a claim to knowledge, we must be able to produce grounds; we must be able to tell how it is we know what we claim to know. But in *normal* circumstances we cannot do this with a proposition such as "I have two hands." It *appears* to be based on the evidence of my senses, but in reality it is not. If in normal circumstances I should look up now and suddenly to my utter surprise see that I have no hands, I should doubt my senses, think I had gone mad, have somehow been dreaming, or the like. What I should *not do* is simply trust the evidence of my senses here. Such an "empiricism" is hardly acceptable.

The kind of commonsense propositions that Moore was pointing to are part of the bedrock in any knowing and acting in which we are engaged. (Here we should think back to the discussion in the previous chapter of that great mass of mundane beliefs, Davidson argues, we could not be mistaken about.) These Moorean propositions stand fast for us. They are just taken as part of an unproblematic background that we hardly think we have a need to articulate. Yet these propositions, which are hardly analytic or conceptual truths and which look like ordinary empirical propositions—at least they have the *form* of such propositions—have a peculiar logical role in our system of empirical propositions. They are not truths I have grasped from study or investigation. I do not discover their truth in the way that I discover that Iceland has warm springs or that Bavaria has many reactionaries. Unlike these last propositions, I do not know how I know (think I know) these Moorean "commonsense" propositions. I cannot give *grounds* for a claim to know them or, in a parallel way, grounds for claiming they are false. And thus they are not knowledge claims or things I can be said to know or for that matter not know, as I cannot give grounds for them or "the grounds" I give are no more certain than the propositions themselves. If these propositions are doubtful, the propositions I offer as evidence would be at least equally doubtful. The concept of knowledge does not apply to the propositions that stand fast come what may that are bedrock in a knowledge situation, background beliefs for the very possibility of our being able to make any knowledge claims at all.

To resist this we would have to speak of "groundless knowing," of "knowing without evidence," "self-evident knowledge," and the like or we would have to show that after all we do have grounds for such bedrock beliefs. The latter seems quite impossible and certainly the former is unpalatable, or at least very puzzling indeed.[6] But so is Wittgenstein's remark that though we are *certain* of these things we can't know them. And it is hardly helpful to characterize them, as von Wright does, as a *Vor-Wissen* (a preknowledge) while keeping firmly in mind that "das Vor-Wissen ist kein Wissen."[7] Yet *Vor-Wissen* is still something Wittgenstein claims we are certain of and must have if we are to have any knowledge or grounded beliefs at all. This certainty is less in our thought than in our practice of judging and acting. It isn't that in the beginning was the word, but that in the beginning was the deed.[8]

Some people, particularly those who have had a certain kind of traditional philosophical training, will continue to feel that such talk of certainty is paradoxical—perhaps even in effect obscurantist— and probably in some way mistaken unless we can show that Moore's type of "commonsense" propositions can be grounded after all and can be shown to rest on evidence. But that is not Wittgenstein's characteristic way of viewing the matter. Rather, again and again, in one context or another, in the twists and turns of his thought, he either asserts or gives to understand that we have in some central and unproblematic parts of our body of beliefs certain ungrounded and indeed even *ungroundable* beliefs we can hardly help having, that are pervasive and necessary if we are to have any knowledge or grounded beliefs at all.[9] These are not esoteric beliefs but are parts of our most mundane commerce with the world. Such reflections, if correct, give considerable force to Wittgenstein's remark, echoed by Norman Malcolm, that "the difficulty is to realize the groundlessness of our believing."[10]

III

It will, our above reservations to the contrary notwithstanding, be useful to adopt von Wright's way of referring to the system of framework beliefs as our *Vor-Wissen*.[11] We cannot state them as a set of axioms in an axiomatic system, for they cannot be enumerated and "laid down" once and for all. We cannot state all the background beliefs that must stand fast for our ordinary knowledge claims to be true. In that respect, as well as in others, our language is not at all like a calculus. Yet the *Vor-Wissen* hangs loosely together into something like a system, a cluster, or nest of sometimes loosely, sometimes more tightly interwoven propositions. But it would be a mistake, à la Colin Lyas, to classify propositions like Moore's "commonsense propositions" as constitutive rules,[12] though it is indeed true that their truth is "fused into the foundations of our language-games."[13] We say—to illustrate—that water boils and does not freeze under such and such circumstances, e.g., when I put the kettle on the stove. Wittgenstein asks, "Is it conceivable that we are wrong? Wouldn't a mistake topple all judgment with it? What could stand if that were to fall? Might someone discover something that made us say 'It was a mistake'?"[14] Our experience of how water has behaved up to now is such that we know it has behaved thus in innumerable instances, and this fact is fused into the foundations of our language, so that, according to Wittgenstein, the proposition "Water boils when a flame is persistently applied to it," though experiential in form, actually behaves in normal circumstances like a rule or a grammatical remark. Yet we can imagine circumstances—wild circumstances but still something we can conceive of—in which it would not be used as a rule and its denial would not be self-contradictory. There seems to be no clear demarcation here between the "analytic" and the "synthetic" or the "constitutive" and the "regulative." "Rule and empirical proposition merge into one another...not everything that has the form of an empirical proposition is one."[15] "Propositions of the form of empirical propositions" as well as "propositions of logic, form the foundation of all operating with language."[16] Von Wright interprets Wittgenstein to be claiming that "beyond everything we know or conjecture or think of as true there is a foundation of accepted truth without which there would be no such thing as knowing or conjecturing or thinking things true."[17] I am not confident that "accepted truth" would be a phrase Wittgenstein would be happy with in such a context, but if we replace that phrase with "foundation of indubitable certainties" or "foundation of groundless but unquestionable beliefs," we do catch his meaning. We are talking about a foundation that must be accepted before we can say of anything that it is known or true. But then it cannot itself be known or true. So we should not speak of accepted truth here.

We have seen that the propositions belonging to our *Vor-Wissen* hang together in a system, albeit a loose system. This system constitutes our *Weltbild*. This world-picture is the common ground we share with others in our culture; it comprises those deeply embedded elements that make communication, understanding, action, and a common life possible within a culture. Without such a shared *Weltbild*, we could not understand either our own words and actions or those of others with whom we come in contact.

I have spoken of the type of propositions, like Moore's propositions, that constitute our *Weltbild*, but if Wittgenstein is right, they cannot be known to be true or false and thus they are not after all, strictly speaking, propositions. The *Vor-Wissen* is prepropositional certainty of action. Our quest for justification comes to an end not in "self-evident knowledge" or necessary truths or "truths of reason" but in *praxis*, in action. It is for this reason that Wittgenstein takes as his slogan Faust's "Im Anfang war die Tat" rather than the biblical "In the beginning was the Word."[18]

Justification, as Wittgenstein remarks, must come to an end; and, when we push back to the point where the structure of our *Weltbild* begins to be revealed, where what is being appealed to is our system of convictions, we must in the end just say, "this is what we do"; "this is the way we act and respond and *we cannot think or act or respond otherwise*." (These are not logical necessities. Are they then necessities of human nature or are they necessities of culture, i.e., of *our* human culture?)[19]

In an attempt to make evident what is involved here, let me note and then comment on some passages in Wittgenstein that attempt to give substance to these dark sayings. I start with #100 on page 15 of *On Certainty.*

100.   The truths which Moore says he knows are such as, roughly speaking, all of us know, if he knows them.

101.   Such a proposition might be e.g. "My body has never disappeared and reappeared again after an interval."

102.   Might I not believe that once, without knowing it, perhaps in a state of unconsciousness, I was taken far away from the earth—that other people even know this, but do not mention it to me? But this would not fit into the rest of my convictions at all.   Not that I could describe the system of these convictions. Yet my convictions do form a system, a structure.

103.   And now if I were to say "It is my unshakable conviction that etc.", this means in the present case too that I have not consciously arrived at the conviction by following a particular line of thought, but that it is anchored in all my questions and answers, so anchored that I cannot touch it.

104.   I am for example also convinced that the sun is not a hole in the vault of heaven.

105.   All testing, all confirmation and disconfirmation of a hypothesis takes place already within a system.   And this system is not a more or less arbitrary and doubtful point of departure for all our arguments: no, it belongs to the essence of what we call an argument.   The system is not so much the point of departure, as the element in which arguments have their life.

106.   Suppose some adult had told a child that he had been on the moon.   The child tells me the story, and I say it was only a joke, the man hadn't been on the moon; no one has ever been on the moon; the moon is a long way off and it is impossible to climb up there or fly there. —If now the child insists, saying perhaps there is a way of getting there which I don't know, etc. what reply could I make to him?   What reply could I make to the adults of a tribe who believe that people sometimes go to the moon (perhaps that is how they interpret their dreams), and who indeed grant that there are no ordinary means of climbing up to it or flying there? —But a child will not ordinarily stick to such a belief and will soon be convinced by what we tell him seriously.

107.   Isn't this altogether like the way one can instruct a child to believe in a God, or that none exists, and it will accordingly be able to produce apparently telling grounds for the one or the other?

108.   "But is there then no objective truth?   Isn't it true, or false, that someone has been on the moon?"   If we are thinking within our system, then it is certain that no one has ever been on the moon.   Not merely is nothing of the sort ever seriously

reported to us by reasonable people, but our whole system of physics forbids us to believe it. For this demands answers to the questions "How did he overcome the force of gravity?" "How could he live without an atmosphere?" and a thousand others which could not be answered. But suppose that instead of all these answers we met the reply: "We don't know *how* one gets to the moon, but those who get there know at once that they are there; and even you can't explain everything." We should feel ourselves intellectually very distant from someone who said this.

109. "An empirical proposition can be *tested*" (we say). But how? and through what?

110. What *counts* as its test? —"But is this an adequate test? And, if so, must it not be recognizable as such in logic?" —As if giving grounds did not come to an end sometime. But the end is not an ungrounded presupposition: it is an ungrounded way of acting.

Our *Vor-Wissen* includes "The sun is not a hole in the vault of heaven," "My body has never disappeared and reappeared again after an interval," and it once did include "No one has ever been on the moon" and still does include "No one has ever been in the Milky Way" and "No one has ever roasted marshmallows on the sun." The remark about the moon might be thought to show that Wittgenstein, like Hegel, was making a priori dicta about the advance of science. But that is a confusion. In #108 above Wittgenstein makes it very evident that where there is no way, utilizing our system of physics, to make any kind of answer to how one overcame the force of gravity or how one could live without the atmosphere and the like, then nothing of this sort could be intelligibly claimed. Now, standing technologically and scientifically where we are now, these questions can be answered and we can sensibly (truly or falsely) say that so and so has or hasn't been on the moon. But without that background—that scientific background—we cannot so speak, just as we cannot now for "I traveled to the Milky Way last night." My not having been in the Milky Way is far more certain that any grounds (evidence) I could give for claiming it to be true or false.[20] Moore's "commonsense" propositions are as sure as any grounds he or we could give for them. There is no finding anything more certain than they are to support them, to show them to be either true or false. And if it is replied that they are not as sure as analytic or necessary truths, it is evident that Wittgenstein's response has not to be taken to heart that "if you are not certain of any fact, you cannot be certain of the meaning of your words either".[21]

With his tough strain of anti-Platonism, Wittgenstein also points out that we cannot lay out the propositions of our *Vor-Wissen*—the framework or hinge beliefs of our system—as we could the axioms, rules, and theorems of an axiomatic system. We cannot discuss the totality of our system of convictions or render a unified, perspicuous display of its structure. In this way we can give no grand or wide-ranging synthesis. But we can describe certain parts of the *Vor-Wissen* and recognize *ambulando* how they are bits of the bedrock of our system and how they relate to each other. We have no idea what the totality of our background beliefs is or even would be like and thus we cannot state that totality.

It is also important to take note of Wittgenstein's claim that "all testing, all confirmation and disconfirmation of a hypothesis takes place already within a system."[22] Our arguments and investigations have their life within that system; there is no possibility of testing, investigating, confirming, disconfirming, or falsifying outside of or without reasoning and categorizing in accordance with some system of categories and some mode of conceptualization with its *Vor-Wissen* or framework propositions that cannot themselves at least on that occasion be tested. They determine within that framework what counts as a test and what is an adequate test. But they themselves cannot be so tested within that system any more than the yardstick can measure itself, though in accordance with *some other* system, with its own distinctive categories and mode of conceptualization, they could, in a way, be tested. But then these other categories in turn are not testable within that system at that time, though they again may be testable in accordance with the norms of yet another system. In the quest for justification, we must eventually come on a cluster of categories and modes of conceptualizing that constitute a part of a *Vor-Wissen*, which are not justified, not tested, not grounded but simply utilized and acted upon. If the need arises—something in one way or another arising out of our lives as a genuinely practical matter—we can, outside that system and in accord with the norms of some other system, assess that system. Or more likely we can, working within a part of the system, criticize and perhaps radically revise or even jettison that part of the system that has become problematic. But we must beware of reifying the system as if it were some entity or fixed reality that did not change or had fixed boundaries. We should also keep in mind what the relevance of the assessment mentioned above is. Moreover, it is not obvious how we can assess whole systems. *At any given time*, we must operate with some cluster of groundless beliefs we accept and do not justify. Wittgenstein puts his core claims tersely in #401 and #402.

> 401. I want to say: propositions of the form of empirical proposi-
> tions, and not only propositions of logic, form the foundation
> of all operating with thoughts....
>
> 402. In this remark the expression "propositions of the form of
> empirical propositions" is itself thoroughly bad; the statements
> in question are statements about material objects. And they
> do not serve as foundations in the same way as hypotheses
> which, if they turn out to be false, are replaced by others.
> "...*und schreibe getrost Im Anfang war die Tat.*"[23]

It is through the certainties of my way of behaving and responding that I gain my most fundamental understanding.

IV

The system of bedrock convictions constituting our *Weltbild* is not, as I have remarked, like an axiomatic system any more than language is like a calculus. It has no fixed boundary; indeed it is crisscrossed and replete with ad hoc additions, so that Wittgenstein's analogy with an ancient city is apt. It is also, as von Wright observes, of a very inhomogeneous composition. It is "an agglomeration of a huge number of subsystems, each with a fluctuating boundary and a 'mixed' content."[24] Knowing, believing, imagining, dreaming, praying, declaiming, asserting, questioning, surmising, pretending, bargaining, negotiating, chiding, contending and promising are all such subsystems and are matched with distinctive language games. ("the concept of knowing is coupled with that of the language-game." #560) Indeed a language game is a distinctive doing things with words, as when we negotiate or claim to know or assert or question or pray or complain. Von Wright remarks, attempting to capture Wittgenstein's meaning, "that every language game has a foundation which is a fragment of the players' *Vor-Wissen*."[25]

Language games are no more rigidly ordered than is an ancient city; indeed they are not even hierarchically ordered, though some language games are either genetically or logically prior to others and some are at least partially parasitic on others and some are more deeply embedded in our *Weltbild* than others. But the diverse bedrock convictions, the *Vor-Wissen*, that lie at the base of these diverse language games are without exception neither true nor false, justified nor unjustified, reasonable nor unreasonable. And our *Weltbild*—the system of such convictions—is neither true nor false.[26] "If the true," Wittgenstein remarks, "is what is grounded, then the ground is not true, nor yet false."[27] Yet why say "the true is what is grounded"? Can't a statement be true, as we found Goldman stressing, even though it is not known to be true or even reasonably believed to be true? That it is true, given that it is thoroughly unreasonable to believe it, is, let us say, astronomically improbable, but still might it not just turn out to be true all the same? Why can't there be ungrounded truths? (This, of course, does not imply that there can be unknowable truths.) Yet, who could justifiably *claim* or assert such ungrounded truths? Does it make any sense at all to speak of "*justifiably* claimed but *ungrounded* truths" or "*warrantedly* asserted but *ungrounded* truths"? But given what Wittgenstein says about testing or knowing bedrock convictions (framework beliefs), and given what he says about our *Weltbild* being neither true nor false, resolving disputes before what John Wisdom calls "the bar of reason" can only take place—or so it would seem at least—within a system and about considerations internal to the framework. We cannot intelligibly argue about the adequacy or the rationality or truth of the framework itself. In a world-picture—a system of bedrock convictions—we find subsystems of convictions that are the various foundations (no one set of things being *the* foundation) of our various language games. The "world-picture-itself, in its prepropositional stage," as von Wright remarks, "could also be called a *form of life*."[28] What form or forms of life we have is shown by what we do and how we respond. It is shown, that is, in our lives. So, simplifying a bit, we can say that a form of life is a loose and indeed homogeneous system of primitive convictions and a language-embedded mode of action that sets the basic outlines of the way the world is viewed for a particular people. The ways of acting that constitute the subdivisions of this form of life are the foundation of those distinctive ways of doing things with words we call language games. Neither the world-picture, the form of life, nor the language games stand in need of justification nor can they be justified. They are appealed to, implicitly or explicitly, in all justification but, Wittgenstein contends, cannot be justified themselves. This does not mean that they are unjustified. Rather, it means that the concepts of being justified or unjustified have no home here.

V

What are we to say when there is either a clash between the adherents of two world-pictures or when, within a given world-picture, a person comes to reject or to try to question that world-picture? Wittgenstein must say that the rejection or overall criticism of a world picture is something that the person or persons in question could not be *justified* in doing, but it is equally the case that he should also say that they are not *unjustified* in doing it either. The consequence of Wittgenstein's position is that the very notions of justification or a lack of justification have no hold or application here. But then there should be no hint of a rebuke by suggesting that the rejection is unjustified. It is a nonrational matter that is neither justified nor unjustified.

However, Wittgenstein also jarringly remarks, hardly in the above spirit, that we would say of a person rejecting his own world-picture that he was mentally deranged, though he is not in error. But isn't that simply using "mentally deranged" as an emotive label? And could it possibly be justified in terms of Wittgenstein's own doctrine about how justification comes to an end? Yet surely isn't there good sense in Wittgenstein's remark that "if Moore were to pronounce the opposite of those propositions which he declares certain, we should not just not share his opinion: we should regard him as demented"?[29] But we need also to realize, as von Wright remarks and Wittgenstein in effect concedes, that in some circumstances the difference in action would not reflect a mental defect on the part of one disputant but would reflect a deep difference in culture. Wittgenstein says that no argument or justification is in order here, though there can be *persuasion* leading to conversion.[30]

(But can't there be *rational* persuasion? But what does *that* come
to in such a context where our *Weltbild* is in conflict with another
and in which one is used to combat the other?) We should also
ask if our *Weltbilder* are ever so discrete, so isolated from each
other. (Here the discussion of Davidson in the previous chapter is
relevant. Putnam, in continuing to defend conceptual relativism
against Davidson, does not give us alternative *Weltbilder* but some
alternative logical systems. But this does not show any kind of
global incommensurability.) We should not think of *Weltbilder* as if
they were axiomatic systems. So what are we to say about these
deep differences in world-views, where both practices and beliefs
seem at least to so diversely conflict, or so deeply go their own
ways, that we do not know how we could make comparative assessments of reasonability? It is understandable, given that, that there
would be a longing for an Archimedean point. But if Wittgenstein
is right we can make no coherent sense of such a desire, for we can
conceive of nothing coherent that would satisfy that desire.

VI

Wittgenstein remarks that "it is so difficult to find the
beginning. Or, better, it is difficult to begin at the beginning. And
not try to go further back."[31] And surely this is the pickle we are
in with what we are trying to do here when we look for foundations
or some fundamental systematizing justificatory perspective. (They
need not, of course, come to the same thing.)
Perhaps one such starting place is with the simple recognition that we indeed unavoidably do learn many things quite uncritically that we do not ground. As Wittgenstein put it: "The child
learns to believe a host of things, i.e., it learns to act according to
those beliefs. Bit by bit there forms a system of what is believed,
and in that system some things stand unshakably fast and some are
more or less liable to shift. What stands just does so, not because
it is intrinsically obvious or convincing; it is rather held fast by what
lies around it."[32] We first learn not single propositions but "a whole
system of propositions."[33] (Here Wittgenstein, Quine, and Davidson
make common cause.) They provide us with the particular interpretation of our experience. We do not read them off from our

experience.[34]   There are certain things in this system—*perhaps* "cluster" would be a better word—that stand fast and are not questioned. Indeed the child, or for that matter the adult who emerges from this socialization, hardly has an understanding of what to do to question these propositions. We know how to question the claim that it is likely that it will snow in the mountains next week and that the elk will begin moving to lower altitudes. But we do not understand what it would be like to query "Things do not disappear without cause." Indeed, if you want, you can say it is abundantly verified—all my experience shows that it is so—but we cannot even conceive of what experiences could count against it, if we were to have them. Verification, if it were to take place, would be quite asymmetrically related to falsification, confirmation to infirmation, and this, of course, makes us wonder if indeed there is or could be any verification or confirmation here at all. Isn't it just a groundless way we have of interpreting our experience?

In that way, among the various propositions we come to believe, a whole host of them with at least the form of empirical propositions stand fast for us, indeed some stand unshakably fast. They may come to have a somewhat puzzling logical status, but nonetheless they are, or at least appear to be, empirical propositions, not conceptual ones. Moore's "commonsense propositions" are among them. They stand unshakably fast for us. Yet Wittgenstein also contends that they do not do so because they are "intrinsically obvious or convincing." They do so because of what lies around them: because they form a web or a system of intermeshing beliefs, though some are deeply embedded hinge beliefs in the system. There is, moreover, no way of "standing outside" this system of beliefs and assessing them as a whole or of even in some reasoned way rejecting the hinge beliefs among them piecemeal. The hinge beliefs are too interlocked with a whole system of belief for this to be possible. We have no idea what it would be like to stand outside the system without concepts and criteria borrowed from the system and to make such appraisals. We live and act and think within systems we simply are socialized into, systems we passively imbibe and learn to take on trust. What we hold fast to "is not *one* proposition but a nest of propositions."[35]

However, could not the skeptic—call him a Cartesian skeptic if you will—say that although for practical purposes these propositions do stand fast with us that there still is no conceptual ban on our questioning them? It might be claimed that we understand perfectly well what we are doing when we do that. And there are plenty of things we do not question that we could at least in principle question. They are in fact groundless beliefs but they are not beliefs concerning which the very idea of finding grounds for them rests on a mistake. Moore's propositions and a host of like propositions, the response goes, are of that sort. We don't have grounds for them, but there is no good reason to think that grounds could not intelligibly be sought out and found.

Wittgenstein thinks this is an illusion. He plainly does not think that experience can have no critical role in the assessment of belief or that, despite the above remarks about socialization, we are utter prisoners of our socialization. He says, what almost all of us would, "I learned an enormous amount and accepted it on human authority, and then I found some things confirmed or disconfirmed by my own experience."[36] And he is not defending, as framework beliefs or hinge beliefs, groundless opinions arbitrarily held. But he also thinks, as we have seen, that framework beliefs have no ground and that there is no way of assessing whole systems of belief and action, or of showing them to be reasonable or unreasonable. So where do we stand here? How do these conceptions fit together? Or is any attempt to fit them a forced fitting?

VII

The following may put them together. We think within an inherited belief system that we just learn and take on trust, and we do not know how to think outside that system. What such thinking "outside that system" would be is utterly opaque. But the system is not fixed and is nothing like a formal, axiomized system. To use Wittgenstein's own analogy, like an ancient city, our culturally inherited belief system is very old and has many layers with many more or less ad hoc additions. It is more or less continuously changing, though slowly. It is not something that we could in some holistic way streamline and make into a modern, geometrically planned city. This does not rule out, for limited, determinant purposes, improvements along the way. But this is a far cry from grand philosophical rational reconstructions that would render the whole system more rational or more perspicuous.

Look at what is involved here from a somewhat different angle. There is no way of challenging this system—this *Weltbild*—as a whole. However, in the interaction of this network of complex parts—which occurs as human beings act and interact—and with the development of thought and with continued human action, some beliefs will come into conflict or at least will not fit well together or there will come to be anomalous situations. With such eventualities, certain beliefs, including sometimes rather central beliefs, though *seriatim*, will come to be questioned. The questioning here, as the pragmatists stressed, will be a live questioning in the context of actual inquiry and not a ritualistic Cartesian questioning. Where beliefs are so queried, it becomes appropriate to ask what evidence we have for them or (where appropriate) what other grounds there are for them. Thus at one point in time it would have been utterly senseless to say someone in Boston talked with someone in London. But as the science and technology was coming on stream that made the invention and the construction of the telephone feasible, such talk came to make perfectly unproblematic sense. (Earlier we saw a similar case about going to the moon.) There are other hinge propositions that are so central, e.g., "TV sets do not disappear into thin air" or "Human beings do not change into toads," that, though these propositions are not analytic, the idea of their being critically assessed and possibly being abandoned makes no sense. We have no understanding at all of what it would be like for such propositions to be disconfirmed or even infirmed. If they went, our whole system of thought would go, and without that system we would have no understanding at all.

There is a great mass of such propositions that all people have whose socialization in societies such as our own has been at all normal. Some of them are so animal, in that way so basic, that all peoples in all societies have had them. And they are propositions (if that is the right word) that people are perfectly certain about. Thus I am certain that I am a human being, have a head, live on the earth, was once a child, will die, need food to live, that a woman gave birth to me, that while still alive I will not turn into stone, and the like. None of these propositions is an analytic or conceptual truth, but *if* I could doubt them I could equally well

doubt that any given, allegedly analytic proposition was really
analytic or that any mathematical calculation was correct or that any
alleged demonstration was really a demonstration.   If someone
brought forth what appeared to be disconfirming evidence for them,
I would, facing that evidence, think I had gone mad rather than
accept such alleged evidence.   If I saw or thought I saw a live
human being turning into stone while still talking and laughing, I
should conclude, even after he was all stone, that I was deranged
rather than to take these appearances at face value.

   There are myriads of such propositions (propositions like the
ones I have just cited)—propositions with a rather empirical look
that seldom (if ever) get expressed—that are objectively certain and
are, at least in practice, taken to be so by normal people within our
culture.   (I do not deny that many of them, perhaps most of them,
have a similar status in other cultures as well.)   These propositions,
to repeat, are not conceptual truths, something true by at least
implicit definition, yet their falsity is inconceivable.   We are certain
of them; they are, whatever their status, not open for us to doubt.
It is not just that we feel certain about them but that for people
such as ourselves their not being in place is an incoherency.

VIII

   Perhaps it is logically possible to *imagine* a culture in which
people had not been socialized into taking such beliefs on trust, but
it is not clear that it is, and there plainly are no actual cultures that
lack those beliefs.   And, to repeat, when we think about them we
realize that to jettison any of them would be in effect to call into
question everything we need to even be able to think and question.
Propositions of which we can be certain are numerous, but how do
we determine which propositions are to have such membership?
We are certain we are human beings and that we have heads, but
we are not certain our toenails will continue to grow after we die or
that we must have a pancreas to live.   The latter two things could
be doubted, and without evidence for them they are hardly
warrantedly assertable; the former do not require evidence but are
still not analytic.   So there are nonanalytic propositions for which
evidence is required and there are nonanalytic propositions that do

not require evidence. Indeed, we do not even know what it would be like to have evidence for them. How do we decide to include or exclude propositions in the list of nonanalytic propositions? The psychological feeling of certainty would surely not do the trick. People can be psychologically certain, what Wittgenstein calls subjectively certain, of the strangest things.[37] I knew someone once who claimed to be certain that plants had feelings. And there are many people with similarly exotic beliefs they sometimes hang on to quite tenaciously. Yet they are beliefs that seem to most of us to be quite unintelligible. (Is that just the big battalions speaking?)

We are not infrequently certain such that we believe that there is no *intelligible option* to what we are certain of for members of our culture or for others that we can envisage as thinking and acting like beings who are recognizably human. (This means that we take them to be something other than culturally conventional matters.) That we can imagine "desert island" cases is of little interest unless we could, filling in the details, imagine the desert island case in concrete detail to be something that could actually obtain. (Recall the moon example.) A word-picture is not sufficient. Thus what would it be like, given our understanding of the world, for us really to be live human beings without heads? Too much of what we understand about being a human being is tied up with our having a head to make this coherently thinkable. But this example aside, how do we decide when this is so? I do not know how to state this generally, though I do not want to deny that this *perhaps* could be done. It may be the case that there is no general demarcation principle here. But it is plain by looking at particular cases in detail that we become aware that some such things are not coherently thinkable for us. There are things about which a mistake is just not possible. We could not be mistaken in our belief that we are human beings.[38] And I could not be mistaken about my belief that the earth has existed a long time before my birth. As Wittgenstein put it, "If I wanted to doubt the existence of the earth long before my birth, I should have to doubt all sorts of things that stand fast for me."[39] Norman Malcolm puts Wittgenstein's central point well when he remarks that Wittgenstein is saying that "there are specific fixed points in my understanding of my life and world, such that if they were taken away I could not think at all."[40]

In thought-experiments Wittgenstein imagines all sorts of wild occurrences that might be employed to put such objective certainties in doubt (beliefs a person might have that could not be mistaken). Where such pressure is put on belief, one of Wittgenstein's responses—a response that seems to me a powerful one—is that if I were told things designed to show that earth had not existed for many years before my birth or that I was really not a human being, there would certainly also be something in those considerations (alleged disconfirming evidence) "that made the grounds of these doubts themselves seem doubtful, and I could therefore decide to retain my old belief."[41]   The claim made by someone that at night in my sleep I turned into a deer and then in the morning turned back into a human being just before I woke up, no matter how many people claimed to have witnessed it, would not be something I had as much reason to accept as the belief that I am a human being and that such things cannot happen to me.

What we do is refuse to accept any of the alleged evidence against our belief that we are human beings or that the world existed for many years before we were born. These claims are not open to disconfirmation. This is not foot-stamping, pig-headed blindness as it would be if we refused to consider any of the alleged evidence that a son of ours had shoplifted or that the sea is becoming increasingly polluted. That would be evasive, though in the shoplifting case understandable. But in the case of such framework beliefs, such hinge beliefs, such a resistance is a mark of sanity: a refusal to be caught up by a beguiling philosophical mythology, a refusal to play a philosopher's game. Skepticism here is senseless.

IX

Yet in spite of this qualified rationally reconstructed defense of Moorean common sense, Wittgenstein is deeply historicist. Unlike Moore, he is skeptical concerning what we can know when it comes to framework beliefs. These framework beliefs are those we—"we" as a people—accept on trust. They are primitive certainties we take on trust, and must take on trust, without question as something in accordance with which we will orient our lives. They are not matters of knowledge or inquiry. Malcolm importantly remarks:

> Let us return to the question of whether we *know* that unheard of events will not occur—events of a kind such that if they were to occur they would at least *seem* to us to contradict some of our fundamental certainties. If we reflect on what Wittgenstein reminds us of—that learning is based on believing: that most of what we know or think we know of history or science rests largely on trust—then it seems clear that not one of us is in a position to *know* that unheard-of occurrences will not take place. As Wittgenstein puts it: if someone declared that he *knows* that it will never seem to him as if anything contradicted some fundamental certainty of his—what would this tell us other than *just* that he is *confident* that this will never happen? Surely no one could *prove* that it could *not* happen.[42]

We have no proof and indeed we do not know what it would be like to get proof here, but we still have utterly firm, primitive certainties, what Wittgenstein calls objective certainties, that we cannot but take on trust. We have no idea of alternatives here. The idea that such beliefs might be mistaken can in no way find feet with us. We do not even understand what it would be like for the assertion of such primitive certainties to be false or their denials to be something we could genuinely entertain. We do not regard ourselves as infallible, but likewise we would regard it as nonsensical to suppose that such assertions might be false or in some other way mistaken.[43]

The distance between Wittgenstein and the confident assertion of a Moorean commonsense realism comes out in this way. We have—as we can see in the appeal of G. E. Moore—an overwhelming temptation to believe that reality must agree with our certainty. Wittgenstein tells us this is a mistake. We can have no knowledge of the kind Moore claims, rather, some things are to be taken on trust without even the possibility of questioning. Our primitive certainties are not bits of knowledge, but we need to recognize our knowledge, resting on them as it does, rests on trust.

However, matters do not stop here, for we also need to understand "how there can be no guarantee that we will not be staggered by unheard occurrences" and how the very "fact that being perfectly or absolutely certain of something is no more than an attitude of ours, and as such does not bind reality."[44] Even where you cannot conceive how we could be wrong, it is nevertheless not impossible that we are wrong. We are not, Wittgenstein stresses, infallible. Being thus mistaken is possible with respect to me as an individual—as it is for any individual—for there may be possibilities that I have not taken into account and could not grasp even if they were pointed out to me. Nonetheless, there are some things, Wittgenstein claims, that we as users of language, as people who play distinctive language games, who enter into forms of life, could not doubt—*collectively* could not doubt. And for those things there is no room for being wrong. If these are called into question, our very capacity to reason—to enter into forms of life, to play language games—would be undermined so that our ability to think coherently would be eroded, eroded so deeply that we would not understand how things stand with us or how it is that we can reason at all. We could not even reflect on our bafflement.

We should not think here of our thoughts, the primitive certainties we have, as either agreeing or failing to agree with reality. We cannot get that far here. There is no room for either realism or antirealism. With respect to many fundamental beliefs, such as the belief that we are human beings and that the earth has existed for many years before we were born, we do not know what it would be like for them to agree or fail to agree with reality. Rather, what we need to recognize is that no clear sense can be given *either* to our thinking that maybe things are other than what we are certain of here *or* to our thinking that maybe in trying to think about "alternatives" to such framework beliefs we are not capable of thinking any coherent thoughts at all.[45] People who have been subject to such language learning—who have simply been so drilled—would be able to see *ambulando* for particular cases that there are things toward which no question of their truth *or* falsity could arise.[46] We have no understanding of what it would be like to set such beliefs aside; are just caught in the web of such beliefs we cannot question.[47] We have no understanding of what it would be like to stand outside them and question them.[48]

X

These primitive certainties give us—or seem to give us—something to break the wheel of a thoroughgoing and uncompromising relativism as well as *philosophical* skepticism.   Moreover, Wittgenstein's account in *On Certainty* enables us to break with the metaphysical tradition and to set aside foundationalist quests as well as grand-scale demands for coherence.   But we also come to see that we have (though they are not foundationalist claims) primitive certainties we cannot coherently deny.   But, as we have seen, this goes with a resolute rejection of classical foundationalist claims to self-evident knowledge, or even to the lesser claims of some "privileged knowledge" of more modest forms of foundationalism. Traditional forms of epistemological inquiry are quite pointless if Wittgenstein's arguments in *On Certainty* are near to the mark.   A worry remains whether, given the way we have these primitive certainties, Wittgenstein's account does not, after all, yield a relativism which is deeply paradoxical and does not square with our reflective expectations. (But perhaps there is something wrong with our reflective expectations?)

XI

Returning to the claims made at the beginning of this chapter, we should note that Wittgenstein does enable us to see both how many perfectly mundane things hang together in an unexceptionally mundane way and that there is no possibility of doing the philosophical thing and doubting these mundane realities, e.g., that live human beings have heads.   But he does this without giving us anything like a synthesis, even an Arnold-like seeing things together and seeing them whole, a moralistic and philosophically unencumbered seeing things whole.   He not only does not attempt this himself, he does nothing to suggest the feasibility of such a project.   The value of his therapeutic philosophical activity comes from the demolishing of the Tradition, that is, demolishing grand philosophical claims and aims as they have been passed on to us from the Tradition of metaphysical speculation and argument.   But they get demolished without our falling into a skepticism or nihilism. These houses of cards come tumbling down, but knowing we have this interlocking cluster of primitive certainties—certainties sufficient to set aside philosophical skepticism—does not yield us a system of beliefs that will enable us to make (moral and human) sense of our

lives together. Getting rid of philosophical skepticism and metaphysical quests is one thing; making sense of our lives together is
another.

Rorty, like a good pragmatist, wished to see philosophy
conceived as a disciplinary matrix replaced by a kind of philosophical
activity that renewed the Socratic quest for making sense of our
lives, though not in the way Wittgenstein found that quest objection-
able.[49] But the Wittgenstein of *On Certainty*, or for that matter of
Philosophical Investigations, is—and self-consciously so—of no help to
us here. Gaining the kind of understanding that would enable us to
break with the Tradition will give us no guidance at all, except
negatively, in making sense of our lives. It will, however, enable us
to live, indeed to flourish, *without a philosophical culture as traditionally conceived* and in that way—taking the fly out of the bottle—
it will help free us and emancipate us from the tyranny of philosophical obsessions.

On Certainty and *Philosophical Investigations* can only help us
negatively here. Negatively, it will tell us that metaphysical quests
(including religio-metaphysical quests) will be of no help with the
problems of life, the problems of our age, problems concerning the
meaning of our lives. However, it is also the case that Wittgenstein's perspicuous representations—reminders assembled for a
particular purpose—will be of no *positive* help to us here either.
But, of course, Wittgenstein never thought that they would, should,
or even could. We could utterly agree with what in effect is
Wittgenstein's metaphilosophy and remain, quite consistently, the
bleakest of nihilists. But there is what Stanley Cavell calls Wittgenstein's philosophy of culture.[50] Yet this side of Wittgenstein (most
fully shown in von Wright's collection of notes called *Culture and
Value*), though compatible with the metaphilosophical account of
Philosophical Investigations and *On Certainty*, does not follow from
it and is not rationalized by it. Someone agreeing with, and taking
to heart, the claims of *Philosophical Investigations* and *On Certainty*
need not accept at all the *Lebensphilosophie* of *Culture and Value*.
One could accept the Enlightenment views that Wittgenstein with
his religiose sensitivities regards as shallow, and still enthusiastically
accept Wittgenstein's dismantling of the Tradition. Wittgenstein, as
philosopher of culture with a *Lebensphilosophie* (to use two preten-
tious philosophical terms), gives us sometimes interesting and

sometimes rather silly views about human destiny and the state of our culture. They place him firmly in a Central European culture that was coming to an end. But these views, whatever their intrinsic merit or demerit, have no ground in or rationale in the powerfully articulated metaphilosophical conceptions of Wittgenstein, his, if you will, antiphilosophical philosophical theses. (Wittgenstein repeatedly denied that he articulated philosophical theses, but this is a posture, a self-deception, for, as the characterization of *On Certainty* in the previous sections brings out, there are philosophical theses galore in Wittgenstein's work.) One could be a happy Neurathian positivist with socialist/communist social views (views Neurath himself had) and yet, without any great shift, come enthusiastically to accept Wittgenstein's metaphilosophy as an advance over a more tradition-bound, holistic positivism. But what such a Neurathian would not accept, could not accept without a wild shift in position beyond smallish technical realignments in the analytic tradition, is Wittgenstein's thoroughly negative and culturally snobbish attitude toward science. But nothing is lost in Wittgenstein's philosophy (philosophy as recognizable in the analytical tradition) if that is set aside.

XII

What is this "philosophy of culture" side of Wittgenstein? Whatever it is, it no more yields, or even tries to yield, a synthetic view of things than does Wittgenstein's metaphilosophy. Cavell rightly stresses that a kind of moral intensity runs through Wittgenstein's work, an intensity that neither your ordinary scientistically oriented or traditionally metaphysically oriented philosopher has.[51] It is equally foreign to both Carl Hempel and David Armstrong. (We should keep in mind that though moral intensity plainly has its place, it may have no proper place in philosophy.) In the service of philosophical therapy, we seek to get a sufficiently perspicuous understanding of things (assembling reminders for a particular purpose) to break philosophical perplexity, but we must all the same live, if Wittgenstein is close to the mark, without either synthesis or foundations. Wittgenstein gives no encouragement at all to the view that we may come by disciplined and nonevasive reflection to one day see things together and as a whole. His moral intensity is not directed toward the achievement of such an Arnold-like vision or toward anything bearing even a family resemblance to that conception of the vocation of an intellectual.

Wittgenstein had—at least given what philosophers typically think—striking cultural attitudes that are not at all that of a happy positivist. Von Wright, quite properly, speaks of his "all too obvious alienation from his times."[52] In *Culture and Value*, in an entry from 1930, Wittgenstein speaks of our time as not being a time of high culture. Indeed, he adds, it is an "age without culture," and he goes on to remark that "I have no sympathy for the current of European civilization and do not understand its goals, if it has any."[53] And in 1949, understandably enough, he speaks of the degradation that has so deeply seeped into our cultural life.[54] He has no sympathy at all for the secularized, progressive, scientistic civilization of Europe and North America with its Enlightenment beliefs in progress and its faith in science and technology.[55] Fascism, communism and U. S. business culture all disgust him. Like Oswald Spengler, who much influenced him in these matters, he thinks Western civilization and its characteristic values of "high culture" are dying out and will be replaced by a barbaric scientistic age.[56]

In 1947 he remarks:

> Science and industry, and their progress, might turn out to be the most enduring thing in the modern world. Perhaps any speculation about a coming collapse of science and industry is, for the present and for a *long* time to come, nothing but a dream; perhaps science and industry, having caused infinite misery in the process, will unite the world—I mean condense it into a *single* unit, though one in which peace is the last thing that will find a home.[57]

This disgust with our age, with its scientism, secularism, Enlightenment belief in progress, and the like, together with a belief that it is unlikely that this state of affairs will soon, if at all, be turned around, made Wittgenstein a cultural pessimist and led to his having a curious attitude toward religion. I shall get at this rather indirectly. His attitudes toward life were deeply religious without his being able to believe. Still, his pessimism and his disgust with and censure of our culture notwithstanding, he did believe that one day there would perhaps be another culture, very different from an Enlightenment culture and with different patterns of life and different values. We are not so much in the iron cage—Wittgenstein's cultural pessimism is not that confining—that we view this change as simply being impossible.[58] Moreover, because he says that perhaps one day this civilization will produce a culture, where culture (*"Kultur"*) is used in T. S. Eliot's sense of "High Culture," it is evident that at least sometimes Wittgenstein thinks that forms of life do not just change but that they change, though not as the Enlightenment would have it, for the better. Yet there is nothing in Wittgenstein's philosophy ("philosophy" now construed analytically) that would justify that. It is a cultural judgment of Wittgenstein's, whatever its worth, that stands or falls on its own.

XIII

His rejection of our modern, technologically oriented civilization runs very deep. The spirit of this civilization is alien and uncongenial to him. There is, as he sees things, no progress, salvation, or even an amelioration of the human condition through the intelligent use of science, and there are no laws of social development, or at least none that we can discover, so that one could plot humanity's progress.[59] Such conceptions are, he would have it, at best mythological. (We see his distance from Marxism.) Wittgenstein, like his Viennese contemporary, Freud, has no vision of the future and, again like Freud, Wittgenstein is a cultural pessimist. But unlike Freud, who was a late Enlightenment thinker, Wittgenstein suffered from a nostalgia for the past.[60]

A philosophy of culture would at the very least, but still essentially, articulate an attitude toward its times. Although *Investigations* and *On Certainty* may obliquely hint at this from time to time, it is surely not their main or even subsidiary or ancillary aim. However, the notes collected in *Culture and Value* do. There are comments, as we have seen, on the decay of our times and the greatness of times past, on progress, the badness of science and technology and of what has come to be called (but not by Wittgenstein) the evils of the ideology of scientism.[61] There are extensive remarks about religion and the meaning of life, about Jewishness, music, architecture, Shakespeare, Mahler, Mendelssohn, and the like. We see through them or by means of them, though not terribly clearly, Wittgenstein's attitude, understanding, and bleak assessment of these times.

One aspect of that—and very different from "happy positivism"—is the attitude toward religion Wittgenstein evinced. Wittgenstein takes a respectful stance toward religion and toward Christianity in particular. He takes Christianity to be perplexing but still of vital significance in making sense of our lives, if this "making sense" is to have any kind of depth. Like Kierkegaard, Wittgenstein believes it is one's sense of worthlessness and despair that drives one to God, and that only in belief in God will one find surcease for that, if indeed one can find surcease at all. The religious person, by contrast with the nonreligious person, has a certain kind of depth and sensitivity. On Wittgenstein's view, atheistic critiques of God and religion, where it is said either that the concept of God is incoherent or that it is a mistake to speak of the reality of God because all such assertions are false (or very probably false), exhibit shallowness, superficiality, and a failure to understand the language games of religion, including what is meant by God. A culture without religion would be a superficial culture that could make no sense of the significance of life.[62] In all these remarks Wittgenstein's way of thinking is in stark contrast with that of Schlick, Neurath, Moore, Russell, Ayer, Carnap, and Quine. It sets him in sharp contrast with the other founding figures of analytical philosophy and, more generally, with the dominant, secular intellectual culture. He has much more in common in this respect with Pascal and Kierkegaard than with Russell and Moore.

Both in his more technically philosophical works and in his remarks on life and culture, Wittgenstein creates a certain ambience that gives a sense of depth one never feels in reading Ayer, for example. Ayer, all through his life, though in slightly modified forms, carried on the foundationalist quest of British empiricism. Here he is a true heir of Hume and Russell. Given the powerful undermining of foundationalism by recent philosophy, Ayer's stance and preoccupations can come to seem rather quaint and distant from what it is now plausible to say as a bit of philosophy. But when Ayer turns to questions of the meaning of life and of religion—and here again he is like Russell—he is a pillar of sturdy Humean common sense, toughness, and nonevasiveness. He comes much closer here to telling it like it is than does Wittgenstein, whose deep underlying attitudes are religiose. Wittgenstein, however, does give us *a sense* of depth that Ayer and Russell do not. Indeed, it may very well be an illusory sense of depth. (In other moods and in other contexts, and rightly, I believe, Wittgenstein makes us suspicious of such claims of depth.) That it is illusory is, I think, true, but still questions are begged here and there is the issue of where the burden of proof lies. I think it lies with Wittgenstein and such defenders of his "depth" as we find in the Swansea philosophers. But to argue and deliberate on such matters would be to try to face carefully and in detail questions about religion and the sense of "the meaning of life," questions Wittgenstein does not touch beyond giving us a few aperçus.[63]

Wittgenstein believes that "there are thoughts which occur deep down and thoughts which bustle about on the surface."[64] On the one hand philosophy is something that aims at "clarity, perspicuity" as things "valuable in themselves"; on the other "someone who philosophizes yearns for...thoughts that are at peace."[65] In the last half of that claim, Wittgenstein is much more like a Stoic or Epicurean and much less like an analytical philosopher. An analytic philosopher will, of course, aim at clarity and perspicuity. But she will find Wittgenstein's belief that such thinking will bring peace or even move in that direction, if really carried through with integrity, intensity, and skill, mildly embarrassing and, what is more important, irrelevant to her philosophical concerns. The thing to be done, she thinks, is to get good arguments and perspicuous representations, peace or no peace. There will also be a perfectly understandable suspicion of Wittgenstein's preoccupation with depth. We need to turn a cold analytical eye (perhaps a psychoanalytical eye as well) on this metaphor, as well as on Wittgenstein's "deep" remarks about "the meaning of life." (See, for example, the entry from 1937 in *Culture and Value*, p. 27.)

Wittgenstein's great cultural distance from the Enlightenment, the spirit of logical positivism, and pragmatism—from the world of Hume and Voltaire, Russell and Ayer, Dewey and Quine—can be vividly seen in a relatively late entry (1944, the particular year should not be lost on us). There Wittgenstein remarks "the Christian religion is only for the man who needs infinite help, solely, that is for the man who experiences infinite torment."[66] He goes on to say, in a Hamannian, Kierkegaardian vein, that "the Christian

faith—as I see it—is a man's refuge in this *ultimate* torment."[67]
Wittgenstein then remarks:

> Anyone in such torment who has the gift of opening his heart, rather than contracting it, accepts the means of salvation in his heart.
>
> Someone who in this way penitently opens his heart to God in confession lays it open for other men too. In doing this he loses the dignity that goes with his personal prestige and becomes like a child. That means without official position, dignity or disparity from others. A man can bare himself before others only out of a particular kind of love. A love which acknowledges, as it were, that we are all wicked children.
>
> We could also say: Hate between men comes from our cutting ourselves off from each other. Because we don't want anyone else to look inside us, since it's not a pretty sight in there.
>
> Of course, you must continue to feel ashamed of what's inside you, but not ashamed of yourself before your fellowmen.
>
> No greater torment can be experienced than One human being can experience. For if a man feels lost, that is the ultimate torment.[68]

Whatever the merits or lack thereof of this passage, this is the world of Pascal, Hamann, and Kierkegaard, not the world of Hume, Hägerström, Schlick, Russell, Ayer, Carnap, Quine, Sellars, Davidson, and Rorty, who, as different in some important respects as they are, are all unalienated and unrepentant children of the Enlightenment.

The earlier figures of the analytic tradition (e.g., Hume through Ayer), with their sense-data theories supposedly giving us the ground of our knowledge or with their conceptions of atomic sentences (all logically distinct) revealing the fundamental structure of the world, would with such foundationalism run into firm conflict with Wittgenstein, but so they would as well with the latter generation of analytic philosophers (e.g., Quine through Rorty). The earlier generation of analytic philosophers seemed at least to think that the underlying rationale for their firm secularism—the thing that would really justify it—lay in their foundationalism. But the latter generation are as antifoundationalist as Wittgenstein while retaining, just as firmly as the earlier analytic philosophers, an underlying secularism. (Rorty picks away at the flattering self-image of analytic philosophy, but he is as thoroughly secularist as Quine. He should not be confused with Alasdair MacIntyre or Charles Taylor.)

My point quite simply is that there is no logical connection at all between Wittgenstein's *Lebensphilosophie*—his attitudes toward life, culture, and religion—and his characteristically philosophical and metaphilosophical stances as set out most powerfully in *Philosophical Investigations* and *On Certainty*. A Quine, Sellars, or Davidson could come to be convinced (though it is hardly likely) of the essential correctness of Wittgenstein's account here and not take on any of his *Lebensphilosophie* or move in any way away from their taken-for-granted secularism. (What Russell and Hägerström had to argue for, Quine and Davidson can just take for granted.) They could very well conclude that that side of Wittgenstein says more about him as a person and the distinctive cultural circumstances in which he came to maturity (though Schlick had similar ones) than anything about his philosophy. They could share what I take to be the correct judgment of Stanley Cavell that Wittgenstein's remarks about culture and life are of interest primarily because it was Wittgenstein who was making them.[69] They are not particularly striking or original and some—his remarks on Jewishness or on Mahler, for example—are almost puerile. If Wittgenstein was not saying them, we could forget about them. They are of interest primarily for what, *if any*, light they may shed on his philosophical work. Cavell is justified, I think, in asserting that they, as remarks on culture, are hardly in a class with the far more perceptive remarks of Theodor Adorno, Walter Benjamin, or Hannah Arendt.[70]

Reflect on the account I gave in explicating Wittgenstein concerning knowledge and *Vor-Wissen*, certainty and forms of life, language games and practices, language and culture, and the like. There is nothing there to favor either a secular approach or a religious one. Certain kinds of Plantingaian philosophical theology attempting to use modal logic in the service of God as well as some metaphysical forms of secularism would be out, set aside as useless cultural artifacts reflecting a cultural malaise or at least a not inconsiderable confusion of mind. In short, Wittgenstein's account would chase away bad philosophy (e.g., metaphysics) leaving cultural space in a world "beyond philosophy" to deliberate over such fundamental matters of life and culture, free now of metaphysical and epistemological intrusions. ("Philosophy" in "beyond philosophy" is taken to mean, as philosophy is in the Tradition, something seeking to be a disciplinary *Fach*.) But unless Wittgenstein's account is given a thoroughly relativistic reading, which I agree with Cavell and Winch should not be done, then it neither supports (as it might not anyway) secularist nor religious orientations.[71] I should add that it supports neither even indirectly or obliquely. It teaches us to reject the giving of philosophical underpinnings for such stances, but it is itself neutral between them. Wittgenstein the man thoroughly rejected Enlightenment secularism, but that says something about *him* and, when we note how the rejection is made, nothing about his *philosophy*.

What Wittgenstein teaches us about culture that has lasting value is indirect. Though he remained tormented by philosophical questions all his life—he never found the peace he hoped philosophizing would give him—he did show us the way for the fly to get out of the bottle. He showed us the unreality of philosophy as the Tradition gives it to us and the senselessness or pointlessness of its questions. We can have neither foundationalism nor any grand synthesis, but we can have our primitive certainties for all of that. And it is not a world (*pace* Feyerabend and Derrida), even if metaphysics as well as God is dead, where anything goes. Wittgenstein found no *Heimat* in such a world, though he relentlessly showed us the way to it: to making, that is, ourselves at home in such a world. The perspicuity (perhaps the genius) and sanity of Rorty is to show something of what it should be like for us unalienated pragmatists, if you will, to live without shallowness, evasion, or inauthenticity in a world that no longer concerns itself with metaphysical questions and the other traditional questions of philosophy.

PART TWO

New Directions

7

Can There Be Progress in Philosophy?

I

Whether there is, or even could be, progress in philosophy is problematic. There is progress in intellectual history, for it is evident enough that human conceptual resources have expanded and developed in the course of history and it is evident as well that these conceptual resources have become material forces in the lives of human beings. However, these things do not entail, or indeed in any way establish, that philosophy has progressed.

"Philosophy" does not name a natural kind. It has denoted various things in the course of its history. In earlier periods philosophy was not clearly distinct from other activities, including science. In the modern era in the West, however, philosophy, as we have seen, became increasingly an epistemologically based activity, claiming a disciplinary matrix that would make it a cultural overseer or adjudicator. With this self-image, it came to make claims to autonomy.

Philosophy, so conceived, as we have noted in Part 1, has not been able to make good its claim to be a cultural overseer or referee. We do not (or so at least it appears) have anything that counts as a distinctively philosophical knowledge. Neither in its epistemological phrasing nor in its successor logico-semantical phrasing has philosophy been able to cash in on its foundationalist

claims.   Yet is important to note that this has been argued—if
"established" is too strong a term—within philosophy itself, so that
philosophy conceived as a distinct foundational discipline with a
distinct disciplinary technique has (or so it is not unnatural to argue)
dug its own grave.

If this is so, we can reasonably see this as part of a development of intellectual history in which there is intellectual progress but
no philosophical progress. (It is question-begging to tie the two
together.)   "Philosophy," however, can be differently construed.
"Philosophy" in an older and looser sense, as an attempt to see
things in a comprehensive way in order to make sense of our lives,
is, as I have noted, as old as the hills, not wedded to a professional
discipline, and not at all about to wither away. To show, in the face
of Wittgenstein's critique, that in a somewhat more rigorous way a
conception of a development of that "philosophy" could be teased
out of a diverse set of activities would be to show that philosophy
could progress. We could, that is, show progress in philosophy if we
could show that something in accordance with that untechnical
conception of philosophy and firmly in its spirit could be developed
along more argument-based and theoretically constrained lines, yet
still effectively serve the same ends with the same rationale. In this
chapter and the next I examine whether anything like this can be
plausibly shown. It must, among other things, demonstrate against
the power of Wittgenstein's counterconception that such an
Enlightenment conception is plausible. I do not think that anything
more than plausibility could be claimed for it.

II

I assume in Part 2 what I have argued for in Part 1, namely,
that Richard Rorty's application of Wittgenstein's dissolution of
philosophy is very close to the mark indeed.[1] More than Wittgenstein or   Wittgenstein's more orthodox followers, someone like
Malcolm, Ambrose, or even Rhees, Rorty has an historical awareness
and sensitivity that he integrates into the way he does philosophy.[2]
Rorty gives us, as an exemplary tale, an intriguing historical
narrative, the correctness of whose details is less important than the
plausibility of its overall picture. (Of course, if too many details are

wrong, then its compelling force should at least be lost.) In the telling of this narrative, Rorty, following Wittgenstein, has shown how philosophy has so developed that any significant formulation of foundationalism has been undermined.[3] The pragmatists and the positivists, if not Kant, had already undermined the traditional "perennial philosophy" and later philosophers—Wittgenstein and those like Quine and Sellars, who pragmatized positivism—have undermined the epistemological   foundationalism of a broadly Cartesian-Kantian sort and its successor programmatic analytical philosophy, to wit, the programs of such philosophers as Carnap, Reichenbach, Gustav Bergmann, and C. I. Lewis. Attempts to respond to Rorty by Kim, Hacking, and Goldman, to take some of the acutest of his critics, have not been, as we have seen, note-worthy for their success, and, even if they had succeeded, given what they have freely conceded to Rorty, there is very little left to make a continued adherence to the Tradition attractive. So laundered, it is, to mix my metaphors, very small potatoes.[4]

I assume all these contentious and perhaps overstated things in the chapters that follow. If I am substantially mistaken in these claims and assumptions, then what would and would not constitute progress in philosophy would have to be looked at rather differently.

So standing, as I do, in essential agreement with the core of Rorty's claims about the end of philosophy as an autonomous disciplinary matrix, I shall turn to an inspection of two at least initially promising directions that a successor subject of philosophy could take or philosophy itself, more broadly conceived, could take. (As John Wisdom might say, take your pick here, for nothing substantial turns on which characterization is adopted.) The first, to get a slogan for it, I shall call philosophy-as-critical-theory, and the second I shall call, in the Deweyan tradition, philosophy-as-piece-meal-social-criticism focusing on what Dewey called the problems of men.[5] After characterizing both views, I argue that as promising as it initially sounds, the philosophy-as-the-problems-of-men approach, unless embedded in a more comprehensive critical theory, comes as philosophy to naught. I also show that critical theory, properly understood, offers us something of a plausible hope either as a radical transformation of philosophy or as a successor subject to philosophy. It also provides us with a basis for believing that there can be progress in philosophy, even with the death of epistemology and traditional analytic philosophy. It may well be that the demise of epistemology and traditional analytic philosophy is a necessary condition for such progress. (It should also be noted that critical theory can and should incorporate the problems-of-men approach.) Whether or not there actually is progress in philosophy will, I argue, depend on whether the complicated and ramified research program of critical theory pans out.

III

Let us start the task by trying to put this into perspective. If we are convinced of the end of philosophy, where philosophy is construed as either epistemology, metaphysics, or conceptual analysis, we might then just close up shop. Maybe such laid-off philosophers should go into computer science or linguistics or mathematics or law or the history of ideas or perhaps even religious studies. However, we might try instead to make something of philosophy, to forge something different from the standard analytic fare, remembering the unproblematic use of "philosophy" as an attempt, in trying to make sense of our lives, to see how things hang together in the broadest sense of that term. (We saw in the previous chapter that it was only relatively unproblematic. Yet in comparison with an epistemologically oriented philosophy there is perhaps some room for development and achievement here.) Starting from this point, but wanting to move to something more determinate, more argument- and theory-based than that popular conception of philosophy, we might naturally ask if there really is any task left for philosophy. Is there, that is, anything reasonable, beyond an imaginative trying to see how things hang together, left for philosophy to be? Is there any way philosophy might reconstruct itself? I want to pursue two distinct but not incompatible ways. Neither is new though both, until rather recently (at least in Anglo-American and Scandinavian philosophical circles), have been in a cultural limbo and have some standard, as well as some not so standard, difficulties. I want to see what, if anything much, of value remains when we have examined these difficulties.

The first reconstruction comes from the pragmatist tradition and was articulated most forcefully by John Dewey. Dewey was, as

Rorty recognizes, as thorough an antifoundationalist as any of the antifoundationalists of a later vintage. He took a naturalistic point of view and resolutely set aside epistemological and metaphysical investigations. (When he himself talked, as in *Experience and Nature*, of developing a metaphysical view, he did not mean what is normally meant.) He rejected the idea that there was any distinctively philosophical knowledge or philosophical way of knowing and he was entirely contextualist about justification.

Dewey believed that neither philosophers nor anyone else could provide any justificatory foundations for science, morality, politics, religion, or anything else. All justification, it is necessary to recognize, is context-bound and inescapably involves reference to existing social practices. Still, we as human beings stand barraged not by "eternal philosophical problems" but by specific problems of life that are not exclusively or at all the problems of a particular discipline. Moreover, though justification appeals to many different things in many different contexts and involves centrally an appeal to a myriad of social practices, social practices not infrequently conflict; we want, if we can, to discriminate the better from the worse. The Deweyan belief is that philosophy, if properly reconstructed, can play a critically constructive role here.[6] And this will, of course, come to trying to provide answers to what Dewey calls "the problems of men." This, for us in our time, means examining the problems of abortion, euthanasia, privacy, pornography, the rights of children, animal rights, sexism, racism, nuclear warfare; the ideological uses of science and the media; exploitation; imperialism; questions about what democracy can come to in our industrial societies; moral questions about the workplace; questions about what education should be at various levels in our societies; questions about inequality and autonomy; broad questions about the choice between socialism and capitalism, reform and revolution; and questions about the ethics of terrorism. These do not, of course, exhaust the problems of men, but they give us a sense of the type of problems that Dewey believes it is the task of a reconstructed philosophy to confront. They are questions that are often treated ideologically, emotionally, and sloppily. It is the task of philosophy, Dewey tells us, to give them a rational and penetrating treatment.

Philosophy's most urgent task, that is, is to deal with present conflicts and confusions. By this Dewey did not mean philosophical puzzles, say, about a brain in a vat, but real confusions that someone might feel about human problems, say, something about what democracy could come to in contemporary life where we seem to be in Max Weber's iron cage. Philosophy's task here is critically normative. It asks what should be said and what should be done about these things.

We have myriads of social practices and frequently conflicting attitudes about their propriety. Think, for example, of the social practice of abortion or the viewing of pornography. Other social practices are solidly accepted but are not shared by some other cultures—indeed they may have conflicting practices, but still they are practices that most of us are not conflicted about, say, our rather passive acceptance of the propriety of capitalism or our strong prohibition of the practice of infanticide. But, as I have just remarked, other cultures have not gone that way. And this can lead us to ask whether our ways are the right ways here. After such reflections, we, and then only some of us, sometimes become conflicted about such matters, typically rather ambivalently. We generally continue to *feel* that our practices are right, but wonder how we could be *justified* in feeling that way given those cultural conflicts.

Dewey's pragmatism takes it to be philosophy's task to provide answers, or to crucially help in the providing of answers, to these problems about social practices by showing which social practices ought to endure, which should be reconstructed, and which should be abandoned. (Dewey's pragmatism contrasts sharply here with Rorty's Dewey-inspired neopragmatism. For Rorty, there is no attaining such a critical vantage point.[7] We will ask later whether that is a more rigorous carrying through of the central conceptions of pragmatism.) Moreover, even if foundationalism is out and there are no "timeless" questions and answers, it does not follow that there cannot be sound, historically determinate arguments for resolving at least some of these questions one way rather than another. That there are no ahistorical standards of rationality or objectivity providing us with ahistorical reasons for acting in a certain way, reasons that can be seen to be good reasons independent of time, place, and circumstance, does not imply that there are no historically determinate reasons that, relative to a distinctive cultural and historical context, can be established to be good reasons for doing one thing rather than another. We should also come to recognize that the issues raised by the problems of men cannot be resolved simply by appealing to existing social practices, context-dependent though justification may be, for the heart of the controversy is the genuine and serious conflict of competing social practices.

There are a series of difficulties concerning such a conception of philosophical activity to which I shall return after I have examined the other alternative I have in mind for a reconstructed conception of philosophy's role. For the nonce, I only want to consider one criticism of that Deweyan turn, a criticism that will lead to the other alternative I want to consider to "perennial philosophy" and to traditional analytic philosophy. One of the things, it will be said, that is wrong with Deweyan philosophy as the-problems-of-men approach is that it is too much like piecemeal social engineering. Philosophy, as we have already seen, has at least one reasonably determinate and relatively unproblematic sense that need have nothing whatsoever to do with foundationalism, a claim to some special philosophical expertise, or anything of the sort. But it is also a conception to which the Deweyan problems-oriented turn is not very well attuned, namely, to the attempt to "understand how things in the broadest possible sense of the term hang together in the broadest possible sense of the term."[8] And this, of course, is our root sense of philosophy. As reflective human beings, we want to see, even if we are firm, nihilistic postmodernists, as far as is reasonably possible, how things hang together. (We may, however, be deeply skeptical about achieving much of anything here. But we would recognize it to be desirable if we could.) Even if there is no epistemological or metaphysical way to do so, and even *if* we have to move in a rather literary or moral-cum-political way or, alternatively, in a rather brutely empirical and historical way, we still want to see if we can understand how things hang together in the broadest possible sense of the term. That impulse, if not possessed too compulsively, is in part what it is to be rational and reflective and, in that broad and untechnical sense, philosophical. Such a conception will survive the death of epistemology and metaphysics and can remain perfectly intact even if it is clearly seen that there is no genuine profession to be professional about designated by the word "philosophy." (There are, of course, techniques that people get taught in graduate school, at least in particular culturally determinate habitations, just as there are techniques theologians learn in certain environments. The interesting question is whether there is much point in learning either of these techniques. Those philosophers who feel quite firmly that there is a not inconsiderable point for philosophy ought to ask themselves how they feel about the case for theology. If they feel there is a genuine difference and that the difference here cuts in favor of philosophy, then they should ask whether they think that because they think philosophy has some access to the truth whereas theology does not. If they really do think that, then they must confront Wittgenstein's and Rorty's probing about how anything like that could be possible.) But even if the Deweyan turn escapes professional deformation, it is still unclear how this piecemeal solving of the problems of men rooted in resolutely viewing them in their problematic situations is going to give us anything like a comprehensive vision. But that is the *Urkantone* of philosophy.

It is such dissatisfaction with the Deweyan approach, along with other dissatisfactions I canvass later, that makes me turn to another approach, which, as I have already noted, might either be viewed as a reconstruction of philosophy or as a successor subject to philosophy. I speak here of philosophy-as-critical-theory.

So let us characterize and run a bit with philosophy-as-critical-theory, where what I have in mind is something more like a Habermasian, quasi-Habermasian, or (perhaps) pseudo-Habermasian enterprise than like the earlier Frankfurt school conception.[9] (Not being in the Habermas explication business, I am not much concerned with its pedigree, though I am vitally interested in what the structure of a sound critical theory would look like.) We want a holistic critical theory—a theory that sees, displays, and explains how things hang together in a comprehensive way—which is in an integrated way a descriptive-explanatory theory, an interpretive theory, and a normative critique. Elements of philosophy, as more traditionally conceived, will be amalgamated with the human sciences with none of the elements claiming hegemony and with philosophy unequivocally giving up all pretensions to somehow autonomously being the "guardian of reason." Critical theory, including its philosophical elements, will, of course, share the fallibilistic attitude of the sciences. Such a holistic theory will provide a comprehensive critique of culture, society, and ideology. In this way it will not only have a descriptive-explanatory thrust but also, and in integral relation to its descriptive-explanatory and interpretive sides, a critical-emancipatory thrust. It will help us not only to better see who we were, are, and might become but also, where there are alternatives, who we might better become and what kind of a society would be a more just society, and not merely a more just society but a more truly human or more humane society. (Talk of justice, plainly, does not exhaust the dimensions of a moral and normative appraisal of society.)

However, such a theory is not just a dramatic narrative or a word-picture, if it is any of these things at all, but a genuinely empirical-cum-theoretical theory that among other things is a descriptive-explanatory theory showing us the structure of society, the range of its feasible transformations, and the mechanics of its transformation. It will also provide (if any such thing is possible) a rational justification (if that isn't pleonastic) for saying of its possible transformations that one is better than the others. It would in the course of such critical-theoretical articulation consider the comparative adequacy of ways of life that might claim our allegiance, including, of course, the various possible capitalisms, socialisms, and technocratic, including authoritarian-technocratic, alternatives.

It is not exactly as if we did not have at least partial models for enterprises something like that. We are not starting completely de novo. In the past, Hobbes, Smith, Condercet, Hume, and Hegel did something like that. And though in our time philosophers have given up doing that, the great sociological trinity of Marx, Weber, and Durkheim did it, and Habermas's work presently exemplifies it. (To say this is not to indicate agreement with its details or even with its basic structure.) It is a definite project of modernity growing out of the Enlightenment—a project presently under postmodernist attack.

However, given what we know now and where we stand, the proof is going to be in the eating, and postmodernist skepticism such as Foucault's, Lyotard's, or Rorty's is not unreasonable. How exactly we should put these elements together in constructing a holistic critical theory is not altogether clear. Before we can justifiably make a claim for progress here in philosophy, we must be reasonably confident that such a research program is going to pan out and that we will not get ideology or Weltschmerz parading as critical theory.

Whether such a critical theory is anything more than a utopian dream that postmodernists can reject as just one more impossible metanarrative will depend on whether in the next few decades critical theory comes to anything.

It is, however, surely appropriate to ask, "What do I mean by saying 'comes to anything'?" I mean that (1) it clearly helps solve some of what Dewey calls the problems of men, (2) it develops a theoretical practice that has a clear emancipatory payoff, (3) its descriptive-explanatory structure actually provides some explanations that are true or approximately true, and (4) these explanations, together with the evaluative and normative claims contained in the theoretical practice, are set together into a well-matching, inter-locking, comprehensive framework that is perspicuously articulated.

It is, of course, possible to be skeptical, as postmodernists are, about the very possibility of such an enterprise. However, as far as I can see, there are no conceptual or a priori roadblocks to carrying out such a program, though there are indeed empirical ones. The obvious difficulty here is the scope. It is, to put it mildly, daunting. Faced with its size, we might respond that such a project is larger than life. To carry it through, we need the talents, drive, and vast knowledge of a Max Weber or Karl Marx. With the contemporary explosion of knowledge, it is surely an understandable scruple to worry if any intellectual or group of intellectuals who could fruitfully work together could play that role again. But, then again, there may be a lot of things we can just cut through. The intellectual—to reason by analogy—who best understands the politics of his time is not necessarily the person who most scrupulously reads a good newspaper every morning. So I think the proof will be in the self-critical carrying out of something like this program of a critical theory. (I say "something like" and "a self-critical carrying out" because it surely will be necessary to repair the ship at sea. To take the program as something written in stone is to utterly abandon the spirit of fallibilism.)

IV

So we have two models for how philosophy (or, if you will, how its successor subject) might progress after the death of traditional epistemologically oriented philosophy and a programmatic analytical philosophy. The models are plainly compatible. The more modest Deweyan one would be subsumed under the critical-theory model, and a Deweyan, understandably skeptical about anything as comprehensive as critical theory, need not, in focusing on the problems of men, deny the very possibility of a critical theory. She can just bracket such considerations. So even if we think the Deweyan model sans critical theory can come to something, we do not have to choose between them. Yet in setting out to do philosophical work under the new philosophical dispensations, how we shall actually proceed will be rather different if, on the one hand, in a Deweyan manner we are skeptical about the feasibility of critical theory or any holistic theory than if, on the other hand, we think we stand in need of a comprehensive critical theory and have a good chance of constructing and then developing a feasible one.

Where should we go? Do we need a critical theory if we can get one? Rorty does not think so.[10] He thinks it is a matter of scratching where it doesn't itch. Someone like Habermas claiming there is a real itch will maintain that without a comprehensive critical theory we will not be able to distinguish theory from ideology. We will not be able to know whether unmaskers like Marx and Freud are not unwittingly wearing a few masks themselves. Without a firm distinction between theory and ideology, we can have no basis for the great hope of the Enlightenment, namely, the making of rational criticisms of our social institutions.[11] There can be no genuine solutions to the problems of men if we do not have such universal rational standards of criticism and validation. If, Habermas argues, we can find nothing like an Archimedean point in virtue of which we can speak of sound or better arguments *sans phrase* as distinct from just having persuasive arguments that convince a given audience at a given time, then we can only have a very relativistic, context-dependent social criticism that, if we reflect on the conditions of its warrant, can hardly count as genuine criticism and is not clearly distinct from ideology. If that is the pickle we are in, we seem no longer to have a distinction between theory and ideology. To get out of this pickle, we need, Habermas argues, a rational consensus as distinct from a purely historically and culturally fortuitous consensus. We need to have such a standard to carry out progressive social criticism and to make a critique of

institutions and ideology.   Otherwise we are mired, he claims, in a
relativistic morass in which only the weakest, ad hoc negative
criticism is possible.

Wittgenstein and Rorty—Rorty doing his Wittgensteinian-
cum-neopragmatist tricks—as well as French postmodernists such as
Lyotard and Foucault, would argue that we have no need for this or
indeed any Archimedean point.   We can't have one anyway, but
even if we could, Rorty argues, we would not need it.   This search
for a grand metanarrative is just more, and by now rather late in the
day, nostalgia for the Absolute.   Criteria for validity and rationality
are in the first-order discourse of our distinct language games, which
in turn are embedded in our forms of life.   What is given there is
a complex cluster of social practices.   It is these practices and the
first-order discourses that are a part of them that set our functioning
criteria for validity and rationality.   There can, Rorty argues, be no
context-independent criteria of rationality and validity.   A search for
a more foundational legitimacy is a search for the color of heat.   But
even with this new sobriety, there is no loss in our not having such
criteria, for we can, Rorty argues, solve the problems of men even
though our criteria of validity and rationality are implicit in and
determined by our diverse language games.   We do not need any
such Habermasian Archimedean point.   Rational argumentation can
only be conducted in accordance with the most reflective and
knowledgeable application of the social practices of a given community at a given time. There can be no getting back of these practices
with their set of conventions to nature's own language, which will
tell us what it really is rational to believe for some supracultural
agents with a God's-eye view.[12]   To think there can be something
like this is just to let the old philosophical superstitions of the
Tradition come in by the back door.   There is no determining what
is rational by some extrahistorical, universal set of criteria.   There is
and can be no such ahistorical legitimation.

It is usual, at least among philosophers and not a few social
theorists as well, to think we have lost something in losing such an
Archimedean point.   Rorty thinks that is misguided.[13]   We are just
frightening ourselves, he believes, perhaps unconsciously pushed by
old religious needs into thinking that we need something more
universal.   That is quite unnecessary, Rorty tells us, for we can
simply rely on the relatively theoretically unramified political speech

used in defense of the liberal vision of Western democracies. It would be better, he tells us, to be frankly ethnocentric here. In solving the problems of men we should just work carefully and reflectively with the criteria built into our actual practices. There aren't any universal, ahistorical criteria anyway, but even if there were, we wouldn't need them. We can live perfectly well and reasonably without the kind of comprehensive unification asked for by critical theory, where we have a unified critical account of norms and facts and of science and society. We need not lose our nerve; we need not be spooked, as Hegel and Habermas are, by the loss of religion in the Enlightenment. Keeping our nerve and avoiding high levels of abstraction (where no one is quite sure what he is talking about), we should continue to use, in a concrete and philosophically unramified way, our creative intelligence *ambulando* to solve our social problems as they come along in the various struggles of life. We do not need anything like a critical theory to realize the hopes, or to make reasonable the hopes, formulated by the Enlightenment.[14]

No matter how much we may be attracted to end-of-philosophy theses, a dialectic putting in question this Rortyan good cheer could start like this: Habermas is surely right in stressing with Hegel that our historical experience is such that we can no longer accept a naive consensus.[15] We—that is we who are part of the ever expanding culture of modernity—are aware of too many different ways of life, points of view, universes of discourse, conflicting ideologies, to possibly just naively and uncritically accept the way things are done in our society.

This "experience of reflection," as Hegel describes it, quite naturally inclines us to what Lyotard calls metanarratives, namely, to "theories of rationality that are supposed to account for why and in what sense we can still connect our convictions and our descriptive, normative, and evaluative statements with a transcending validity claim that goes beyond merely local contexts."[16] Must or should a critical theory be a metanarrative or rely on a metanarrative? Habermas denies that his critical theory is or contains such a narrative, though, without providing a metanarrative, he believes that his account "preserves the possibility of speaking of rationality in the singular."[17] But he is not, he maintains, even attempting to provide any "foundational ultimate groundings" for society or a "totalizing philosophy of history." People who do this are people who write metanarratives, though note this is doing something wilder, or at least far more ambitious, than what is licensed by the above initial characterization of a metanarrative. Given the structure of his account, there is no place in it for metanarratives in the sense, as we find in Hegel or Spengler, of giving some totalizing philosophy of history.[18] His critical theory, as a theory of communicative action, is in part philosophical and in part empirical, involving a nonexclusive division of labor between philosophy and the human sciences. "It has the aim of clarifying the presuppositions of the rationality of processes of reaching understanding which may be presumed to be universal because they are unavoidable."[19] This whole critical account, like any scientific theory, has empirical testing constraints. It can be confirmed or infirmed.[20]

Habermas also believes that he is not committed to any form of absolutism or "pure transcendentalism." He thinks that if one has a good understanding of the modern world, one can neither accept absolutism on the one hand, nor relativism or pure historicism on the other. The last two, he believes, carry "the burden of self-referential, pragmatic contradictions and paradoxes that violate our need for consistency," and the first is "burdened with a foundationalism that conflicts with our consciousness of the fallibility of human knowledge."[21] He remarks, it seems to me rightly enough, that no "one who gives this situation much thought would want to be left in this bind."[22]

Critical theory provides a third way. What is this third way? Let me initially come at this indirectly. We are participants in arguments; there are problems of life that are *our* problems, where we are not just ethnological, neutral observers of the actual and predictors of the probably possible, but participants. As participants we need to maintain, as Habermas puts it, the distinction Rorty wants to retract, namely, the distinction "between valid and socially accepted views, between good arguments and those which are merely successful for a certain audience at a certain time."[23] It is, of course, a beginning philosophy point that there is a difference between winning an argument, at least in the sense of getting your opponent to go along with you, and making a sound argument, that is, making a valid argument with true premises. Moreover, views can be soundly reasoned yet need not be identical with views currently accepted. Someone, for example, might argue that lesbian couples should have the same access as anyone else to sperm donor programs, and that view might be soundly argued even though it was fiercely resisted in the community in which it was argued. Indeed, presently in North America, that is, it is sad to record, exactly what one would expect.

Rorty is, of course, perfectly aware of these elementary if, for all that, not unimportant points. His view is that when we push deep for our canons of validity and for what it is rational to believe, we will find, as Wittgenstein argues, that they are rooted in our use of language, which in turn is given in our various language games rooted in our forms of life. Critical theory, at least on Habermas's reading and probably on any plausible reading, cannot rest content just with saying that. Critical theory, as Habermas puts it, is aware that there are in the modern world a not inconsiderable number of competing convictions, some of them running very deep. We are people who have some of these convictions, and a number of us are aware of alternatives to these convictions. We are not, as I remarked, merely neutral observers of the actual. We have an interest, as Habermas puts it, in seeing "social practices of justification as more than just such practices."[24] To establish that they are more has been philosophy's traditional interest in reason, and it at least partially explains, the "stubbornness with which philosophy clings to the role of the 'guardian of reason'."[25]

Critical theory tries in a more realistic and empirically oriented way to carry on this guardian role. It preserves philosophy's interest in reason and tries, *pace* Wittgenstein, Winch, and Rorty, to preserve "the possibility of speaking of rationality in the singular."[26] In transforming philosophy into critical theory with its amalgam of aspects of traditionally oriented philosophy (particularly analytical philosophy) and the human sciences, critical theory seeks, in a systematic but fallibilistic and nontranscendental way, "to cope with the entire spectrum of aspects of rationality."[27]

There are at least two principal types of difficulty that face such a grand holistic theory. One is a quite persistent, and indeed insistent, postmodernist Rortyan skepticism, though in one sense it is a rather "unskeptical skepticism." It argues that however natural it may be to want such rational standards—to want to show and believe that social practices of justification are more than just such practices—that nonetheless it is the case that no such standards are available.[28] (Salt could be poured on these wounds through the argument that the very idea that there could be such standards is incoherent.) The other difficulty—a difficulty we have already gestured at—is quite different and quite un-Rortyan. It is not, it argues, that such a project is in principle impossible, i.e., conceptually incoherent. Rather, the real concern is that there is in fact not much chance that such a program is going to be carried out. It is, after all, just too daunting. Where there is this doubt it is not unreasonable to form the considered judgment that belief in critical theory can come to little more than a pious wish, and, this being so, it is better to stick to piecemeal social criticism and to an intelligent coping, rather *seriatim*, with the problems of men. This need not be reformist naivete, as it was not with Bertrand Russell and is not with Noam Chomsky, but instead a realistic recognition of the limits of human capacities in the domain of the social.[29]

V

So let us return to the Deweyan problems-of-men conception of philosophy and to difficulties that will reasonably be felt about it beyond the one I stated that led us into our discussion of philosophy-as-critical-theory. Dewey wants us *as philosophers* to face actual problematic situations and in facing them to somehow use our philosophical abilities to solve or substantially help solve the stressing problems of human beings, e.g., problems of abortion, sexism, racism, questions about the justification of socialism, and the like. It is possible to care very much about those problems yet still feel quite helpless here *as a philosopher*. How can philosophy, or *can* philosophy, contribute anything here? We talk, from this Deweyan perspective, of giving these social problems a rational and penetrating treatment. But that may be little more than chatter. Remember we have given up the claim that philosophy can do anything foundational, that philosophy can somehow know the truth about these matters because it knows what knowledge or what warranted belief really is or because, with its understanding of meaning, it can command a clear view of the essence of the concepts of abortion, sexism, racism, socialism, and the like. Philosophy, we are now granting, cannot play such a role as a cultural overseer. But what then can our talk of giving these problems a rational and penetrating treatment come to? With the death of epistemology and the abandonment of the claims of programmatic analytical philosophy, or for that matter "perennial philosophy," we have abandoned the idea that philosophers have some special expertise, such as logical analysis, conceptual analysis, linguistic analysis, or whatnot, such that they can resolve these questions or provide the basis for the resolution of these questions in a way that tolerably educated, concerned, and thoughtful people cannot.

We might try saying, like Rawls, Dworkin, Gauthier, or Nozick, that the philosopher can do critical moral theory in a clearheaded way, and this is what a rational and penetrating treatment would come to here. But what is behind the nice phrase "critical moral theory"? If there is no epistemology, there certainly is no moral epistemology. If there can be no foundational work in epistemology, then talk of the foundations of morals or the foundations of politics will come to nothing. We should recall that Rorty's claim that talk of conceptual foundations gets us nowhere. At best, it is a pedantic and sometimes arcane redescription, perhaps in the formal mode or perhaps in some bizarre or quasi metatalk, of what we already know. We learn from Rawls and Dworkin about matters such as social justice because they are informed, reflective human beings who know the history of social thought (the history of moral philosophy being a part of it), the relevant legal, factual, and social science considerations surrounding the issues they discuss, and because they have thought deeply about these social issues for years. But there is nothing in the way of philosophical expertise, technique, knowledge, or bright new analytical tools they trot out or that are available to the philosopher to enable her to get a purchase on these problems in the way that a political scientist, a literary critic, a novelist, a lawyer, a sociologist, a political economist, or a historian cannot or can only with a kind of difficulty from which the properly equipped philosopher is free. With the death of foundationalism, such a claim on the philosopher's part is pure hubris. Both the capacities and character traits as well as the type of knowledge that I attributed to Rawls and Dworkin are vital. Part of this knowledge is a knowledge of the history of moral and social philosophy, but there is little, if anything, in this historiographical knowledge that is technically philosophical that is not fairly readily open to a whole range of academics and, beyond them, to persons who have a reasonably good education, a not inconsiderable amount of leisure, and the inclination to have a go at these texts. There are no analytical techniques needed or available here comparable to something we would have to learn in studying physics, micro-economics, linguistics, modal logic, or computer science, that must be mastered to understand what is going on here or to make the arguments or essential points that Rawls and Dworkin make.

The Deweyan will not be disturbed that there is no "philo-sophical way of knowing" or logical technique that will give a philosopher much purchase in tackling these problems. But then, if the problems of men become the problems of philosophers, how do these persons, working *as philosophers*, aid in their solution? Apart from the fact that not a few people in the past who were called philosophers intelligently talked about them, what do we, *as philosophers*, now contribute? And was it really very different in the past? Spinoza, for example, says some powerful things about our fate. Are those powerful things, or at least their import, really tied in any important way to the technical aspects of his philosophy so that such remarks about our fate would lack that power if they were not tied to that machinery? And could not similar things be said about Plato and Schopenhauer?

That there does not appear to be anything for *philosophy* to do here with the problems of men is perhaps what is behind the inclination of both traditional philosophers of the old days—philo-sophers of the genteel tradition—and analytic philosophers of a more or less orthodox sort to say that there is very little philosophy in Dewey. He, for the most part, either talks grandiloquently about the unfolding of the history of human thought or rolls up his sleeves and goes at certain concrete social problems, sometimes in a rather peculiar vocabulary, a vocabulary that probably does more harm than good. (The sensible things that Dewey often says seem to come through in spite of his cumbersome way of writing.)

There is, of course, in both Dewey and his followers a lot of talk of scientific method. It is easy for us now, standing where we stand, to dismiss this, saying it comes to little more than instrumental commonsense recipes that any sensible person would follow. But this misses that it was directed at philosophy as a kind of uncontrolled speculation à la Whitehead, Royce, Bergson, or Tillich, to take once influential examples. That not many philosophers go on like that today we may thank to the kind of critical stress put on such recipes that we got from the pragmatists and their positivist allies. Such talk of scientific method is valuable in the face of such indiscipline or Brand Blanshard's disciplined rationalism. This, as Habermas stresses, is an important thing to do, but we hardly have anything here that should be inflated into the methodological foundations of philosophical or scientific inquiry or even of critical theory.

There is a natural response that should be made at this point. Why, keeping the same problems-of-men approach, cannot contemporary Deweyans say that what philosophers qua philosophers can legitimately do, if they have this Deweyan concern, is the traditional analytical philosophical job of helping people troubled by these problems of men command a clearer view of the key concepts involved, display the relevant considerations in a more perspicuous manner, and seek to state the relevant arguments in valid patterns of argument and in a clear and compelling way? Issues such as abortion, sexism, racism, and questions about the viability of socialism, as much public discussion reveals, are typically debated in a wild, undisciplined, and propagandistic manner. A philosopher, aware of the relevant factual and moral issues and of the underlying ideological forces at play, can bring clarity and discipline to these problems and, approaching them in this modest underlaborer's way, assist in their resolution. Here is something distinctively philosophical that a philosopher can contribute even after the demise of epistemology and programmatic analytical philosophy.

I do think these are useful virtues, and I hope philosophers in their day-to-day activities in the classroom, on forums, in writing articles, and the like will display them. Nevertheless, I think Rorty is right in arguing, as it comes out with particular force in his "Philosophy in America," that when properly separated from the trumpeting philosophers make about such virtues, they (1) will be seen not to be as distinctively philosophical as philosophers are wont to think, and (2) though indeed valuable, these virtues will accomplish far less than most philosophers flatter themselves into believing.[30]

In arguing the first point, Rorty argues that there is no distinctive mode of argumentation possessed by philosophers that others (say, economists or lawyers) do not have. Moreover, it has become increasingly clear, since the breakdown of programmatic analytical philosophy like that of Reichenbach, Carnap, or C. I. Lewis, that there are no distinct philosophical methodology or analytical tools that can be appealed to that give distinctive force to a philosopher's often clear and to-the-point argumentation. Philosophers frequently (indeed, almost invariably) cloak their arguments in some currently fashionable philosophical jargon, but that jargon quickly goes out of fashion—the whirligig, as Rorty points out, goes more rapidly nowadays—and it is not essential to the, theoretically speaking, rather low-level arguments for taking a certain position about these human problems. (That, theoretically speaking, they are rather low-level arguments does not even suggest that there is anything wrong with them.) The soundness of the arguments need not be affected by their level of abstraction or by a dropping of the jargon. Indeed, in dealing with these common human problems, the reasonable expectation would be that the level of abstraction would and should be rather low. (Suspicion of technocratese is not the same as love of obscurity. Quite to the contrary, it is concern with clarity and the closure of argument, where that is a reasonable expectation, that fuels that suspicion.) The important thing to see is that these arguments about the problems of men could have been formulated by any clearheaded, well-informed person with a sense of relevance and a reasonable measure of critically reflective common sense. (People without such a sense, e.g., clever sillies or people with utterly unrealistic obsessions, have repeatedly been the scourge of philosophy.) Philosophers' concepts are no more essential here than those of lawyers, economists, or anthropologists, though in certain contexts any of these concepts may turn out to be useful shorthands. In other circumstances, they block understanding—block the road to inquiry. Talk of powerful analytical tools that a philosopher can lay his hands on to bring to the problems of men is just arm waving.

It is like an appeal to magic. There is no reason to believe that philosophers have some special expertise with concepts such that they command, or can come to command, a clearer view of the conceptual terrain surrounding these problems so that they then have an deeper grasp of the issues than do others. People who think clearly, have a good knowledge of the relevant factual issues and are morally sensitive are very likely going to have more reasonable views about human problems than others. But these virtues are not the private property of philosophers. Philosophers neither have some distinctive concepts to deploy in the service of strengthening arguments nor, as Rorty puts it, some "special, privileged knowledge about concepts" that puts them in a privileged position to assess the problems of life or of culture. They at most have a similar argumentative style, though even in this there is a world of difference between Carnap and Wittgenstein, between Quine and Austin, between Lewis and Cavell.

The false but still flattering philosophical image—an image consoling to many contemporary philosophers—is that philosophers have some mastery of "conceptual questions" that others lack, or that they have up their sleeves some superconcepts that gives them in some way or ways special expertise in the articulation and critique of the forms of life and assessment of culture. The reality is, as the array of arguments of Part 1 was designed to show, that philosophers neither have some special skill nor something distinctive they can be skillful at. Philosophers cannot tell us what makes our ideas really clear, what we really mean, or what we are really justified in believing.

The Deweyan approach that a reconstructed philosophy should concern itself with the problems of men seems to founder on the fact that there is nothing distinctive that a philosopher qua philosopher can do to resolve such human problems. This is not likely to become evident until the philosopher recognizes the nonviability of the orthodox conception of philosophy as an autonomous discipline with a special understanding of what warranted belief or coherent discourse consists in or as a discipline with a special methodology. She can, of course, pitch in like any other concerned citizen, activist, or intellectual and help with the resolution of these human problems. But any non-arm-waving appeal to philosophy drops out.

We wanted to use philosophy, if we took the Deweyan turn, to come to establish which social practices ought to endure, which are to be reconstructed, and which ought to be abandoned. The Deweyan way, just as much as traditional analytic philosophy, seems quite incapable of showing how philosophy has anything distinctive to contribute here. If we could, like John Rawls, Alan Gewirth, or perhaps even Alasdair MacIntyre, construct a systematic, substantive ethical theory that would give us an Archimedean point with the intellectual resources to help make, in some nonideological and nonethnocentric way, such cultural assessments, then philosophy would have a new lease on life.[31] But it should be clear from the history of the critical examinations of their work that none of these philosophers succeeded in giving us such an Archimedean point and that Rawls, whose account is far and away the most impressive, concedes just that in writings subsequent to *A Theory of Justice*.[32] Their efforts are the latest in a long history of failures, some of which have been very impressive. Previous great failures—the high point of such failures (to which Rawls's work is comparable)—have as their peaks the great systematic ethical theories of J. S. Mill, Kant, and Sidgwick. Programmatic analytical philosophy of a generally positivist sort, say, that of Hägerström, Ayer, or Stevenson, warned us against the very possibility of such attempts, as did, in a quite different way, cultural criticism of a broadly Hegelian sort. It should be evident by now, if we have our heads neither in the clouds nor in the sand, that others are not going to succeed in constructing systematic ethical theories yielding an Archimedean point where Sidgwick and Rawls have failed. We should no more expect to succeed in trying to construct foundational ethical theories than we should expect to succeed in trying to construct foundational epistemological theories.

VI

The Deweyan program, where it cannot be effectively supplemented with critical social theory, perennial philosophy, or analytical philosophy, cannot deliver the goods about philosophy reconstructing itself by dealing with the vital existential problems of human beings. It cannot, if my arguments are generally sound, give any clear sense as to how *philosophy* can deal with these problems. But it is also true, if my previous criticisms are near to the mark, that perennial philosophy has been undermined in both its Cartesian-Kantian epistemological turn and in its (generally speaking) Thomist metaphysical turn. Critical theory, a fallibilistic systematic theoretical-cum-empirical social theory, as a successor to philosophy traditionally conceived, seems to be the most plausible candidate for the kind of turn that would make philosophy as a theory and practice of social criticism viable. A Deweyan stress linked with critical theory would no longer be piecemeal. The two accounts would supplement each other. Moreover, such a linked account would ensure that social criticism so inspired is not slapdash. With social science techniques linked with analytic philosophy's traditional concern for analysis and clarity, and with philosophy's traditional concern to be self-consciously reflective about what one is doing, there would be some disciplinary expertise deployed (albeit principally—perhaps entirely—from a cluster of the social sciences). It would have some theoretical purchase by virtue of which it could criticize culture, provide a rationale for criticizing culture, and help us render some tolerably objective judgments about which social practices ought to endure, which should be reconstructed, and which should be abandoned. It would not, of course, give us "timeless answers" that would put answers or responses to vital issues beyond serious question. There is no room for appeals to self-evidence or absoluteness in such a fallibilistic perspective. Truth may in some trivial sense (à la Tarski and Carnap) be eternal, but our judgments as to what is or is not true, let alone what is "the truth" (if that has any sense at all), are not. We should recognize with Dewey, and as Davidson approvingly quotes, that truth is a collection of truths.[33] However, the acceptance of fallibilism and the recognition of such truisms does not mean that sound, historically determinate answers could not be given to questions we have about abortion or the desirability of capitalism and the like. Also, in a way a piecemeal approach could not answer to, we would have with the articulation of a critical theory, a comprehensive theory capable of distinguishing between theory and ideology, and with such a distinction we would have found conceptual space for the core Enlightenment notion of a rational criticism of existing institutions. If such an account is well grounded, we are no longer subject to the nihilistic challenges of postmodernity.

I have already noted a series of problems that such an account faces. I have, as well, given my reasons for thinking that the difficulties in such an account are perhaps not crippling and that critical theory, as a successor subject to philosophy, is our best hope for answering to some of the traditional concerns, human and explanatory, of philosophy after the end of philosophy. Here there is both important agreement and important divergence with Rorty. Rorty wants to see a world in which there ceased to be a distinct discipline called "philosophy."[34] Philosophy would, on his account, become a kind of learned and witty kibitzing, the playing of a gadfly role in the conversations of humankind. Alternatively, and in contrast, I want "philosophy," except in the colloquial sense of reflectively taking a comprehensive look at things, either to cease to have a use and for critical theory to become its successor subject, or (what is substantially the same thing) for its denotation and connotation to extensively change so that "philosophy" comes to refer to and to connote critical social theory, where critical social theory, with its emancipatory thrust, would be vitally concerned with the problems of men, though in a more holistic way than were the Deweyans.

The type of activity I am recommending would not be philosophy as usually understood, for it would, while continuing to have its conceptual side, be through and through empirical, the conceptual side integrated into and parasitical on the empirical side. But neither would it be just pure social science, as traditionally understood, for it would have a critically normative and emancipatory thrust. It would, that is, not just be descriptive-explanatory and interpretive but would also say something about what is to be done and what sort of world we should try to bring into being. It would, of course, not try to say "just one big thing" (whatever that means), but, in a Deweyan spirit, say a lot of little things that it would try to connect together along with some reasonably high-level generalizations and remarks about how these relate to what they are generalizations about. It would not have a single disciplinary matrix but an amalgam of disciplinary matrices that, as the critical theory developed, would become more unified. In that way it is very different from Rorty's advocacy in *Philosophy and the Mirror of Nature* of learned and witty kibitzing. Perhaps critical theory is a research program that will not pan out. If it remains too vague and does not, even as it is developed, provide any critical guidance, it will be politically impotent and without emancipatory thrust. And, what is probably much the same thing, if it does not help solve the problems of men, then it will turn out to be, what not a few fear, a vapid utopia. To be *critical* theory it must be effectively critical. The next four or five decades will put it to the test.

VII

To bring this chapter to a close, I want to show, in the light of all this, what should be said about my title topic for this chapter ("Can There Be Progress in Philosophy?") and, in doing this, to point to what seems at least to be a central flaw in Rorty's avowedly postmodernist "pragmatism without method," a pragmatism that seems to me very unpragmatic. I will turn to the second topic first.

Rorty's postmodernist stance comes out most clearly in his "Habermas and Lyotard on Postmodernity" and his "Postmodernist Bourgeois Liberalism."[35] If what Rorty maintains in these two articles is approximately right, it is not just philosophy that is threatened but something rather more important. That is, perhaps the core ideals and expectations of the Enlightenment have been undermined or at least effectively challenged. Rorty thinks, as is clear in his "Priority of Democracy to Philosophy," that that is overly dramatized hyperbole and in effect responds that all he is doing is realistically cutting these ideals and expectations down to size and freeing them from metanarratives. Let us see if we can sort this out.

In "Habermas and Lyotard on Postmodernity," Rorty develops an owl-of-Minerva theme. Our "emancipatory consciousness" always arrives too late on the scene after the social change has taken place. Intellectuals, including, of course, critical theorists, even if they are in tune with a substantial working-class movement, cannot form a revolutionary vanguard.[36] If they try to play such a role, they will just end up writing groundless metanarratives (a pleonasm) that they will unwittingly inflate into critical theories. We can at best only reasonably give genuine historical narratives that will include "scenarios about what is likely to happen in certain future contingencies," presumably of a rather short range. What we should avoid like the plague, Rorty follows Lyotard in claiming, are genuine metanarratives, i.e., "narratives which describe or predict the activities of such entities as the noumenal self or the Absolute Spirit or the

Proletariat."[37]   They are grand-scale just-so stories rather than
genuine historical narratives operating under empirical constraints.
They "purport to justify loyalty to, or breaks with, certain contemporary communities."[38]   But they do not succeed in this.   They
neither succeed in telling us "about what these or other communities
have done in the past" nor in giving us "scenarios about what they
might do in the future."[39]   They are bits of ideological myth-making
that distort our knowledge of ourselves and the societies in which we
live.   Attempts to give ourselves some picture of substantive,
noninstrumental rationality—the dream of a Horkheimer—that will
tell us what a rational, emancipated community would look like will
produce a picture of undistorted communication that accords with
the desires that presently obtain in the society toward which the
putatively emancipatory activity is directed.   If we start with
bourgeois ideals, we will end with bourgeois ideals; if we start with
communist ideals, we will end with communist ideals; if we start with
fascist ideals, we will end with fascist ideals.   We, Rorty remarks in
referring to his own community, have the good luck to live in liberal
bourgeois democracies.   (He might even regard "liberal bourgeois"
as pleonastic.)   It is better, he tells us, to be "frankly ethnocentric"
and stick with and evince loyalty to "those untheoretical sorts of
narrative discourse which make up the political speech of the
Western democracies."[40]   The bourgeoisie have developed a number
of social practices that reveal "the social virtues of the bourgeoisie."[41]
We intellectuals can show how such practices link up with other
practices of the same group or other groups.   We can engage in a
kind of impressionistic, piecemeal criticism here with our contrasts
and linkages, though this "criticism" sounds to me more like
ethnographical description.   But we cannot go beyond this to critical
theory and criticize the whole shebang.

     Our reasoning about what should be done, Rorty argues,
should always be with reference to a certain historically determinate
community with a certain historically determinate set of values.
There is no supercommunity such as humanity itself with whom we
can identify.   We cannot reasonably break or transcend our
particular loyalties by invoking a conflicting loyalty to humanity as
such.   Against universalists of a Kantian stripe, such as John Rawls
or Ronald Dworkin, Rorty takes humanity to be "a biological rather
than a moral notion"; there is, he claims "no human dignity that is

not derivative from the dignity of some specific community, and no appeal beyond the relative merits of various actual or proposed communities to impartial criteria which will help us weigh those merits."[42]   It is an illusion, Rorty tells us, to think that we can abstract "from any historical community and adjudicate the rights of communities vis-à-vis those of individuals."[43]   He accepts Michael Walzer's view that a "given society is just if its substantive life is lived in a way faithful to the shared understanding of the members."[44]   Liberal society under the influence of the groundless theories of Kantians has tried to ground liberal institutions on something "more than mere solidarity." But that is a myth. The only genuine basis is solidarity with one's tribe, in their case—that is, in Rorty's own case—the actual liberal community.[45]   Kantians such as Rawls and Dworkin, along with their Continental counterparts, Habermas and Albrecht Wellmer, as well their Marxist critics, Alan Gilbert and Kai Nielsen, think that one can give an account of "rationality" and "morality" in transcultural and ahistorical terms. But that is an illusion.[46]

The thing to do, Rorty tells us, is " to disentangle bourgeois liberal institutions from the vocabulary that these institutions inherited from the Enlightenment—e.g. the eighteenth-century vocabulary of natural rights."[47] We should come to recognize in our society, Rorty stresses, "that loyalty to itself is morality" enough. We need no such rational grounding as Kantian or Millian liberals tried to provide. We need to be responsible only to our "own traditions and not to the moral law as well."[48]

I do not want to argue with this historicized relativism here. I will, though, on some other occasion, as I will argue with the extensive elaboration of a similar view in Michael Sandel's *Liberalism and the Limits of Justice*. For now, I wish only to argue (1) that despite Rorty's explicit denial to the contrary, it is a form of historicized relativism and (2) if Rorty's account here really is a telling it like it is, it is not nearly as benign as Rorty cheerily takes it to be. It would not protect liberalism or a humane individualism, for it would undermine the hopes that not only fuel what I take to be one of liberalism's legitimate heirs, Marxism, but it would also undermine the hopes of liberalism itself, including the progressive social democratic versions we find in Deweyan pragmatism. (My criticism here applies most aptly to his "Habermas and Lyotard on

Postmodernity" and to his "Postmodernist Bourgeois Liberalism." By
the time we get to "The Priority of Democracy to Philosophy" he has
shifted to a much less relativistic and more historicized view closer
to the those I articulate and defend in Chapters 9 and 10.)

Let us turn to the issue of relativism first. Rorty, in the
closing passage of his "Postmodernist Bourgeois Liberalism," denies
that he is a relativist or that his views commit him to relativism.
This seems to me to be another example of the backing and shifting
that philosophers not infrequently engage in that is so well characterized by J. L. Austin's "First you say it and then you take it all
back."

Rorty's closing passage where he does just this—or so I claim
he does—should be quoted in full:

> The second objection is that what I have been calling "postmodernism"
> is better named "relativism," and that relativism is self-refuting.
> Relativism certainly is self-refuting, but there is a difference between
> saying that every community is as good as every other and saying that we
> have to work out from the networks we are, from the communities with
> which we presently identify. Postmodernism is no more relativistic than
> Hilary Putnam's suggestion that we stop trying for a "God's-eye view" and
> realize that "We can only hope to produce a more rational conception of
> rationality or a better conception of morality if we operate from within
> our tradition". The view that every tradition is as rational or as moral
> as every other could be held only by a god, someone who had no need
> to use (but only to mention) the terms "rational" or "moral," because she
> had no need to inquire or deliberate. Such a being would have escaped
> from history and conversation into contemplation and metanarrative. To
> accuse postmodernism of relativism is to try to put a metanarrative in the
> postmodernist's mouth. One will do this if one identifies "holding a
> philosophical position" with having a metanarrative available. If we insist
> on such a definition of "philosophy," then postmodernism is postphilo-
> sophical. But it would be better to change the definition.[49]

To accuse Rorty, a postmodernist, of relativism, as I would,
need not be to accuse Rorty of being committed, however unwittingly, to a metanarrative, even if what is intended now is something
rather more humble than "narratives which describe or predict the
activities of such entities as the noumenal self or the Absolute Spirit
or the Proletariat."[50] In attributing relativism to Rorty, we need not
attribute to him anything very grandiose or theoretical that should
be dressed up by a label such as "having a metanarrative."

That Rorty is engaging in the backing and shifting that
comes to first saying it and then taking it all back comes out in the

first part of the long quotation given above. When what he says in the main body of his text is compared with that first part of the quotation it will be evident that he is indeed backing and shifting. Of course, to say as he does in the passage quoted, "we have to work out from the networks we are, from the communities with which we presently identify" is not to commit oneself to relativism, for the first word need not be the last word. We might very well work out, as did Bayers Naude, from the community with which we presently identify to a wider community, perhaps (*pace* Rorty) even to humanity at large. To say we must work out from the networks we are says something reasonable about the points from which we start and, perhaps, even about the points from which we *must* start, but it says nothing about being contained within or constrained to remain within the parameters of that starting point or about the possibility of getting our beliefs in wide reflective equilibrium and the like. It does not even suggest that we are caught within the perspective of our tribe. There is indeed nothing supportive of relativism in *that* claim of Rorty's.

However, his statements in the main body of the text are much stronger than that and they are recognizably relativist. (Rorty, in trying to avoid the charge of relativism, makes a similar move to that of Peter Winch in trying to avoid the same charge, namely, he takes one very vulnerable formulation of relativism and insists that that is just what it is to be a relativist and then denies, correctly enough, given that characterization, that he is such a relativist. But that is just playing with words.)[51]

The remarks in the main body of his text, as well as in his article on Habermas and Lyotard, that show he (at least at the time of writing these essays) was a relativist in a perfectly recognizable and uncontroversial sense are as follows:

1. Rorty says there is no supercommunity such as humanity itself with whom we can identify. What we should do is be frankly ethnocentric and take the standards of our community as the standards to be accepted because there can be no more objective set of moral values to which our loyalties can be directed. There just are no supercultural standards to be appealed to nor can there be.

2.   There is in morality "no appeal beyond the relative merits of various actual or proposed communities to impartial criteria which help us weight those merits."[52]

3.   A "given society is just if its substantive life is lived in a way faithful to the shared understanding of the members."[53] This clearly entails that for any society X, X is just if its substantive life is so lived no matter what the content of that life is. Thus many different societies even with conflicting practices and principles of justice must all be said to be just if they meet that condition.

4.   Solidarity with one's tribe in a sufficient basis for solidarity, and indeed it is the only basis for solidarity.

These are all recognizably relativist views. (Dworkin, as Rorty recognizes, calls the third view relativism.) None of them are skeptical views. They all tell us, without any vacillation, what we ought to do. They say what is just or right or good. None suggests that we cannot know what we ought to do or what is good. They tell us that what is right, desirable, or what we ought to do is relative to the standards extant in different communities and that there are no standards beyond those of the community to which we can appeal to correct any of those views. This is as recognizably relativistic as is the form of relativism Rorty says he is *not* committed to, namely, the "self-refuting view that every community is as good as every other." They share a family resemblance, though the first view is less plainly vulnerable than the second. Rorty, like most critics of relativism, takes an absurd form of relativism and says that he is not that. (Refuting this absurd form of relativism is a standard classroom exercise that I doubt ever satisfies any bright student worried about relativism.) But other forms of relativism are more plausible, including the one I just attributed to Rorty. So, if that attribution is correct, Rorty cannot rightly deny that, at least in the two articles under consideration, he is a relativist.

Rorty is a relativist and (particularly where solidarity is taken as it is by Rorty to have a not inconsiderable value) relativism takes the form of maintaining that solidarity with one's tribe is a sufficient (and indeed the only) basis for solidarity. That view seems, at the very least, to have some rather worrisome implications. Some of them run like this: If one is an Afrikaner then one should stick to that solidarity, if one is a Zulu one should also stick to that solidarity, and if one is a North American liberal one should also stick to that solidarity. Whatever our tribe we should remain in solidarity with it, otherwise we are rootless individuals without solidarity. Sticking with that solidarity will bring the liberal into conflict with the Afrikaner, though it will give him no rational basis with which to criticize the Africaker. The Afrikaner, the Zulu, or the North American liberal can only just pit their solidarities against each other and, should anyone prevail over the other, power and a willingness to stick it out will be the relevant deciding factors, if Rorty's account is right. And indeed, if we accept his account, these will be rationally uncriticizable deciding factors. There will be nothing to criticize in their holding sway. Similar characteristics obtain for the other three formulations of relativism I elicited from Rorty. They raise, if we reflect on them, old, well-canvassed difficulties with relativism.

Perhaps relativism is, after all, unassailable, though Rorty does not show this. Perhaps the standards of our tribe are the only possible standards for us, and our own standards for what is sound moral belief are given, in a way ideology obscures from us, in the network of our social practices—social practices beyond which we cannot coherently make a moral or rational appeal. Perhaps it is not even really a matter that we *should* be frankly ethnocentric but that we *cannot* but be ethnocentric: We have no other alternative. Our conceptual imprisonment here is too deep. Perhaps in reality we can only have loyalties to our own tribe and stand in solidarity with our tribe. Impartial cross-cultural moral criteria may be a Holmes-less Watson or, worse still, an incoherency. There may be no coherent way of speaking of the just society or of even saying that contemporary Sweden is a more just society than contemporary Saudi Arabia so long as the substantive life lived in Saudi Arabia is lived in as faithful a way to the shared understanding of its members as is the case in Sweden. *By that criterion*, Saudi Arabia is probably a more just society than Sweden. Indeed, there are, given its liberalism and disinclination to ethnocentrism, more nay-sayers to Swedish culture among Swedes than nay-sayers to Saudi Arabian culture among the Saudis.

Solidarity may be essential in the moral life and it may be, *pace* Kantian or utilitarian universalists, that the only basis for solidarity is solidarity with one's tribe. No matter that the Afrikaners are brutalizing and exploiting blacks, one should, given the importance of solidarity, stand in solidarity with them if one is an Afrikaner and one can, if that is where one starts, have no reasonable ground for ceasing to be an Afrikaner. No matter that Hitler is murdering millions of Jews, one should stand in solidarity with him if one is a Nazi and, again, one can, if that is where one starts, have no reasonable ground for ceasing to be a Nazi. Rorty, as a good conservative liberal, cannot, of course, mean, and surely does not mean, to assert any of that. Yet such views seem plainly to be entailed by what he says about morality. Whether he likes it or not, he is, with such views, in that iron cage. Seeing himself as a social democrat, as he does, he plainly should regard that as a reductio.

What made liberalism attractive in the first place is that it seemed to leave a place for humanistic values that could take one beyond ethnocentrism and tribalism. This is one of the attractive features of Dewey's pragmatism that was a part of the humanistic, Enlightenment tradition of modernism. It is the same underlying commitment that, in their controversy, set Habermas apart from Rorty. Rorty's postmodernist neopragmatism gives us very different hopes and commitments than we find embedded in Dewey's pragmatism or in what Habermas endorses in that pragmatism.[54] Rorty's democratic liberalism, at least as he characterizes it, does not rest on a critical moral understanding or on a rational assessment of our social condition and historical possibilities, but on an accident of cultural history. These views, Rorty is in effect saying, just happen to be the views that got socialized into him as he grew up in the moderately comfortable, protected, and somewhat open-minded circumstances of North America rather than in the significantly different circumstances of Saudi Arabia, Nazi Germany, or in the Orange Free State. It is only a rationalist ideology, Rorty in effect gives to understand, that makes us think that there is such a thing as a cross-cultural, rational moral understanding. There just are those cultural differences with their different social practices and with their different standards of validity and rationality embedded in distinct and indeed often quite different forms of life. Like good ethnographers, we can note them, but there is no way of assessing them without begging the question. This, whatever we want to say about its truth, is light-years away from Dewey's expectations and those of progressive social democratic liberalism generally. This is, at best, liberalism in retreat.

Perhaps Rorty is right and his postmodernism is really telling it like it is. Perhaps this is indeed the tough-minded view. But, all that notwithstanding, Rorty's pragmatism is an eviscerated pragmatism rejecting the deeply embedded Enlightenment hopes that made pragmatism so attractive in the first place. If one really is to be a postmodernist—if this view of things is on the mark—then it seems to me that it would be less evasive to say with another postmodernist, Michel Foucault, that for "modern thought, no morality is possible" than to accept Rorty's cheery, "liberal" tribal moralism.

VIII

Let me return by this circuitous route to the question, "Can There Be Progress in Philosophy?" I have sought to give a reading to this question, and, if that reading is allowed to stand, I can answer the question conditionally in the affirmative. *If* the research program that is critical theory pans out, that is, *if* critical theory gets progressively and better defined and *if* a body of intellectual practices develops that yields empirical and normative results confirming their central claims and *if* disconfirming evidence does not mount that cannot be plausibly accounted for, then philosophy, construed in the broad way I chose, will have strikingly progressed. This is, however, a very chancy claim, for such an ambitious, holistic research program may well come to nought. If this happens, if critical theory comes to nought, it seems to me that the prospects for progress in philosophy are bleak. I believe that Rorty is essentially right in maintaining that in Wittgenstein and in pragmatism, when those intellectual orientations are thought through, as well as in the pragmatization of positivism that is in much of Quine and Sellars, we have, when we consider the force of these contemporary developments taken together, an account that thoroughly undermines foundationalism in its traditional forms in Cartesian-Kantian epistemological moves, in metaphysical "perennial philosophy," or in systematic analytic philosophy. Moreover, there is nothing significant in the Tradition that has come along to replace these with accounts that still effectively make the strong claims these various programmatic accounts made for philosophy.[55] I argued extensively for these claims in Part 1 and again, briefly, in a different way in this chapter.

With the end of philosophy, where "philosophy" is construed in the traditional professional ways, a Deweyan problems-of-men approach with a resolute rejection of any disciplinary matrix for philosophy seemed initially promising. I argued, in some detail, however, that it could not make good on its promise that *philosophy* could provide a rational and penetrating treatment of the problems of men. Shorn from the Tradition, and particularly from analytic philosophy and its differently vulnerable claims, it does not even give any clear sense to what *philosophy's* giving the problems of men a rational and penetrating treatment could come to. This, together with its piecemeal quality, undermines its initial attractiveness. We are pushed back to some form of critical theory, if we are to have anything of a theoretical sort, to refurbish the hopes and aspirations of the Enlightenment.

Suppose we go back, as Rorty argues we should, to an old, untechnical sense of "philosophy" in which "philosophy" does not name a distinct discipline but refers instead to the endeavor to see things in a comprehensive way in an attempt to make sense of our lives. "Philosophy," on that reading, simply refers to the endeavor to so see things for such a purpose and may or may not involve the employment of a discipline or a cluster of disciplines. If we so view philosophy, and I believe we should, then we can see critical theory as an attempt, now in a reasonably disciplined way, to do just that, i.e., to be philosophy in just that way. In doing that, it develops a cluster of disciplinary matrices to carry out in a more disciplined way the very conception of what philosophy is about built into philosophy in that ancient, relatively unproblematic and nondisciplinary sense.

Perhaps, as Rorty believes, nothing like this can be done, and critical theory will be no more an effective instrument in the realization of the endeavor to see things in a comprehensive way and thus make sense of our lives, than were the various ways the Tradition gave us. This is very possible and perhaps even likely. Critical theory is indeed a Pascalian wager. But it does not seem to me much of an exaggeration to say that vital human hopes turn on the outcome of that wager. And with this wager, or so it seems to me, go the prospects for progress in philosophy. If the wager works out, we have progress; if not, we do not.

I would like, however, to add a bit of an anticlimax. I have for the most part described critical theory in such a way as to make it sound as if it were springing fresh from the forehead of Zeus. That impression is misleading. I think critical theory as I have characterized it is new, but it has forerunners in the work—to take prominent examples—of Thomas Hobbes, Adam Smith, J. S. Mill, and, though rather differently, in the work of G. W. F. Hegel. We get closest of all to something like it in the work of Karl Marx and more generally in the Marxian tradition, on the one hand, and in the work of Max Weber, on the other. Critical theorists, as I remarked initially, in working out a critical theory do not have to start, and indeed should not try to start, de novo. Indeed, it seems to me that the best place to start is with the careful, rational reconstructions one gets of Marx by such analytical thinkers as G. A. Cohen, Allen Wood, Alan Gilbert, Richard Miller, Jon Elster, and Robert Paul Wolff and in the developments of Marxian theory found in Andrew Levine, Erick Olin Wright, Alison Jaggar, Harry Braverman, Herbert Gentis, Richard Edwards, Göran Therborn, Jeffrey Reiman, John Roemer, Joseph McCarney, and Claus Offe, to name a few. These rational reconstructions of Marx and developments of Marxian theory may, when taken together, give us the kind of critical theory we need—something we can develop, refine, and apply. Alternatively, we may need a far more thorough synthesizing of Weber and Marx to get the beginnings of a more adequate critical theory. Perhaps Habermas's still greater departure from Marx with his melding of many different traditions in philosophy and social theory, as we find in his mammoth and monumental *Theory of Communicative Action*, is what we need? Perhaps, instead, what we need is something closer to the approach of Anthony Giddens or perhaps it should be something linked more closely with the work of Durkheim or Pareto or perhaps it will be something that takes a strikingly original line. Still, we have plenty of models here—models with family resemblances.

I have my own Marxian hunches here, but they are little more than hunches. What I have been concerned to do in this chapter is to delineate the outlines, in a very general way, of what a critical theory could be and should be and to defend it as a coherent and plausible possibility of what the successor subject of philosophy should be after the end of philosophy as traditionally conceived.

Let me conclude with just one more twist of the dialectic. Bertrand Russell and Noam Chomsky have done some superb social criticism with a progressive emancipatory thrust, and Joshua Cohen and Joel Rogers have recently followed brilliantly in their footsteps with their little book *On Democracy*. Many who are not even in Russell's or Chomsky's intellectual ballpark have made sport of the untheoretical and nonsystematic side of their social criticism. Indeed, their work has been rather brutely empirical and normative with little theoretical baggage invoked, and it has not made systematic claims. Chomsky makes it clear that he does not think social theory is in a position to attain such a systematic scientific status.[56] Yet their social criticism has typically been acute and probing. Many of us would like it to have a more determinate theoretical under-pinning, but *perhaps* it is in the very nature of social criticism that it cannot have such an underpinning? When we try to impose it, it is not unreasonable (though I hope a mistake) to believe that we will get what we do not want, namely, a metanarrative. *If* that is so, then a good critical theory would be far less theoretically ramified and holistic then I have characterized it, but it still would be subject to empirical constraints, fallibilistic, and have an emancipatory thrust. With these various features, it would remain a good successor subject to philosophy. However this Russellian-Chomskyan thing would have at least some of the problems of the Deweyan problems-of-men approach. Indeed, such a minimalist conception of critical theory is hardly distinct from the problems-of-men-approach. The two models seem to blend into each other here.[57] Be that as it may, it is natural to ask just what is *philosophical* about what they do? *Perhaps* what should be said is that this cut-down critical theory just is what counts as philosophy here. But then this answer is available to the Deweyan problems-of-men approach too.

If along any of these rather various lines we can get a sound critical theory, we can then say that philosophy, construed as critical theory, has progressed. If critical theory, along all these lines, comes to nought, then the prognosis for progress in philosophy is very bleak, given the power of the end-of-philosophy theses that Rorty, linking Wittgenstein with a historical narrative about the evolution of modern philosophy, has powerfully thrust on our reflective consciousness.

8

Scientism, Pragmatism, and
the Fate of Philosophy

I

Many have taken the real object of Richard Rorty's attack
on systematic philosophy to be an attack on analytical philosophy.
That is a mistake.[1] He is ranging much wider than that. Husserl,
in his estimation, has taken a wrong turning as much as Russell or
Popper, and (coming to our time) Habermas (or at least Apel) as
much as Dummett, to the extent that the former, as much as the
latter, relies on transcendental arguments or takes a transcendental
turn. It is the very taking of any transcendental turn and turning
philosophy into a distinctive discipline with specialized form of
knowledge that Rorty sets out to undermine. Richard Bernstein
puts it well when he remarks that "Rorty's primary object of attack
is any form of systematic philosophy which shares the conviction that
there are real foundations that philosophy must discover and that
philosophy as a discipline can transcend history and adumbrate a
permanent neutral matrix for assessing all forms of inquiry and all
types of knowledge."[2]
What if (as Rorty has argued and I have argued) there is no
defending the Tradition, and systematic analytical philosophy and its

Continental cousins along with traditional metaphysical philosophy
(e.g., Thomism or idealism) must be given up? We will then want
to know "what function, if any, philosophers can perform and what
type of self-understanding of philosophy emerges if we give up the
various 'self-deceptions' that Rorty exposes."[3]

From a reading of *Philosophy and the Mirror of Nature* it is
very easy to get the impression that Rorty is telling us we should go
from epistemology to hermeneutics, from systematic philosophy to
edifying philosophy, giving us a new kind of philosophical theory.[4]
This is a mistake, but a revealing mistake. The phrase "edifying
philosophy" is, I think, unfortunate, but not the concept—a concept
borrowed from Kierkegaard—that underlies it.[5] The phrase suggests
that philosophers are to pour on the sweet syrup of consolation or
moral encouragement (perhaps even moral rearmament) urging us
either to accept life as it is or to go on, Faust-like, to still greater
heights of achievement. Rorty has nothing like this in mind. Nor,
for that matter, did Kierkegaard. For Rorty, "edifying philosophy"
is reactive, debunking philosophy—the sort of thing done with genius
in the nineteenth century by Kierkegaard and Nietzsche and in the
twentieth century by Wittgenstein and (Rorty says) Heidegger. It is
always a reactive philosophy parasitic upon the pretensions of
systematic philosophy. Edifying philosophers direct an assorted
battery of reductio arguments against systematic philosophy. They
satirize and scorn the Tradition in various ways. They are the
masters of indirect discourse. With such techniques they mock the
grand Either/Or: "Either there is some basic foundational constraint
or we are confronted with intellectual and moral chaos."[6] But they
do not offer us a new method or new foundations; instead, they
produce a mocking critique of both the need for foundations or a
method and the very possibility of foundations or a new method, or
indeed any kind of method, that would give us the rationale for a
critique of culture. Systematic philosophy purports to give us a more
rational picture of the world and an Archimedean point for the
critique of our institutions. Edifying philosophy, with its hermeneutical turn, sees philosophy not as a rational inquiry but as conversation, as one of the many voices in the conversation of humankind.
Philosophy should no longer be seen as argument and attempted
proof but as conversation that can "be civilized, illuminating,
intelligent, revealing, exciting."[7] We move from a scientific style (or

at least an attempted scientific style) to something like a literary style. Philosophy is no longer to be viewed as an inquiry into truth or an attempted discovery of foundations. Yet considerations of truth do not simply drop out. They enter, along with many other elements, into the conversation, for Rorty does think that there is something called practical wisdom, which is necessary to participate effectively in the conversation, that philosophy is partner to.[8] But the attainment of this practical wisdom means abandoning the persistent philosophical illusion that really good philosophers are people who know "something about knowing which nobody else knows so well."[9]

II

This alternative conception of Rorty's is not clearly or perhaps even consistently articulated. There are philosophers who, generally in agreement with Rorty's critique of the Tradition, find his alternative unpalatable.[10] Richard Bernstein is one of these. He believes that "Rorty himself does not quite see where his best insights and arguments are leading him" and that, more like Wittgenstein and less like Dewey, he remains too obsessed with the very tradition he would reject.[11] Indeed, claims Bernstein, a version of the Either/Or still haunts him: "Either we are ineluctably tempted by foundational metaphors and the desperate attempt to escape from history *or* we must frankly recognize that philosophy itself is at best a form of 'kibitzing'."[12] Bernstein, using a technique that is Rorty's, prods us to ask: "Suppose, however, that Rorty's therapy were really successful; suppose we were no longer held captive by metaphors of 'our glassy essence' and 'mirroring', suppose we accepted that knowledge claims can never be justified in any other way than by an appeal to social practices, suppose we were purged of the desire for constraint and compulsion, what then?"[13] He thinks that if that were so, the cultural scene and the voice of philosophy in the conversation of mankind would look very different from those Rorty proposes.[14]

Dewey sees further and deeper than does Rorty or Wittgenstein, Bernstein argues, as to what a reconstructed philosophy would look like on the other side of a liberation from the Tradition and its

eternal "problems of philosophy."[15]   For Dewey, philosophy recon-
structs itself when it turns the problems of philosophy into the
problems of men:

> Dewey would certainly agree with Rorty that all justification involves
> reference to existing social practices and that philosophy is not a
> discipline that has any special knowledge of knowing or access to more
> fundamental foundations. But for Dewey this is where the real problems
> begin. What are the social practices to which we should appeal? How
> do we discriminate the better from the worse? Which ones need to be
> discarded, criticized, and reconstructed? Dewey sought to deal with these
> problems without any appeal to "our glassy essence," "mirroring," or
> foundational metaphors. According to Rorty's own analysis, these are
> genuine problems, but Rorty never gets around to asking these and
> related questions. He tells us, of course, that there is no special
> philosophical method for dealing with such issues and no ahistorical
> matrix to which we can appeal. But accepting this claim does not make
> these issues disappear. Whatever our final judgment of Dewey's success
> or failure in dealing with what he called the "problems of men," Dewey
> constantly struggled with questions which Rorty never quite faces—
> although his whole reading of modern philosophy is one that points to
> the need for reflective intellectuals to examine them. Sometimes Rorty
> writes as if any philosophic attempt to sort out the better from the worse,
> the rational from the irrational (even assuming that this is historically
> relative) must lead us back to foundationalism and the search for an
> ahistorical perspective. But Rorty has also shown us that there is nothing
> inevitable about such a move. Following Rorty, we do not have to see
> this enterprise as finding a successor foundational discipline to
> epistemology, but rather as changing the direction of philosophy, of giving
> the conversation a different turn. Ironically, for all his critique of the
> desire of philosophers to escape from history and to see the world *sub
> specie aeternitatis*, there is a curious way in which Rorty himself slides
> into this stance. He keeps telling us that the history of philosophy, like
> the history of all culture, is a series of contingencies, accidents, of the
> rise and demise of various language games and forms of life.   But
> suppose we place ourselves back into our historical situation. Then a
> primary task is one of trying to deal with present conflicts and confu-
> sions, of trying to sort out the better from the worse, of focusing on
> which social practices ought to endure and which demand reconstruction,
> of what types of justification are acceptable and which are not. Rorty
> might reply that there is no reason to think that the professional
> philosopher is more suited for such a task than representatives of other
> aspects of culture. But even this need not be disputed. We can
> nevertheless recognize the importance and the legitimacy of the task of
> "understanding how things in the broadest sense of the term hang
> together in the broadest sense of the term."[16]

Rorty does indeed leave conceptual space for these problems, but he does not grapple with them himself or, like Dewey,
direct philosophers, at long last free from the Tradition, to grapple

with these problems, let alone indicate how they might successfully do so. His own account, unlike Dewey's, remains an "aesthetic pragmatism." That there are no ahistorical standards of rationality or objectivity providing us with ahistorical reasons for acting, reasons that can be seen to be good reasons independently of time, place, and circumstance, does not imply that there are no historically determinate reasons—"historical reasons" if you will—that, relative to a distinct cultural and historical context, can be established to be good reasons for doing or not doing one thing rather than another.[17] Moreover, the issues *cannot* be resolved simply by appealing to existing social practices, for "the heart of the controversy is the genuine and serious conflict of competing social practices."[18]

There may be very good reasons indeed—at least on some readings—for accepting Rorty's historicism and for claiming that all justification, scientific and moral, is social and historically determinate. What else, it is natural to ask, could it be? In that way there is no escaping history. Still, we can accept this quite unequivocally while quite consistently believing that as human beings acting at a particular time and place, with an historically conditioned consciousness, we still need, firmly in situ, to try to determine among conflicting social practices which ones are to be acted in accordance with or which to be modified and in what way so that we can attain, in a determinate context and for a determinate time, a rational consensus. The method of wide reflective equilibrium is, I think, a very good general characterization of how we are to go about achieving such a rational consensus—and it squares nicely with what Rorty commends as a "pragmatism without method."[19] (I explicate it, argue for it, and defend it from criticisms in Chapters 9, 10, and 11.)

In so reasoning here, we are going to get, if anything, *phronesis* (a type of practical reasoning that doesn't attempt to appeal to ultimate foundations, eternal standards, or algorithms) rather than the foundationalist's *noesis*. The rationality available to us within this contextualistic fallibilism "is always a form of rational persuasion which can never attain a definitive ahistorical closure." (The rationalist's search for such a closure is a further flight from reality—a dreaming of the dream of the Absolute.) But reflective understanding and assessment of our situation does not require such an Archimedean point. Rather than searching for foundations, we should see philosophy as reflective conversation, playing its part in a larger conversation, in which we attempt to hammer out for a particular time and place a rational consensus concerning how to realign conflicting social practices so that they form a more reasonable social whole.

III

Rorty takes not only talk about conceptual foundations but talk of methodology as his nemesis. Such talk, he believes, will always lead us down the garden path. There are, however, ways and ways of raising methodological considerations and of stressing the importance of method. In a way that is commensurate with but still importantly distinct from Bernstein's remarks about Dewey and Rorty, Isaac Levi shows that Rorty badly misappropriates one of his three great heroes here, i.e., Dewey.[20] For Dewey (*pace* Rorty), considerations of method were central. He sought to articulate something he called "logic, the theory of inquiry," which showed the social activity of science, construed broadly and flexibly, to be continuous with ways of commonsense reasoning that are cross-culturally pervasive. This picture of how to fix belief—or so I would claim against Rorty—was not scientistic and did not fix scientific method in stone as something called the hypothetico-deductive method. But it did afford the general outlines of a way in which the institutions of society—including its moral stance—and various forms of life could be understood and rationally criticized, and it did firmly stand against what we would now call Kuhnian or Winchian incommensurability claims—claims Rorty takes over holus-bolus. Levi is at least as thorough an antifoundationalist as Rorty, yet he does not accept incommensurability theses. "Opposition to foundationalism," Levi remarks, "ought to be the philosophical equivalent of resistance to sin."[21] But, he argues, Rorty confuses "anti-foundationalism, anti-representationalism, and opposition to glassy essences"—all good things in Levi's view (as well as mine)—with the Kuhnian doctrine of "anti-commensurabilism," and all of these "with opposition to recognizing truth as an important desideratum in inquiry."[22] Levi thinks that if we think through key aspects of what

Dewey says about method, we will come to see that we can be, and indeed should be, antifoundationalists, all the while rejecting Kuhnian and Rortyan incommensurability theses. We will also recognize without the mystification of the correspondence theory of truth the importance of the search for and the attainment of some measure of truth or warranted assertability in our struggle to see how things hang together in the most inclusive sense of that word. Rorty's stress on literary sensibilities, and a literary rather than scientific style in the writing of philosophy, is a good antidote to *scientistic* thinking and styles of philosophical writing, but it also underplays the role of what Dewey called scientific inquiry in all domains of our life. In rightly reacting to scientism, Rorty, like Wittgenstein, is too inclined to see science as but one form of life among others.[23] Dewey, we need to remember, construes "science" very broadly. "Rational deliberative inquiry" might be a better phrase for what Dewey has taken scientific method to be. But perhaps not much turns on this beyond the fate, shifting in different cultural contexts, of "science" as an *honorific* term. (More of this later.)

Applying certain Deweyan ideas, Levi argues that there are "no incommensurable abysses worth bridging." We are not caught up in various incommensurable hermeneutical circles or, at the very least, it has not been shown that we are so trapped, let alone that we must be so trapped. Rorty, it is important to remember, generalizes Kuhn's incommensurability theses not only to different scientific paradigms or disciplinary matrices but to different political and economic arrangements, aesthetic stances, conceptions of philosophy, religions, world-views, and the like. What Levi seeks to undermine is the claim that rival points of view concerning the truth or falsity, warrantability or unwarrantability of scientific theories, the propriety of political arrangements or the aesthetic qualities of works of art are in their core aspects incommensurable in the sense that they are incapable of being, as Rorty puts it, "brought under a set of rules which will tell us how rational agreement can be reached or what would settle the issue on every point where statements seem to conflict."[24]

Levi, roughly following Dewey, sets forth a procedure (a method, if you will) for avoiding the block to inquiry in incommensurability claims. Prima facie when one finds oneself in the sort of situation where Rorty or Kuhn would say we have incommensurability claims (claims concerning that we must just choose—or so the notion goes) what we should do is bracket those claims and conceptions that at least seem to be incommensurable and essentially contestable and seek to isolate, between the contending parties, "those assumptions and procedures which are noncontroversial in the context of the controversy and move to a point of view where only these assumptions and procedures are taken for granted in the inquiry, deliberation or discourse."[25]   We bracket or suspend judgment on the contested issue (the putatively incommensurable claims) for the nonce and, working with and from the issues on which we agree, see if by drawing implications from them we can ascertain, working from that consensus and by considering how it can be uncontentiously expanded, which of the contested positions or courses of action ought to be adopted.   Using a coherentist model, we seek to see which of these contested claims fits best with what we do agree on.   It will usually be the case that one will fit better than the other alternatives, and when this obtains we will have good grounds for accepting the better-fitting one.   Where they both fit equally well (something that will seldom, if ever, obtain) we can say that there is no significant difference between them.   Where the at least putative incommensurabilities are so indeterminate that we cannot ascertain which makes the better fit, we can, and will if we are reasonable, work (operating from our prior consensus) to make them more determinate until we can ascertain either which makes the better fit or whether they both fit equally well.   In no instance are we just struck with incommensurabilities, though sometimes, of course, which makes the better fit will be very difficult to determine.   What we need to recognize is that by proceeding in this way, we can avoid begging questions at the outset, blocking the road to inquiry, and findings ourselves trapped with two or more distinct theories or practices with no rational grounds for adjudicating between them.

However, there is, as Levi is fully aware, an evident enough objection to such a procedure: "It is not always sensible to suspend judgment in the face of disagreement in order to give other views a hearing."[26] As Levi puts it, "Feyerabend to the contrary notwithstanding, it is silly to give a serious hearing to every fool proposal that comes along."[27]   Must astronomers pay attention to flat-earthers?   Ideological struggles aside, should scientists pay any attention at all to creationists?   If, standing where we are, someone tries to start a movement in physics with the slogan "Back to Aristotle," should we pay any attention at all?   It was relevant for Galileo but not for us.   We may find it difficult to define criteria for scientific advance.   But at least in the hard sciences, isn't there plainly such an advance?[28]   I do not think it is undue dogmatism—or indeed dogmatism at all—on my part to say that these questions are all rhetorical and that it is plainly not the case that everything goes. We should not, because of some philosophical or ideological dogma, pretend to doubt what we do not really doubt after careful and knowledgeable reflection.

What bothers me here a little as a philosopher—though I don't lose much sleep over it—is that I do not know how in any very comprehensive or even satisfactory way to explain *why* this is so.   And I think it *may* be a worthwhile task to do so, though it no doubt has a lower order of priority than not a few philosophers are wont to believe.   But in the interim, while we are awaiting such an account, if indeed we ever get one, I would take a Moorean turn and say of any philosophical account that says there has been no scientific development or claims that "anything goes," that it is far more reasonable to reject it than it would be to reject claims of the ordinary sort to scientific development and claims such as Levi's that some views are just too silly to deserve a hearing.   Christian Science would be a case in point.   Must we solemnly study Mary Baker Eddy?   It is an unserious sort of relativism that tells us we must.

Still there are problems here about the boundaries.   I was about to write "Must we listen to Nazis?" when I reminded myself that there are chaps in our culture—even educated chaps—who would have as readily used the example "Must we listen to Communists?"   And, as Noam Chomsky has forcefully brought to our attention, those who are thought to be beyond the pale of academic responsibility (particularly when social issues are discussed) and those who are thought to deserve a hearing in the domain of politics get defined very conservatively and very ideologically indeed.[29]   So although it is clear enough that some things are beyond the pale—something we recognize *ambulando*—and it is silly to seek a consensus that would bring everyone under the net, it remains, as Levi puts it,

an interesting and important question when one should and should not
open up one's mind to rival points of view concerning the truth of
scientific theories, the rightness or wrongness of actions, the legitimacy
of political constitutions, or the qualities of works of art. It is just as
indefensible to answer "always" as "never"; and no alternative context
independent principle applicable on all occasions and regardless of the
nature of the dispute and its participants will prove better.[30]

It looks, at least in the meantime, that what we have to do is rely
on our own judgments—indeed our very fallible, sometimes ideologically distorted judgments—aided, of course, by our background
knowledge, affected by where we stand in history and in the society
in which we live and dependent on our capacities both to empathize
and to distance ourselves. Sometimes, for some of us, that can put
us in a fine ideological pickle indeed.

In trying to find some viewpoint from which we could
criticize social institutions or practices or even whole ways of life in
some manner that does not beg the question, we do not need to
find a point of view neutral to *all* controversies—that indeed is an
impossibility—but a point of view neutral to the particular issues
under scrutiny, even when those issues are as broad as comparing
the relative merits of capitalism and socialism in the twentieth
century.[31] To transcend an ideological treatment of the matter, it is
important to find such a neutral ground if we can. And there is no
good reason in advance of inquiry not to think that if we work hard
we can find such a neutral ground. It might, in this instance,
depend on there being a consensus on the possibility and (if
possible) the importance of such holistic assessments, or on what
good explanations in the social sciences would look like, or on at
least some of the conditions necessary for there to be undistorted
communication. But to do these things and feasibly to engage in
social critique or use this Deweyan method in such critique, we do
not have to be able to give a coherent account of what is probably
not itself coherent, namely, the idea of moving to a point of view
that is neutral vis-à-vis all controversies.[32] In attempting to solve
the problems of people (real-life problems, when the engine isn't
idling) and when faced with seemingly intractable conflict, we only
need (to keep reasoned argument alive and not block inquiry) to be
able to move to "a point of view neutral for the issues under

scrutiny."[33] We do not have to be able to move to "a point of view neutral for all controversies."[34]

There may very well be no way to prove the nonexistence of incommensurabilities. But failure of proof here does not even remotely mean that we should assume that there are incommensurabilities so that there are some issues concerning which there just is no possibility of reasoning through to a better or worse conclusion. Still, we should not become too optimistic about the *actual* powers of reason and critical inquiry to provide the engines of sound social critique and the critique of ideology. Even if we are always able to suspend judgment for the sake of argument over some genuinely contested issue without begging questions, still, as Levi well puts it, this will itself not "guarantee that enough will survive [when we set aside initially the contested issues] in the way of noncontroversial assumptions and methods to secure resolution in a reasonable and definite manner."[35] However, faced with such possibilities we may always reasonably *hope*, as the pragmatists stressed, that "proceeding with inquiry will yield resources for resolving disputes."[36] The resolution may not be immediate and sometimes may be only resolution in the longer run, but, even so, we need not, and indeed should not, assume that we just run up against stark incommensurabilities concerning which we can only take a stance.[37] We do not have to assume, nor is it the direction in which reason (that is, the use of our rational powers, our intelligence) pushes us, that there are situations in which our intellects cannot give us guidance and decision becomes king. Such decisionalism is Kierkegaardian, Harean, Sartrean, Popperian romanticism, not something a realistic understanding of our lot forces us to accept. There are times when the practicalities of the situation simply require action under great unclarity. Any revolutionary knows the pathos of this. But if we counterfactually had the time for further deliberation and investigation, nothing in the nature of the case tells us that we will run up against situations in which we can *know* that nothing more is to be said and we must just plump one way or the other without justification. Such secular Lutheranism has not been established, though we can, of course, have no guarantees that there will always be a determinate solution either.

To view things in this manner is not a touching or benighted faith in reason, but just a refusal to place roadblocks in the path of inquiry. If we are thorough antifoundationalist coherentists, we will not postulate incommensurable conceptual frameworks or even assume any sharp distinction between issues concerning conceptual frameworks and those concerning nonconceptual frameworks. That should go with the rejection of any sharp, nonrelativized distinction between analytic and synthetic. These considerations are strongly reinforced by the Davidsonian arguments against the conceptual relativism I articulated in Chapter 5.

Following Kuhn, Rorty rightly sees, Levi claims, that controversies in the sciences do not differ in kind from controversies in politics and morals. But, according to Levi, Rorty gives this the wrong twist. The reason they do not differ in kind is rooted in the implications of the fact that actual "scientific inquiry is goal or problem oriented."[38] This being so, what constitutes an optimal solution in science as well as politics "depends on the nature of the problem and, hence, on the aims and values of the inquiry."[39] This makes scientific discourse in certain important respects like practical deliberation. *Phronesis* rather than *noesis* applies here as much as in the art of politics or in morality. Between these different forms of life our canons for rational goal attainment are not very different, let alone incommensurable.

Dewey does not exaggerate when he speaks of the "fundamental unity of the structure of commonsense and science."[40] Without reducing or attempting to reduce values to facts or factual claims to normative claims, we can use a common method for their rational resolution yet not see morals and science or normative and factual claims as having the same subject matter or giving normative and factual claims the same logical status. Moreover, recognizing the importance of the claim that a fundamental unity of the structure of common sense and science yields a common method of inquiry is perfectly compatible with the acceptance of a reasonable reading of Antonio Gramsci's claim that what is the common sense is certain bits of the ideology of the ruling class of a particular time.

Although bracketing any consideration concerning the various philosophical contenders for the best analysis of what "true" or "truth" means, we can take truth, or at least warranted assertability, quite seriously as something to be judged relative to the development of what Dewey calls, treating the term generally, scientific method.[41] When we look at the various belief systems strewn around over cultural and historical space and time, we are not caught with incommensurable, fundamentally unarguable, distinct world views. In this context it is particularly important to keep in mind Levi's contention that neither Rorty nor Kuhn, or for that matter neither Winch nor Wittgenstein, have given us anything like adequate reasons for believing "that incommensurability ever has obtained or does obtain."[42] Morals, the arts, politics, and science may very well be different forms of life with different ends and distinct rationales, but they are all in important respects goal-oriented, and because of this they share some common norms of rational inquiry and thus are not incommensurable activities with incommensurable norms of appropriateness.[43]

Without reducing ethics and politics to science, or engaging in any kind of reduction either way, we can (*pace* Rorty) still stress the availability of a common method of inquiry and common norms of rationality. And these norms and that method undermine nihilism and at least certain forms of relativism. However, Levi stresses even here, following Dewey, both the centrality and the strategic nature of scientific inquiry. The fruits of scientific inquiry "serve as resources for further information gathering inquiry, as standards for judging possibility in guiding policy and furnishing technologies for policy and the arts."[44] Truth (rational investigation) here takes priority over style. What is crucial to recognize is that our moral and political conceptions—including our values—can be made "subject to critical control in inquiries which bear marks of rationality similar to those exhibited by properly conducted scientific inquiries."[45] It isn't that we can rely without supplementation on these general standards of rationality and scientific method for resolving all, or even most, of the various problems of men. The "method must be supplemented by additional assumptions and rules, by special objectives which differentiate branches of scientific inquiry from one another and these from activities focused on problems of 'use and enjoyment'."[46] But an underlying, commonly required method with common standards of rationality undercuts incommensurability claims and extreme forms of relativism.

There is, it is not unnatural to argue, a dual role for philosophy after the demise of the Tradition. It is (a) one voice among others in the goal-directed carrying out of this inquiry and in the critique of the problems of men, and (b) a critical reflection on this very ongoing inquiry—a kind of, as Dewey put it, criticism of criticisms—designed incrementally and in a fallibilistic manner to sharpen, improve, and, where desirable, systematize our problem-solving abilities. This reconstruction of philosophy or, if you will, this successor to philosophy, is neither systematic or unsystematic analytic philosophy nor edifying philosophy, though on occasion it will use bits and pieces of both for its own purposes. And it will be philosophy (if that is the right name for it) more closely inter-locked with the human sciences than the philosophy coming out of the Tradition or Rorty's aestheticized neopragmatism. It also nicely meshes, on a more general level, with the Deweyan conception of philosophy as social critique, defended by Bernstein.

IV

There are three changes—all moving in the direction of Dewey, one of Rorty's heroes—that I have urged on Rorty. Recognizing (as does Rorty) that "philosophy" is not a word standing for a natural kind, I have argued (a) that Rorty fails to recognize the role of philosophy, after the death of epistemology, as social criticism or criticism of ideology in the service of the problems of men; (b) that Rorty too readily follows the trend of a rather uncritical acceptance of incommensurability theses; and (c) that Rorty does not see, taking now the wide sense of "science," the importance of the Peircean-Deweyan conception of the role of scientific method in the fixing of belief.

Rorty has shown a remarkable, and to my mind commend-able, flexibility in response to criticisms and a readiness to rethink positions and abandon claims without losing the profound, and to some unsettling, underlying conception he is spinning of the development of philosophy and its role in our intellectual and social history. It seems to me that if Rorty were to go in the more pragmatist direction gestured at here, nothing would be lost of his overall conception of the nonspecialist, nondisciplinary conception of how philosophy should develop after the demise of the Tradition and of what the role of this "new philosophy" should be in our intellectual life. At most he would, though in an utterly nonscien-tistic way, have to give to science and to systematic social critique more, and a somewhat different, weight in the conversation of humankind than he seems willing to do now. He could—or so it seems to me—with these emendations and without abandoning historicism, deflect frequent charges of nihilism and relativism, charges he in fact wants to deflect.[47] (With such changes, this would include my charges about relativism made in the previous chapter.)

There are, however, some remarks in Rorty's important and revealing "Reply to Six Critics," as well as in his "Pragmatism Without Method," which might indicate grounds for resistance about incommensurability and scientific method.[48] In the former he faces Alasdair MacIntyre's challenge that to write the kind of narrative about philosophy that Rorty intends, he must have available standards of objectivity and rationality beyond anything he thinks is available to him. Rorty responds to this in two passages:

> As I see it, those who, like MacIntyre and myself, write revisionist history in the form of what MacIntyre has called "dramatic narratives," no more appeal to "standards of objectivity and rationality" than novelists appeal to "standards of good novel writing" or than Newton appeals to "standards of scientific inquiry." Typically a new history or a new theory or a new novel succeeds by striking its readers as "just what we needed." Later, perhaps, somebody may come and construct some "standards" which the latest successes satisfy, but that is just ad hoc pedagogy. If there were such things as "standards of objectivity and rationality" which determined what counted as a good argument about the nature of objectivity and rationality, then they would either be forever immune to change, for their critic would be convicted either of self-referential inconsistency by invoking them or of irrationality by not invoking them. So I take it that there are no such standards. There are just communities of informed readers who are open to persuasion.[49]

> Here we can recognize the same artificial problem as came up in connection with MacIntyre's "objective and rational standards." If there were such standards, or if there were a vocabulary the employment of which constituted rationality, then they would be uncriticizable. There would be no way "rationally" to substitute some new standards or some new vocabulary. I call this an artificial problem because I think that it is solved every day, *ambulando*, by people gradually becoming bored with old platitudes, beginning to treat as "literal" what they had once treated as "metaphorical" and conversely and insensibly ceasing to discuss Q not because they doubt its presupposition P but merely because they have found better things to discuss. The changes from pagan to Christian, from Christian to Enlightenment, and from Enlightenment to romantic and historicist ways of speaking cannot be analyzed as "rational," if that means that a speaker of 4th century B.C. Attica would "in principle" have been able to formulate the arguments for and against making these

changes. But nobody wants to say that this sequence of changes in the
Western mind was "irrational." The opposition between "rational
argument" and "irrational persuasion" is simply too coarse to describe
what happens in intellectual history.[50]

Rorty is right in claiming that a variety of specific and
diverse contextually embedded factors in the main determine how at
any specific time it is reasonable to proceed.[51] He is also right in
claiming that very specific, putatively contextless conceptions of
substantive canons of rationality would, if treated seriously as
rational guides, hamstring the development of thought. But Levi's
pragmatist conceptions are procedural and would not so block
thought. Indeed, they make conceptual space for openness in a way
that should be congenial to Rorty. Even substantive canons of
rationality need not have either the self-defeating features or the
antifallibilistic features Rorty ascribes to them. They can and should
be put forth as putative canons of rationality and as such, along with
more contextual factors, guide without hobbling. We have with
them a sense that not everything goes and we can specify, if pressed,
why a given view is in cloud-cuckoo-land without putting our alleged
standards beyond criticism.

Rorty might well counter that so construed they are harmless
enough but also useless because they are always being corrected by
our concrete practices. But there is no warrant for saying this.
What is true is that sometimes the practices correct the standards
and sometimes the standards are used to correct the practices. We
shuttle back and forth until we gain what for a time is an equilibrium. Theory corrects practice and practice corrects theory.
Correction goes both ways as it does in the relation between
considered judgments and general principles in seeking wide reflective equilibrium. Sometimes the specific considered judgments give
rise to an alteration or abandonment of general principles, and
sometimes general principles (particularly when taken in conjunction
with other considered judgments) give rise to a modification or an
abandonment of certain judgments. We make adjustments at either
end and, indeed, often in the middle, no algorithm telling us what
we must always do. It seems to me that the relations between
particular practices and general canons of rationality are the same.
And such a method of reflective equilibrium is fully in the spirit of
fallibilism that Rorty, like Levi, rightly prizes. It is not that when

people write revisionist history they must appeal to such standards. They may or may not do so.   But in subsequent justificatory arguments the standards are among the considerations that can relevantly be brought to bear, as can Levi-type standards of procedural rationality.

We have incommensurability problems and problems about the limits of rationality when adherents of large and comprehensive points of view have systematic disagreements that extend not only to how these disagreements should be resolved but, more fundamentally, to how they are to be correctly characterized.   The problem that Rorty, following Kuhn and MacIntyre here, feels—and feels as the problem of incommensurability—is how it is possible, if indeed it is possible, to rationally and objectively, without something like ideological distortion, adjudicate such rival claims, including the comparative appraisal of claims embedded in contexts so different that apparently no neutral criterion or standard of argument is available.   Because of these (putative) incommensurabilities, there appear at least to be vital, large-scale disagreements in many domains that are rationally irresolvable.   The power of Levi's suggestions is to show that if we follow his fundamentally Deweyan procedures (as it is always open for us to do), we have no good grounds for denying, at least in advance of determined and repeated attempts, that at some relevant level we will be able to find neutral criteria that (if we have the will) will give us the bases to adjudicate the rival claims of any putative incommensurability.   There may be all sorts of practical reasons why we will not, and indeed should not, always so reason things out.   But that is not because reason is wanton and because we do not have the intellectual resources for such reasoning.

V

Rorty may balk at this Deweyan conception of philosophy as criticism of criticisms, for Rorty (a) is wary of methodological turns, (b) rejects claims that philosophy can provide an Archimedean point to assess the rest of culture, and (c) rejects the claim that the term philosophy "names a natural kind—a distinctive sort of inquiry with a continuous history since the Greeks."[52]   He neither laments that fact, if it is a fact, nor feels that it deprives philosophy, now to be construed more broadly, of a useful cultural function.

I argued in Part 1 that Rorty is right, and indeed deeply and insightfully right, in his rejection of the Tradition and its conception of philosophy as expressed in (b) and (c) above. I also think he is right to be wary of methodological turns. They often just reduplicate in a foreign jargon familiar problems at a metalevel and serve as an excuse—often an ideologically convenient excuse—for failing to come to grips with pressing substantive problems. But that they often do does not mean that they always must. The Deweyan turn is not such arm waving. Moreover, philosophy conceived as a "criticism of criticisms" and Dewey's talk of method can take various readings, but I do not think the reading Levi puts on it conflicts with the rejection of the Tradition pressed by Rorty. "Philosophy," on this conception, does not name a natural kind. It is not a distinctive professional discipline operating autonomously from science and our various reflective practices. It is not a discipline that, functioning autonomously, perspicuously displays the "foundations of knowledge" and gives us the rational basis for the adjudication of cultural claims.

Dewey always links philosophy closely to the social sciences and to social criticism and the reflective activity of socially engaged human beings. Rejecting bifurcations as he does, Dewey would not think of philosophy as sharply distinct from social science or social criticism. And his intellectual practice does not differ much in kind from that of Max Weber, George Herbert Mead, Erich Fromm, and C. Wright Mills. Indeed, what seems perplexing both to many traditional philosophers and analytic philosophers and a mistake to not a few is that Dewey often does not appear to be even trying to do philosophy. He does say some sensible things, but they do not seem to be philosophical or even to be of any particular philosophic interest. His work in ethics, for example, looks very different from that of Henry Sidgwick or G. E. Moore on the one hand or R. M. Hare and Philippa Foot on the other.

Dewey is quite self-conscious about this. He does not think that there is, or even could be, anything distinct from commonsense knowledge or scientific knowledge (something he took to be continuous with common sense) that would give philosophers an Archimedean point from which to assess culture. A "criticism of criticisms" has no such exalted or specialized role. It is, rather, an on-site, reflexive activity where philosophers, concerned with the problems of men, reflect, as part of a continuous operation, on what they are doing and use any general critical categories and norms that are germane to the human problem at hand. The methodological component is so integrally linked to the practical critique that it is hardly the eviscerated methodological turn that Rorty found evasive.

VI

However, in making these points I have ignored his revealing essay "Pragmatism Without Method" in a festschrift for Sidney Hook.[53] Rorty seems in effect to say things there about scientific method contrary both to what I have argued and to what Levi argued. My surmise is that Rorty would regard our reading of pragmatism as being as scientistic as he sees Sidney Hook's, for in respect to what is at issue here our views are very similar. What we say about pragmatism and the scientific method is very close to what Hook says, as well as to remarks by Levi's mentor, Ernest Nagel.[54]

What exactly does Rorty find wrong with such pragmatism? While agreeing that this stress on scientific method was a prominent side of Dewey's many-faceted thought, Rorty believes that Hook is mistaken in opting "for the 'let's bring the scientific method to bear throughout culture' side of pragmatism, as opposed to the 'let's recognize a pre-existent continuity between science, art, politics, and religion' side."[55] Peirce's programmatic "Fixation of Belief" is the prototype and model here for those taking Hook's option. The scientific method (broadly conceived) and methods continuous with it in common sense are the sole way of gaining knowledge or reliable beliefs. Cartesian a priori methods will gain us nothing. There is no distinctively philosophical way of coming to know anything, and there are no such things as "philosophical knowledge" or philosophically grounded justified belief, though there is, of course, historiographical knowledge of philosophy. But the latter is a form of scientific knowledge. Rorty agrees with this claim about philosophy, but that notwithstanding, he argues that Hook is being too positivistic in stressing, as did Dewey, that scientific method (broadly construed) is the sole reliable method for fixing belief and that the creative use of intelligence in all cognitive domains requires such a commitment.[56] This, Rorty believes, entirely misses the force of those developments of postpositive philosophy of science that criticize the idea that there is anything very determinate called the "scientific method." Hook, and Nagel as well, and by implication Levi, give us, as Rorty sees it, a scientistic pragmatism against which Rorty poses a "pragmatism without method." Recent developments in the philosophy of science, Rorty contends, show that we cannot hold theory and evidence apart in the relatively sharp way that Hook and Nagel require.[57] There is no theory-independent objective *given* that we can just take as the evidence to confirm or disconfirm competing theories. One should not think of pragmatism, Rorty argues, in this scientistic, positivist way as a view that has shown that the scientific method is the one reliable method for reaching the truth about the nature of things. Rather, Rorty argues, one should take pragmatism in Quine's way, and *sometimes* Dewey's, as a holistic and syncretic theory, the core conception of which is an attempt to replace the notion of true beliefs as representations of "the nature of things" with a conception of successful rules of action.[58] We must come to recognize that appealing to evidence or citing evidence is not a "very useful notion when trying to decide what one thinks of the world as a whole."[59] We need, instead, and in all kinds of different ways, to make adjustments from time to time in our intricate web of belief. And in dropping the claim for something called "the evidence" that is our common ground for adjusting our beliefs, we do not need to conclude that one person's web or even one culture's web is as good as another's.[60]

What Rorty takes to be a scientistic form of pragmatism assumes that we have "a duty to have a general view about the nature of rational inquiry and a universal method for fixing belief."[61] Rorty rightly doubts that we have any such *duty*. We have a duty to talk to one another, to listen to arguments and the like, and to converse, but it is far from clear (to put it minimally) that we have a duty to adopt such a methodological principle for fixing belief. But, contra Rorty, what might not be a duty might still be a good thing to do.

Rorty claims that we very seldom have by way of methodological principles anything more than platitudes gimmicked up to look like algorithms. We cannot, he says, isolate anything useful from science and common sense called "the scientific method" for fixing belief. We can "only know what counts as being 'scientific' in a given area, what counts as a good reason for theory-change, by immersing ourselves in the details of the problematic situation."[62] It is this rather than an ahistorical, contextless appeal to that ersatz something calling "*the* scientific method" that is vital in appraising our practices, but if we go this way we will have no method or principle or set of principles for determining what to do. We will have nothing like the hypothetico-deductive observational method to fix for us in all domains what is reasonable to believe or to do. A thoroughgoing fallibilist will avoid this methodological fix—this shortcut—just as definitely as he will avoid a metaphysical fix; he will unequivocally abandon "the metaphysical urge to find some ultimate, total, final context within which all our activities could be placed." And with that he will abandon philosophy as traditionally conceived.

VII

I agree that this nostalgia for the Absolute, this waiting for Godot, this longing for some ultimate, total, final context in which our deepest hopes will be met and our perplexities resolved is something pragmatists have long since set aside. I also agree that this is a good thing. Indeed, I am inclined to think such a fallibilistic notion would be part of the attitude set of anyone who had thoroughly ingested the attitudes of modernity. But to return to Bernstein's Deweyan criticism of Rorty cited earlier, someone who had thoroughly accepted such a fallibilism might still wish to recognize that big human problems (Dewey called them the problems of men) still stand before us, with or without the end of philosophy as a professional discipline, in every bit as demanding a way. Without metaphysical comfort they may seem to some even more demanding. Even with the demise of the Tradition, philosophy, as social critique and ideology critique, would still be very much to the point in setting out to answer such problems. There remain, that is, as I remarked in the previous chapter, the problems of abortion, euthanasia, pornography, privacy, the rights of children, animal rights, exploitation, imperialism, the ideological use of science and the media, nuclear threats, sexism, racism, questions about inequality and autonomy, and broad questions about the choice between socialism and capitalism, reform and revolution, the ethics of terrorism, questions about what democracy can come to in our industrial society, and questions about the coherence, approximate truth, and social import of historical materialism and other theories of social change.

These and related human questions remain in need of both penetrating and rational treatment. It would indeed be desirable if we could say some true things about these matters. And there may very well be some telling and relatively objective remarks that can be made about these matters, even if the realism and antirealism debate and debates of that sort require, as Rorty believes, dissolution rather than resolution. And it may be that some answers come closer to being right than others, or even that some of the answers for some of these questions or facets of these questions are the right answers and others are the wrong answers—period. Rorty ought to be quite willing to assert that we can have no a priori or general philosophical guarantees here. We can have no guarantees that we *cannot* have such answers to such questions. And it is premature to say that research programs organized around such questions have not panned out. Moreover, to reasonably assert that there can be answers to such human questions, that important true or false statements about them can be made, we need not have any views about how truth is to be characterized or defined, or as to what, if anything, truth adds to warranted assertability. Like Rorty, we may regard these as bad questions, comparable to "What does moral rightness add to being the best thing to do in the circumstances?"[63]

I doubt that Rorty would deny that some answers to these human questions are more reasonable than others, though sometimes he sounds as if he were denying that anything with any argumentative rigor could be done to resolve such questions. But that is not embedded in his position. It is perhaps (to be deliberately *ad hominem*) a defense on his part to preserve his rather easy-going conservative liberalism from critique.[64] But Rorty would no doubt reply that a sense of how to go about things here requires specific contextual responses and not broad generalizations about method, including scientific method.

I think such a response is too antinomian. Certainly recent work in the philosophy of science and in the history of science should disabuse us of any penchant for reifying scientific procedures into something called *the* scientific method. Sciences are various, and even parts of the same science are often very different, employing different methodologies. Although Dewey did talk, as do Hook and Nagel, about the scientific method, it was usually quite clear from how they did so that they saw it as something quite flexible and that would *in part* require a contextual, discipline-by-discipline specification. (The general things he said about incommensurability notwithstanding, this is also true of Levi.) But they also recognized that certain general things could and should be said as well. Rorty in effect recognizes them, too, but rather dismissively refers to them as platitudes. But what is or is not a platitude is itself very contextual. It depends on what is being denied or assumed. What Rorty calls platitudes were once important to assert against a certain kind of resistance to science and a certain kind of metaphysical or theological stance. Because such stances among Western intelligentsia have now nearly withered away makes it boring and platitudinous to assert these things now. (However, before we too quickly forget about these platitudes we should remember, particularly in North America, that there has been, strangely enough, a return among some analytic philosophers to a traditional metaphysical Christian philosophical theology. Modernity has not quite yet swept these away.) But where modernity and postmodernity have made themselves felt, there are more interesting things to assert and to argue for than such banalities. Rorty is surely right about that. But platitudes can be, and typically are, true or (where considerations of truth do not arise) reasonable to assume and to employ as guides in situations where they cannot go without saying. Faced with an extreme relativistic stance about what science can come to or what it commits us to or what its aims are, such platitudes are not infrequently worth asserting. They are also perhaps worth asserting against arcane claims about what knowledge of factual matters can come to. There is, moreover, reason to think that in thinking about science and our commonsense ways of knowing, science requires certain ways of reasoning and viewing things. They may be platitudes, they may be banal, but we cannot just dismiss them. We cannot, for example, if we are reasoning scientifically, just ignore the results of a well-conducted experiment. Moreover and distinctly, the "platitudes" here (*pace* Rorty) need not come to a statement of epistemic principles or to the making of any foundationalist claims.

There are certain straightforward, factual questions, e.g., "Are there blue jays in Australia?" And there are well-known ways of answering such questions. If we do not know the answer to such a question, we know perfectly well how to go about finding out the answer. If Rorty's historicist belief that our categories, no matter who we are, are a function of our era and are essentially formed through a historically localized tradition is meant to deny that there are determinate ways of answering such questions, then such a historicist thesis must be mistaken. Though this, of course, does not mean that anyone just situated in any culture anywhere in history can answer them.

There are, in this same determinate way, other questions like "Could German shepherds survive outside in ordinary kennels in the Arctic in winter?" which also admit of a perfectly determinate method for grinding out answers. We know how to set out the hypothesis and how to test it, though I would hope for that particular hypothesis moral considerations would keep us from doing so. Popper may call these "banal" rational routines, but they are routines, they are rational, and we do use them. Moreover, there are less mundane questions that could be answered as adequately using the same routine, determinate method. A certain determinate scientific method for a range of questions, that is, works by amending or discarding hypotheses when the predictions drawn from them fail. Experience and evidence have an indispensable role here, as they have throughout science. That they often do not function in the simple and direct way in which they were traditionally depicted as functioning in empiricist epistemologies does not gainsay that.[65]

No matter what the story we tell about the theory dependence of observations, it just is the case that there are indefinitely many facts that could be established if we were willing to use our imaginations and such techniques of discovery as we might devise and if we employed our techniques of validation starting with the mundane techniques I have described. Other issues, however, are not so straightforwardly *simply* matters of fact, regardless of how we conceptualize. But in stressing this we should not forget that there are sticks and stones, hills and rivers, night and day, that people get born and die and sometimes are in pain, and that most people speak some language whereas earthworms do not. In that important way, there just is a world out there independent of what we believe about it, whose features are for certain sorts of belief an ultimate and objective test of what we believe. (I did not say of everything we *rightly* believe.) Whether we think of ourselves as realists or antirealists, there is no denying that.

However, not all matters of fact are so bluntly and uncontroversially factual. As Martin Hollis nicely puts it, there is "a blurred edge to the idea of a matter of fact."[66] Suppose—to use his example—the map of Alpha Centauri records "Here be gaseous cuboids," as the map of Australia might record "Here be blue jays." But in the Alpha Centauri case, observation may still leave undecided whether the cuboids are life forms or conscious. It is no longer evident that there is a clear fact of the matter that will settle this. Much turns in such a case on questions that cannot be settled by just looking and seeing what is to count as conscious life. What is at issue is no longer independent of our thought as it is in the question of whether there are blue jays in Australia. We have plenty of concepts that do not function as mere labels. "Concepts," as Hobbes put it, "also enter into how we perceive, before we interpret and explain. Indeed, in perceiving, we are often already interpreting and explaining."[67] And we can make that Hobbesian point without entering into any dogma of scheme and content.

Such complexities complicate the description of what scientific method will come to in some contexts. Given the present development of medicine (to take an example), there is a division of expert opinion concerning what, if any definite factor or cluster of factors, are the underlying causes of schizophrenia. Some think it is caused by a chemical imbalance in the brain, and others think it is caused by mental disturbances linked to our psychosexual histories. There are, of course, other views as well. No simple and unequivocal pointing to evidence would settle the matter. The evidence we appeal to can be read in different ways, and there is a parallel dispute as to what is to count as controlling or curing schizophrenia. If a patient takes drugs and this has a calming effect, is that just a suppression of symptoms or is it a way of treating the underlying condition? Psychiatrists disagree about this, and, again, no simple set of observations will settle the matter. There is perhaps no escaping the need for interpretation here, but in assessing the various interpretations, hypotheses will be formed and predictions will be derived from them that in turn be tested by evidence. This is not all that will go on, but it is typically a vital part of what does. There will also be a putting things together in coherent rationales, but this will go on with appeal to evidence and, where possible, experiment. Nothing will be decisive in appealing to evidence and making tests, but this does not mean that there are no methodological constraints and that evidence and often experiment will not have a vital role.

Bas van Fraassen may well be right in claiming that scientific method cannot adequately be characterized in terms of the hypothetico-deductive observational method, but there is all the same in science a loose family of methods that constrain and help define scientific activity and distinguish it from uncontrolled speculation and various a priori and intuitive methods. Rorty's "Pragmatism Without Method" fails to see the central role that scientific method (construed broadly) plays in our understanding of the world and tends to treat science too much as just one language game among others.[68] Whatever may be true of philosophy as an epistemological or logico-semantical enterprise, science does at least in its own self-image aim to represent the world accurately. That is an essential part of its self-image. Philosophy, if Rorty is right, cannot do anything like that, but it has to be shown as well that science in certain domains cannot do it. It has to be shown that it is a naive scientistic faith to think that it can. (Surely with Rorty's Quinean beliefs about the a priori, he can hardly riposte by saying that if there is a seemingly good transcendental argument against its very possibility, then no matter what scientists think they can do they cannot do it. Rorty will not claim such rationalist powers of reason.)

There indeed is no such thing as nature's own language or a particular privileged vocabulary in which the world demands to be described. But that by itself is not enough to make it senseless or even mistaken to speak of there being an independent world that we try to describe with varying degrees of success. Pragmatists, like positivists and other figures of the Enlightenment, were aware that there was something special about science, both in our attempts to understand the world and in our attempts to obtain reliable beliefs. Rorty, in a very unpragmatist manner, seems to think that there is nothing special or particularly interesting or significant about science. One need not be a science worshipper, caught up in scientistic fetishes, to consider that view not only very unpragmatist but also very fishy.

Even if (*pace* what I have been arguing) Rorty is right in believing that characterizations of scientific method can only give us platitudes (banal truisms) about how to go on in rationally fixing belief, still, as Bernard Williams has remarked, the very success of science invites or at least permits a description of what yields such success.[69] In doing this, even if we cannot say anything very useful about scientific method, we might, as Popper believes, be able to say something nonmythological about the objective progress of science in finding out what the world is like. Perhaps Feyerabend is right and there is neither scientific method nor scientific progress in finding out what the world is like. Perhaps our scientists know no more about the world than the best-informed ancients did. (Is that really credible?) But that there is no scientific progress is counterintuitive indeed and would take a not inconsiderable showing. Rorty seems just blandly to assume that there is no such progress.

Science, independently of philosophy, has its own self-image. The sort of representationalist idioms that Rorty thinks are mythmaking come not only from philosophy but from science itself. As Williams observes, "Science itself moves the boundaries of what counts as observation."[70] Scientific theory can create and constitute new forms of observation. A given scientific theory can, for example, explain how "such an elaborately constructed image as an electron micrograph can be a record of an observation."[71] Science, without relying on philosophy, explains the reliability of its own observations and the truth of its conjectures. Indeed, scientific theory is cumulative in that it often can explain why some of the predictions of previous theories were true and others false and by doing this it does something to mark out the record of scientific advance. Science can even explain itself and explain how it is that creatures like ourselves understand a world that has the characteristics science says it has. It is an evasion, perhaps propped up by an incessant preoccupation with the language of language games, to say that evolutionary biology and neurological theory are just some vocabularies among others and that it is an illusion that they contribute to a conception of the world as it is, independently of our inquiries. Representationist epistemologies may fall to Wittgensteinian demythologization, but it is something else to say that the claims of science are similarly known to be illusory. Science's essential self-image, as Williams well puts it, is that one is "not locked in a world of books" or in a hermeneutical circle of interpretations of interpretations, but that in one's scientific work one is "confronting 'the world'," and that one's scientific "work is made hard or easy by what is actually there."[72] Whatever it is appropriate to say about the social sciences, in the biological and physical sciences this belief is central. It is, as Williams remarks, difficult to believe that science could go on without such an image of itself. Perhaps science's own self-conception rests on a mistake—though Rorty has not shown that (it would be extraordinary to show that)—but if it is a mistake engendering illusions, it at least sounds as if it engenders illusions necessary to keep the activity of science going.

This conception of science and its self-image is radically different from the conception Rorty would like to see philosophy come to have of itself. The stress would be the old one of trying to see how things hang together. But the new manner of doing this would be the hermeneutical one of "seeing how all the various vocabularies of all the various epochs and cultures hang together."[73] To try to take such a turn in science as distinct from philosophy would, if it became institutionalized, undermine at least natural science, for its driving force is the attempt to confront the world and find out how it really works. Without that impulse there would be no physics, chemistry, geology, or archaeology. (Or so it seems. It is logically possible that, operationally, science could go on in the same old way while people had different metabeliefs about what they were doing. My point, and Williams's as well, is that it is likely that these metabeliefs would in fact cripple the impulse to go on doing science.)

Pragmatism thought of itself as generalizing and applying in new domains—most particularly in the domains of morals and politics—scientific rationality and a number of methods distinctive of both common sense engaged in purposive activity and science. Even if viewed by someone who is thoroughly absorbed into a scientific culture, they are taken to be banal recipes of rational procedure; they still provide general constraints on how reasonable people imbued with the scientific spirit would reason and act in the purposive direction of their lives and in trying to understand their condition. Such people would believe, when the issue was clearly and forcefully brought to them, "that science offers one of the most effective ways in which we can be led out of the web of texts...in which Rorty finds himself imprisoned along with the 'bookish intellectuals of recent times'."[74]   Rorty's "pragmatism without method" hermeneutically enmeshes us in a web of words. Whatever its intrinsic merits, it should be classified as "pragmatism" in scare quotes. The classical pragmatists, Peirce, James, and Dewey; their middle-period expositors, appliers and developers such as Hook and Nagel; and their contemporary representatives such as Levi and Morgenbesser, whatever their other differences, saw a central role for science and scientific method in our cultural life and in a reconstructed philosophy. They believed it is a way out of the cell of words and the imprisonment in language that can result from philosophy and, in a quite different way, from cultivating a *certain kind* of literary sensibility. (It is mercifully not the case that all literary sensibility generates such a belief set. But some of it does take the worst, most obscurantist sides of Derridian postmodernism.) Pushed in a certain way, such a pragmatism can become scientistic dogma. (Any intellectual stance can be frozen into dogma.) A cure for that is to cultivate the kind of intellectual sensibilities Rorty, following Wittgenstein, cultivates, but in reacting to scientism it, too, can blind in turn itself, as it seems to in Rorty's case, to the fundamental understanding that science, with its conception of inquiry and truthfulness, can give us.

VIII

In this last section I turn to an examination of the relation between what I have just argued and a Deweyan conception of what post-Philosophical philosophy should look like when Philosophy, conceived as a professional undertaking that in one way or another is to be the overseer of culture, has finally been set aside, when we have finally given up the belief that there is a discipline that makes our ideas really clear, tells us what we really mean, and what in any domain we are really justified in believing. What, we are asking, is left for philosophy after such claims have been seen through as pretensions resting on illusion? Many, including those in various ways generally sympathetic to Rorty, have thought his positive suggestions for a "post-Philosophy philosophy" sketchy at best. Even to see it as cultural criticism for which there is no very distinctive expertise is rather empty, for it seems, given Rorty's way of conceptualizing cultural criticism, to lack any critical thrust. It just sounds like a way, sometimes a rather elegant and learned way, of kibitzing.

Here the conception of going about things that pragmatism stresses—the real pragmatism *with* method that Rorty eschews—is vital. Firmly rejecting with Rorty any conception of philosophy as a discipline with a special knowledge or as a discipline that somehow "lays the foundations for life" (as if we understood what that means), pragmatism sees philosophy as a somewhat distinctive form of social critique. So conceived, philosophy, both *ambulando* and systematically, will set itself the Sisyphean task of answering, or at least coming to grips with, the problems of men. That is, it will set about answering the sort of large-scale social problems mentioned earlier. (How they get settled is, of course, a matter of social struggle, but which answers are the best answers is not. The correct resolution— where there is a correct resolution—may not be the resolution that prevails.)

By utilizing methods of conceptual analysis (indeed typically rather commonsensical methods) and the articulateness and concern for consistency and truthfulness that goes with it, by utilizing scientific methods, by attending closely to the best-founded claims of science (particularly social science), and by engaging in careful moral reflection using the method of wide reflective equilibrium, this nonphilosophical philosophy can give us, in determinate contexts without a thought to epistemology, metaphysics, or even metaethics, the standards needed for a critique of culture and ideology and for facing the problems of men with care and decent intellectual resources. In doing this, philosophers, or as I would rather put it, reflective, informed, and intellectually disciplined intellectuals, need also to recover the art lost at least to Anglo-American and Scandinavian philosophers of writing broad philosophical narratives similar in type, though not necessarily in content, to Rorty's own *Philosophy and the Mirror of Nature* or MacIntyre's *After Virtue* or Charles Taylor's *Sources of the Self.* (I speak of intellectuals because it is to be hoped that the philosopher, as a kind of specialist, will go the way one hopes theologians are going.)   These narratives will, however, be worked into our critical theory (the successor subject of philosophy) by way of giving that critical theory a perspective, though, in turn, our critical activities may lead, and characteristically would lead, to new or reworked narratives of our philosophical, intellectual, and social history.   (Here again we have something analogous to the method of wide reflective equilibrium.) This would mean that never again could any reflective person who had a good understanding of what he was saying say with Quine that there are those people who are interested in philosophy and those people who are interested in the history of philosophy.[75] It would be impossible, on this post-Philosophy conception of philosophy, to be intelligently interested in philosophy without being interested in its history. Still, this new turn in philosophy or this replacement of philosophy (this critical theory), call it what you will, would have the critical bite, the commitment to engage in rational elucidation and criticism, that was behind Quine's misguided quip.

9

Searching for an Emancipatory Perspective: Wide Reflective Equilibrium and the Hermeneutical Circle

I

We have seen in the last two chapters how we might construe philosophy-as-critical-theory. It would utilize conceptions from pragmatism, but it would also be holistic and would utilize narrative in setting out its claims. Narrative would be an essential part of its structure. That is to say, critical theory, as I construe it, will in ways broadly similar to the ways Habermas, MacIntyre, Taylor, and Rorty have done (themselves only broadly similar ways), place its philosophical arguments and claims in the context of setting forth a story of the development of philosophy and (more generally) of human thought and other human activities as well. The weight given to these different activities (e.g., how we farm, build, organize labor, what our kinship structures are, how our intellectual history goes) will depend on the particular sort and rationale of the narrative given. (Historical materialist narratives will be rather different from liberal and conservative narratives or narratives with a religious rationale.)

It is as well a philosophy embedded in the human sciences and affording a rather holistic descriptive-explanatory-interpretive account of our condition. It would attempt to say something about who we were, are, and might become. In the course of this, a genuine critical theory would say something about how our societies are likely to go and what feasible courses of action are open to human beings. However, as we have also seen, critical theory will not only be descriptive-explanatory-interpretive, it will also be normative. It will not only say something about how we live and could live but about how, within range of feasible possibilities, we ought to live and about what a just and humane society would look like. It will in short give an account of what a good life for human beings would be like.

This normative endeavor will involve a critical theory yielding as an integral part of itself a theory, or at least an account, of morality that is in some sense critical, an account that would show what a critical morality would be like and proceed to develop one as a core part of a critical theory. To do this it will utilize a method, though it will (as Goodman and Putnam do) use this method more broadly as well. Following Norman Daniels I have called this the method of wide reflective equilibrium. I now turn to its articulation (particularly in setting out a moral theory as part of a critical theory), use, and defense. And in the course of doing this, I will comment on the place of reflection and deliberation in morality and how we are to test the soundness of moral practices, beliefs, and theories.

II

Let us start indirectly by asking how to begin in thinking reflectively about ethics and, more generally, thinking about what sort of people we would like to be and what sort of society and world order we would like to see. To look about us at what has been said, and indeed said on such grand themes by people who are knowledgeable and reflective, is enough to give us a kind of vertigo. We have varieties of utilitarianism, varieties of contractarianism, duty-based theories, rights-based theories, perfectionist theories (some harking back to Aristotle), varieties of relativism or conventionalism, projectivist error theories, new forms of subjectivism, and new forms of noncognitivism. All these theories are in themselves very different in many ways at a number of levels, and all get articulated within the dominant Anglo-American analytic tradition.[1] When we step out of that ambience to traditions that tend to look at ethics rather more broadly and not so much as a distinct philosophical subject matter to be pursued as a distinct branch of philosophy, the motley of voices is even more motley. Jürgen Habermas's communicative ethics integrally linked with his systematic critical theory of society is one thing; Michel Foucault's ethics of "practices of the self" as he resolutely turns his back on the project of constructing systematic moral foundations is quite another thing. So, too, is Hans-Georg Gadamer's still very different hermeneutical placement of such matters, the pragmatist approach of John Dewey, Wittgenstein's approach to such matters, or Rorty's contextualist, neopragmatist, neo-Wittgensteinian approach in the service of a somewhat conservative form of liberalism.

The differences here, both substantive and methodological, often run very deep. It isn't that these theorists more or less agree about what is at issue and give different answers to roughly the same questions as, say, Richard Brandt, Robert Nozick, David Gauthier, and John Harsanyi do. Rather, the differences are sometimes so profound that it is not at all clear that these philosophers have a common subject matter. The differences in conception are such that it may well be the case that no comparisons can be usefully made, not to mention the scouting out of anything like a unified project. What is there in common among R. M. Hare, Gadamer, Dewey, and Foucault that would make such scouting and such a comparison fruitful? Is this not just a tower of Babel?

I want to suggest that perhaps it is not. I think if we look carefully at what is involved in what I call an appeal to considered judgments in *wide* reflective equilibrium—a conception central to the work of John Rawls but one that others, myself included, have adopted, adapted, modified, and argued to be a central underlying methodology in setting out an account of morality or of ethics—we see a way in which diverse strands in thinking about ethics can be brought together into a unified whole.[2] When the method of wide reflective equilibrium (WRE) is integrated with a substantive critical theory of society developed with an emancipatory intent, we *may* have a project that can articulate a legitimate conception of a normatively acceptable order to set against the reality of what is now disorder and illegitimacy. Such a project in a fruitful articulation would use insights (valuable in themselves) drawn from Rawls, Williams, Foucault, Gadamer, and Habermas in a unified account that makes sense of the moral terrain and gives us a coherently integrated set of normative criteria to appeal to in social assessment and criticism and for making sense of our lives, lives that often, particularly under contemporary conditions, have the look of being senseless.

This, if it has any chance at all of coming to something, cannot be an eclectic hodge-podge of diverse and incommensurable parts. The components are indeed diverse and are stressed by their authors for very different purposes and often under very different frameworks. But collected and unified by WRE, the elements can be seen to fit together into a coherent whole.

III

In coming to see this, we need to see what WRE comes to and how it fits in with a critical theory of society. We cannot, in responding morally and reasoning morally, avoid starting from tradition and some consensus. In this fundamental sense, we always and unavoidably start from morality as *Sittlichkeit* and, however far back we go in a reformist or even in a revolutionary or iconoclastic direction, refer back to that *Sittlichkeit*. Back, that is, to a cluster of institutions and institutionalized norms sanctioned by custom through which the members of an actual social order fulfill the social demands of the social whole to which they belong. This must not be mistaken for an implicit defense of conservativism. The reflective moral agent, starting with a distinctive *Sittlichkeit*, can and will reject certain—indeed perhaps whole blocks of such—institutional norms or she will refashion some of these culturally given norms or perhaps forge some new ones. But she cannot coherently reject or stand aside from the whole cluster of institutional norms of the life-world in which she comes to consciousness and, so to say, start afresh. We cannot avoid starting from our, culturally speaking, deeply embedded norms that go with our interlocked set of institutions.

The norms, starting from our own culturally derived *Sittlich-keit*, that we would most resist abandoning—the ones that humanly speaking are bedrock for us—are those John Rawls takes to be our firmest considered judgments (convictions) with a very strategic but still nonfoundationalist place in our moral reasoning and conceptions of how we would justify our moral beliefs.[3]   In spite of what are otherwise enormous differences, Rawls and a hermeneuticist such as Gadamer have a common point of departure here.

Starting with our firmest considered judgments and then turning a Rawlsian trick by utilizing a coherentist model of justification and rationalization, we will seek to get these considered judgments into *wide* reflective equilibrium.   This would involve, in our reasoning from such a *Sittlichkeit*, a winnowing out of these culturally received norms.   Some, perhaps by far the most, would be retained, though sometimes rather considerably modified.   Others would be rejected, sometimes to be replaced by quite different norms.   The *Sittlichkeit* of a society is not eternal.   Rawls, like Habermas, in the tradition of the Enlightenment, will not stick with tradition—what R. M. Hare called "received opinion."[4]   (The Enlightenment is a tradition bent on repeatedly questioning and revising tradition.)

Let us see a little more exactly what wide reflective equilibrium comes to.   Narrow or partial reflective equilibrium, the inadequate method used by contemporary intuitionists, consists in getting a match between our considered particular moral convictions (judgments) and a moral principle or cluster of moral principles (which may themselves be more general considered convictions) that systematize the more particular considered convictions so that we can see how they all could be derived from that principle or those principles, or at least come to recognize that they are thereby best explained and rationalized so that together the more particular moral convictions and more generalized moral principles form a consistent whole perspicuously displayed.   Principles that do not so match with the great mass of our specific considered judgments will be rejected. Also to be rejected are specific considered judgments significantly different from the mass of specific considered judgments *and* in conflict with moral principles widely held.   (Such moral principles will also be considered judgments of more abstract sort.   We get considered judgments at all levels of generality.)

Wide reflective equilibrium, which I defend, is also a coherence theory of justification and moral reasoning. But it casts a wider net than narrow reflective equilibrium. It seeks to produce and perspicuously display coherence among (a) our considered moral convictions, (b) a set or at least a cluster of moral principles, (c) a cluster of background theories including most centrally moral theories and social theories, among them social theories that are quite definitely empirical theories about our social world and how we function in it, and (d) an empirically based, broadly scientific conception and account of human nature. (There will be an overlap between [c] and [d], for surely any even reasonably adequate account of human nature will be an account of how we are social animals through and through. But, of course, we are part of the animal kingdom as well and what kind of biological creatures we are and how that relates to our sociality needs a careful accounting.)

We cannot take the point of view from nowhere or see ourselves as purely rational, noumenal beings with no local attachments or enculturations.[5] Such Kantianism, as Hegel saw, affords us no foundation of morals. If we self-consciously seek to place ourselves vis-à-vis our considered moral convictions and our overall moral and intellectual views in the perspective of some radically different time and place, we will fail. Whether we like it or not, we are children of modernity and are deeply affected by its conditioning and the dominant consensus in the considered convictions of modernity. (Even Islamic fundamentalists extensively educated in the West are not free of it. In certain key respects their reaction is more like the Counter-Enlightenment reaction of the German romantics to the Enlightenment.) It is true, looking at the Western industrial or (as some say) postindustrial world, that this is a matter of degree. Some strata and subcultures of society are more influenced than others by modernity, but the point is that all are deeply influenced by modernity. And as the demystification of the world runs apace, we are becoming increasingly and more pervasively so influenced. Postmodernist reactions to modernity are themselves a kind of carrying through of modernity and not at all a return to premodernity.

It is also true that within the culture of modernity there is disagreement as well as consensus, but what is important for wide reflective equilibrium is that there is consensus and, as in any

justificatory venture, it is unavoidable that we start from there.[6]
Questions of justification arise when we disagree among ourselves or
when we as individuals are of two minds. To resolve problems we
must proceed from what everyone involved in the dispute holds in
common.[7] Indeed, even when as individuals we are ambivalent
about an issue, we need to retreat to some relevant set of beliefs
that for the time at least holds fast for us.

So we start in WRE from what we have a firm consensus
about. Fortunately, there is in the broad cluster of the cultures of
modernity an overlap of considered convictions, including agreement
in what I have called moral truisms, e.g., judgments such as it is
wrong to torture the innocent, to break faith with people, to fail to
keep one's promises, and the like. It isn't that these can never be
done, no matter what the circumstances. Rather, to do any of these
things is ceteris paribus wrong. There is always a presumption
against doing them and, particularly in the case of torturing the
innocent, that presumption is very stringent indeed. These are
deontic considerations. But the consensus includes as well moral
truisms or at least evaluative truisms such as pleasure is good and
pain is bad, or it is good to develop one's powers, to have meaningful work, and to have meaningful human relationships. ("Meaningful" in its two occurrences in the last sentence is not crystal clear
but is also not so vague that there is no agreement about what
meaningful work and meaningful relationships come to.) To the list
of items over which there is now a firm consensus we should add
what Charles Taylor says we have developed a particular concern for
since the eighteenth century, namely, "a concern for the preservation
of life, for the fulfilling of human need, and above all for the relief
of suffering."[8] This moral consensus, as the above illustrates, not
only consists in a consensus about rights and obligations—about what
we must do; there is also a consensus about some teleological
judgments.

There is, as the above illustrates, an extensive consensus
about such moral truisms, both deontological and teleological; all
ethical theories, ethical skepticism and its country cousins aside,
accept these judgments and compete to show who best reveals their
underlying rationale and how they can reasonably be seen to
constitute a coherent cluster of beliefs. Moreover, ethical skepticism
rejects them only because ethical skeptics reject *all* moral judgments

as somehow unjustified, perhaps because there is and can be, as J. L. Mackie put it, no objective prescriptivity.[9] They do not, however, single out these particular moral conceptions (the above truisms) for rejection because of their having some distinctive defect.   They reject them because they do not think any moral beliefs at all can be objectively warranted.   (In its very *generality* such moral skepticism is suspect.) But this judgment does not rest on any particular worry about any specific moral judgment.   Rather, the whole category is to be rejected as being in error. It does not matter in the slightest for such a skeptic that there is firm consensus about a moral judgment and that it is reflectively sustained. It is enough for it to be in error that it is a moral judgment.   But that is like rejecting all inductive inferences because they are not and cannot be deductive inferences. These are pointless and arbitrary philosophical complaints. What is more to the point are actual disagreements, if such there be, that remain after sustained and informed reflection utilizing WRE.   There are, of course, where we have not got our beliefs in WRE, deep disagreements among us over the right and the good. But there is plainly much agreement as well, and we can and should *start* from the consensus in trying to rationalize morality and in trying to show against nihilism how the very institution of morality has a purpose and a point. To show this we need not show that we can always gain moral agreement. There may be nothing like a principle of sufficient reason in ethics, and morality could still have a point and an objective rationale. Moreover, there could still be some moral beliefs for which there are good reasons and concerning which there is an informed consensus that there are such reasons.

   We start with our firmly fixed considered convictions filtered for convictions that we would only have under conditions in which we would plainly make errors in judgment, such as the errors we would typically make when we are out of control, enraged, depressed, drunk, fatigued, under stress, in the grip of an ideology, and the like. In our first filtering we excise convictions so rooted. But we do not rest content, as an intuitionist would, with simply making a fit between our particular moral convictions so screened and our more general moral principles.   WRE, unlike partial or narrow equilibrium, is not just the attaining of a fit between the considered judgments and the moral principles we remain committed to on reflection or the simplest set of principles from which we could derive most of those considered convictions. Beyond that, WRE remains committed to a fit that includes matching the principles that not only satisfy the conditions just mentioned but also match best with ethical theories, theories which are the most carefully elaborated and rationalized and which fit best with what we know about the world and the full range of our considered convictions – including convictions appealed to in defense of these theories or relevant background social theories. Some of these moral convictions are distinct from and logically independent of the considered convictions with which and from which we started. We shuttle back and forth between considered convictions, moral principles, ethical theories, social theories, and other background empirical theories and those considered judgments of which some at least must be distinct from the first cluster of considered judgments associated with or constitutive of or partially constitutive of the moral principles, social theories, or other background theories. (The association will be such that they are standardly appealed to in justifying those principles or theories.) In such shuttling we sometimes modify or even abandon a particular considered conviction; at other times we abandon or modify a moral principle or come to adopt some new principles. Sometimes we modify or (though more rarely) abandon a social theory or other background theory or even come to construct a new one. We move back and forth rebuilding the ship at sea, modifying and adjusting here and there until we get a coherent and consistent set of beliefs. When we have done, we have for a time attained wide reflective equilibrium. (It is important in such coherence accounts that we have a large circle involving many considerations rather than a small one.)

Put another way, the account of morality is the most adequate that most perspicuously displays the conceptions we would reflectively accept and act in accordance with. And that is the account that (a) fits together into a coherent whole at least the provisional fixed points in our considered convictions better than alternative accounts, (b) squares best with our best knowledge and most plausible hypotheses about the world (including, of course, our social world), and (c) most adequately (of the alternative accounts of morality) provides guidance when we are, without recourse to a reflective application of WRE, not confident of what particular moral judgments to make or, in more extreme cases, at a loss in knowing what to do. Where we come to be unsure about a considered moral judgment, WRE will help us decide whether to continue accepting it or how to revise it. In new situations (say, in arguments about nuclear matters), WRE will also guide us better than alternative accounts of moral method in making extrapolations from the judgments at hand. Such an account will show us best what extrapolations to make in such situations from our stock of considered judgments in the light of what we know or reasonably believe about the world. Accounts that do these things best are the best accounts, that is, the accounts that are for the nonce in reflective equilibrium.

A given account of morality might be better in one of these dimensions and worse in another. Where this obtains and we cannot devise an account that unites these virtues for a time, we will not have achieved wide reflective equilibrium. Furthermore, we should also note that it is the case, as Rawls puts it, that a Socratic element remains in all such reasonings. We unavoidably make reflective contextual judgments all along the line in thinking about particular considered moral judgments, moral principles, ethical theories, rationalizing particular judgments and principles, making assessments of the facts, and considering critical social theories with an emancipatory intent. In all those contexts we make reflective judgments about what to do or be. There will also be in choosing ethical and social theories an appeal to considered judgments and a reliance on location, so to say, on our particular reflective judgments. Nowhere along the coherentist path do we get something utterly value-free; there is no avoiding the necessity of making reflective judgments. If we say, rather counterfactually, that for a given population at a given time and place they have put their judgments into wide reflective equilibrium and thus have shown they are justified, their reflective equilibrium will not be one that could have been attained without their making such reflective judgments. We cannot get around that; we can have no algorithms here.

Our justificatory account of morality, in keeping with our programmatic articulation of a critical theory, will be a holistic, antifoundationalist coherentism. It is an account designed to yield an adequate conception of critical morality and to provide the methodological component for representing a sound moral point of view or, reasonably and morally speaking, the best moral point of view that we can garner at a given time. This is not a matter of *per impossible* getting a conception derived from or in some other way based on unchallengeable general principles or a matter of deriving such principles from a set of self-evident propositions or squaring this moral point of view with a set of particular considered judgments that are not even in principle revisable or challengeable. No such quest for certainty, no such tacit appeal to foundationalism is in order. Instead, the justification of a claim that we have such a moral point of view is "a matter of the mutual support of many considerations, of everything fitting together into a coherent view."[10] Unlike in intuitionism or in another view that would stick with narrow reflective equilibrium, our sense of what is right and wrong or good and bad, while starting from tradition, may undergo extensive change and change at the behest of critical reasoning and investigation starting from our considered convictions. On this thoroughly fallibilistic coherentist account, where all claims, including any considered judgments at any level, are at least in theory revisable, there is no foundationalist appeal to some moral beliefs (say, some of our concrete considered convictions) or some very abstract principles à la Sidgwick as basic or self-warranting. Our grounds for accepting the moral principles that we accept are not that they systematize pretheoretical considered judgments that carry epistemological privilege. None of the moral judgments, moral principles, moral theories, or background social theories carry such privilege or indeed any privilege. The point is to get these diverse elements into a coherent whole that does justice to the importance and relevance of our firmest convictions, to our best rationalized social and moral theories, and to what we know or reasonably believe about the world. But none of these elements is uncriticizable: None forms a justificatory base we simply must accept, though some of them may never actually be doubted or subjected to criticism. But it is, as the pragmatists stressed, utterly impossible to doubt them all at once. Something must for the nonce stand fast while we doubt other beliefs. But this, as Peirce showed against Descartes, does not mean that any belief is permanently indubitable. Indeed, for some of them it is astronomically unlikely that there will be any point at all in doubting them, but this does not mean they are indubitable. To doubt and then come to reject some of them, such as giving no account to the suffering of the innocent or to the keeping of promises, would (if such a rejection actually took place) shake our moral universe. We would have no understanding of what it would be like to have a morality without them as a proper part. But we can perhaps conceive of a people *without a morality* not caring about the suffering of others at all and taking no account of promises. These moral truisms, unlike the primitive certainties of Wittgenstein's *Vor Wissen* discussed in Chapter 6, are things we can conceive of a people not holding, but they nevertheless still constitutive of the moral point of view.

At no place along the line is there a foundationalist claim (modest or classical), not even with our firmest considered convictions. WRE is not employed with the purpose of trying to find or construct such an Archimedean point but rather to gain for a time and always subject to future revision the most coherent package of beliefs relevant to how our life in society is to be ordered and how we are to care for our lives as individuals. Justification in ethics and the having of a critical morality comes to getting these beliefs in wide reflective equilibrium.

IV

A persistent worry about WRE is that, starting where it does from a particular agreement in considered judgments at a particular time and place, it will in one way or another be ethnocentric: It will be skewed from the beginning along class lines, gender lines, or otherwise along the lines of a particular culture. Such unavoidable starting points in local attachments cannot, the claim goes, but skew the outcome.

This worry does not take seriously enough what WRE is or attend carefully enough to how it works. We *may* possibly get such cultural skewing in the end just as we had it at the beginning, even after we have achieved our best obtainable approximation of WRE. But this is not a necessity, and I would predict that it is rather unlikely, particularly if we resolutely reason in accordance with WRE. We cannot, of course, have any guarantees here—again we should avoid taking an a priori or transcendental road—and we would not know whether we had avoided this skewing until we had carried through such reasoning thoroughly and had reflectively reconsidered it. But we can have good hunches here about the critical potential of WRE.

To illustrate, suppose we started not from a consensus we could actually attain in a Westernized society such as ours, but from a *Sittlichkeit* that was definitely of an Anscombeish-Donaganish, Hebrew-Christian morality that actually might have been our *Sittlichkeit* in an earlier period. The considered convictions that would be a part of our consensus in the initial situation in such a life-world would be: Voluntary sterilization is impermissible because it is a form of self-mutilation; casual sex must be evil because it cannot but be exploitative; and abortion, suicide, euthanasia, and sex outside of marriage are all *categorically* impermissible. These would be core considered convictions in such a life-world. But starting with such a consensus in such a life-world does not mean that we would end with it after protracted cultural debate *where the contestants would be committed to using WRE.* To have such a commitment means not only appealing to a partial reflective equilibrium that might take it as sufficient to get our considered judgments to fit with the first principles of the natural moral law, but also, more radically and more extensively, to get them into equilibrium with the best rationalized moral theories, social theories, and other relevant empirical-cum-theoretical theories and with the best factual knowledge we have about the world. It is very doubtful whether such an initial consensus in considered judgments could survive the justificatory demand that we get such judgments into the most coherent package of this whole range of beliefs. We unavoidably start with local attachments—firm bits of our culture—and we can never break out of the hermeneutical circle or the web of belief and see things as they are *sub specie aeternitatis.* We never get to a view from nowhere. But we can always rebuild the ship at sea. WRE gives us the conceptual and empirical equipment to criticize the initial considered convictions from which we start. Nothing in that starting point justifies metaphors of conceptual or cultural imprisonment. And wide reflective equilibrium is not a disguised form of intuitionism with the subjectivist and ethnocentric quality of intuitionism, even though intuitionism views itself, self-deceptively, as a form of objectivism. Moreover, we need have no views about moral truth or accept either moral realism or antirealism. We will not, of course,

get certainty. But knowledge with certainty is not pleonastic and
fallibilism is not skepticism or subjectivism. It is rather late in the
day to have nostalgia for the Absolute, though perhaps such
nostalgia is a kind of recurrent Philosophical disease.

V

        WRE yields a coherent triple of clusters of beliefs concerning
which there is or could be extensive informed consensus in a given
society or cluster of societies at a particular time.   That triple
consists of (1) a cluster of specific considered moral convictions, (2)
a cluster of moral principles (some of which may be general
considered convictions), and (3) a cluster of relevant background
theories that may, and normally will, include both moral and
nonmoral theories. Like Rawls, Norman Daniels, to whom my own
account is indebted and whose account is in some significant respects
like mine, gives too traditionalist an account of the relevant
background theories, though traditional moral (normative ethical)
theories do have a considerable role in the setting forth of such
background theories, as does a conception of a well-ordered
society.[11] I also agree with Rawls and Daniels that at the next level
of WRE there should be an appeal to a theory of the role of
morality in society, a theory of persons, and a theory of procedural
justice.   And finally, furthest in the background as vital feasibility
tests for the other claims, there should be, again I agree, a general
social theory and a theory of moral development.   In assessing
proposed moral principles such as a self-realizationist (perfectionist)
principle, the principle of utility or Rawls's two principles of justice,
it is surely vital to closely examine, in first achieving on the way to
WRE a partial equilibrium, the claims and rationales of various
moral theories and to see what they can say for the principles they
propose and against the principles they criticize. In assessing these
theories, we need a theory of the role of morality in society. So far
so good.   But in his account, in finding ways of assessing moral
positions and moral theories, Daniels places too much stress on the
working out of a theory of persons and a theory of procedural
justice. He focuses more than necessary on typical philosophical and
legal concerns and not enough on characterizing and exploring the

role of general social theory in such contexts and on specifying what kind of social theory we need. He directs too much attention to philosophy as traditionally conceived and not enough to sociology and critical theory. (Here my arguments of the previous two chapters are crucial.)

I shall proceed indirectly in showing—now moving from another direction—that this is so. Foucault, in responding to why he should be interested in politics, said:

> What blindness, what deafness, what density of ideology would have to weigh me down to prevent me from being interested in what is probably the most crucial subject to our existence, that is to say the society in which we live, the economic relations within which it functions, and the system of power which defines the regular forms and regular permissions and prohibitions of our conduct. The essence of our life consists, after all, of the political functioning of the society in which we find ourselves.[12]

To be seriously interested in ethics, at least in societies such as our own, is to be deeply interested in politics. In ethics we care about the quality of our lives and our relations to others, and we know, in thinking in a theoretical way about ethics, that this is a central object of concern of the moral life. That this is so much a part of the moral life means that if we care about morality (which, given our conditioning, most of us will), we must also care about the society in which we live, because the very care of ourselves, the the quality of our lives, and the kinds of relations we can have with others is deeply and pervasively affected by the kind of society in which we live. Our hopes for human enhancement, for the extensive and equitable satisfaction of our needs, and for self-development are importantly tied to what it is reasonable to hope for concerning the possibilities for social change and the kind of society we can reasonably expect and sensibly struggle for. To have any reasonable understanding here, we must at least see how our society works and, even better, how societies generally work. We need to understand our society's social and economic structure, its structures of legitimation, what holds it together, what could change it, what the direction and limits of change are, and how permanent those changes are likely to be.

We need as much knowledge of these things as we can get to help us in our coming to know what we should strive for, how

we are to live, and what is right and wrong. Ethics and politics
(*pace* Henry Sidgwick) are inextricably intertwined. But traditional
ethical theories (including traditional contemporary ethical theories)
are of little help here.[13] Indeed, it is very likely that ethical theory,
at least as traditionally understood, is more of an impediment than
an aid to understanding the society we live in and possibilities for
change and to a reasonable advocacy of certain changes, and that
metaethical theories are of no help at all except to explode the
myths of ethical rationalism or its alter ego, ethical subjectivism.
So it is in developing an adequate WRE that we must look to social
theory and to the social sciences. We need more sociology and less
philosophy (at least as traditionally understood), for though in the
past figures such as Aristotle, Augustine, Montesquieu, and Hobbes
were of central importance in such matters, among our near
contemporaries social thinkers in the mold of Marx, Weber, and
Durkheim should be our models of what kind of social theory we
need, not philosophers. (John Dewey is a partial exception, but he,
as we have seen, is an odd sort of philosopher, someone who did
not march lockstep with the Tradition.   It is not uncommon for
philosophers to think that he was hardly a philosopher at all.)

VI

Given such a conception of WRE, it is vital to see if we can
develop anything intellectually respectable that counts as a holistic
critical theory of society with an emancipatory intent. As I have
remarked, I am largely indifferent to whether this critical social
theory is to be called philosophy or a part of a successor subject to
philosophy. If "philosophy" is construed broadly as an attempt to
see things in a comprehensive way to make sense of our lives, then
a critical theory of society is also a part of philosophy. But, as we
have seen, many would want to construe "philosophy" more narrowly
as a distinct and autonomous disciplinary matrix. On that construal
critical theory, where conceptual analysis is integrally linked with the
social sciences, has a philosophical component but is not itself
philosophy, though it might be regarded as a successor to philosophy. What is crucial is not whether a critical theory of society is
or is not philosophy, but whether it makes a disciplined set of claims

that can be warrantedly asserted and will provide us with an adequate account of what society is like, what sorts of changes are possible and desirable, and how it can change.[14] Critical theory wants to help us understand how things hang together and how some of the ways in which things could hang together answer more adequately to human needs and are more liberating of human powers than others. In seeking WRE, having a social theory that really did such things is of considerable importance. If such a theory is not to be had it would considerably diminish the force of WRE. What it could achieve without such a theory would be far less than what could be achieved with a viable critical theory.

The critical theory we are seeking on the perhaps illusory hope that it is attainable is a holistic theory that will display and explain how things hang together. It is, as we have noted, a descriptive-explanatory theory, an interpretive theory, and a normative critique. Elements of philosophy as more traditionally conceived will in such a theory be amalgamated with the human and social sciences, with none of the elements claiming hegemony and with philosophy unequivocally giving up all pretensions to somehow being autonomously the "guardian of reason." (To claim this is not to defend irrationalism or to rage against reason, though it is to reject philosophical rationalism. Friedrich Waismann's dictum that the heart of rationalism is irrational is salutary.)

Critical theory, while remaining descriptive-explanatory, will also provide a comprehensive critique of culture, society, and ideology. And in this it will have its critical-emancipatory thrust, though it will be to a great extent indirect, by way of its descriptive-explanatory and interpretive power. It will help us see not only who we were, are, and who we might become but also, where there are alternatives, who we might better become and what kind of society would be not merely a more just society but also a more humane society that more adequately meets human needs and aspirations. WRE is integral to a critical theory of society here, just as critical theory is integral to WRE. They mutually require each other, at least if we are to have anything more than a rather impoverished WRE. But it is important to recognize that critical theory is not a fancy word-picture—a grand philosophical-social vision or metanarrative—but rather an empirical-cum-theoretical theory that must meet empirical constraints.[15] It is, we must not forget, a descriptive-explanatory theory showing us the structure of society and the range and mechanics of its feasible transformation. Tradition-bound analytic philosophers will think this carries us out of philosophy into an altogether different kind of activity. But this is pure conservative dogmatism, and if analytic philosophy is as broken-backed as Putnam and Rorty believe, and as I have argued in Part 1, it is a very unfortunate dogmatism indeed.

Critical theory is a definite project of modernity growing out of the Enlightenment, which is now under postmodernist attack. It is, to give postmodernism its due, surely not unreasonable to be skeptical about whether social theories on such a grand scale can meet anything like reasonable empirical constraints. They may, their author's intentions to the contrary notwithstanding, be just grand theories or metanarratives providing us with accounts which are nothing more than dressed-up word-pictures. Whether critical theory can be something more, that is, can be a genuine critical theory, will depend on whether it proves able to importantly contribute to the solving of some determinate human problems, e.g., whether it gives us guidance for what to say and do about abortion or terrorism or sexism. What is important is whether it develops a theoretical practice that has a clear emancipatory payoff, whether it is a theory whose descriptive-explanatory structure actually can be utilized so as to yield some true or approximately true explanations, and, finally, whether these explanations, together with the evaluative and normative claims contained in the theoretical practice, are set together into a well-matching, interlocking, comprehensive framework that is perspicuously articulated. This is, of course, a portion of WRE, for it requires a theory of society; it is also unsettlingly the case that the prospects of carrying such grand theory to successful completion or even to a promising temporary closure are daunting. (Perhaps talk of "completion" for such a program is a mistake.) It is, however, one thing to say this about the prospects for carrying it out and quite another to say there is something incoherent about the very idea of such a grand theory. But that latter conceptual stopper has not been made out. It has not been shown that there is something incoherent about the very idea of a comprehensive critical theory of society. The difficulties concerning scope, the problems posed by the knowledge explosion, the complexity of the social world, and the like appear to be empirical difficulties and not difficulties in the very idea of a holistic social theory. The proof of the viability of critical theory will be in the self-critical carrying out of something like this program, one which, if achievable, would provide the appropriate social theory for WRE and, more generally, have an emancipatory potential.

Postmodernists will resist such claims to theory. Not a few will claim that the incommensurability of competing theories and forms of life runs too deep for grand theories to be possible. Despite good intentions, what we get instead is ideology disguised as theory. Great unmaskers like Marx and Freud are, the claim goes, unwittingly wearing a few masks themselves. Habermas, in responding to postmodernism and in effect defending the ideals of the Enlightenment, argues correctly that critical theory requires a firm distinction between theory and ideology. Without it the very possibility of social critique is threatened.[16] Beyond that such a postmodernist critique seems at least to require the acceptance of a belief in incommensurability, but, as we have seen in Chapters 5, 7, and 8, claims to there being such incommensurabilities are not, to understate it, unproblematic. We seem at least to have no good reason to accept strong incommensurability theses. Conceptual relativism in its global form appears to be incoherent, and more restricted forms have not been established.

Critical theory, in arguing for a distinction between theory and ideology, argues that embedded in our life-world is a whole array of distorted legitimating beliefs that, taken together, provide us with legitimating myths. (Talk of "legitimation" here is in a sociological sense only.) These false beliefs and their associated mistaken attitudes are the norms and attitudes that in no small measure make up our world-picture and our social consciousness, and they prompt us to commend as legitimate, or at least accept as necessary, a network of institutions and practices of a highly repressive kind, including certain conservative political attitudes and an authoritarian work discipline. These are central, ideologically distorted beliefs—a system of legitimating myths—that underwrite our repressive social system of coercion. Even if we accept Davidson's belief (as I argued that we should in Chapter 5) about how the mass of mundane beliefs must be (objectively) true, we could still accept this Habermasian conception about ideology and its extent. Even with this massive agreement, there could be differences aplenty and some of them could be ideological differences rooted in a distorted understanding of ourselves.

Given this, a critique of ideology is a vital element in a critical theory. But this claim also dramatically underscores the need to be able clearly to distinguish critical theory from ideology and, more generally, ideology from nonideology, distorted discourse from undistorted discourse. What, in fine, would a cluster of nonideological legitimating beliefs look like? What would it be for us to have a true account of society where, against postmodernist irony and a pervasive skepticism, we would come to have a correct picture of our needs and their proper scheduling and an ideologically cleared up self-understanding, enabling us in this important way to see the world rightly? (Postmodernists will, of course, challenge the very idea of seeing the world rightly.)

Let us see, roughly following Habermas, whether we can characterize a set of circumstances in which the beliefs that would be standardly held could be plausibly said to be nonideological beliefs. This is, of course, a model, and we are talking about counterfactual circumstances and not about our class-divided and pervasively sexist societies. It is important for their coherence that counterfactual circumstances characterized are not so "otherworldly" that we could not conceive what it would be like for them to obtain. (Indeed, if that were so there could hardly be a genuine characterization.) But having this empirical significance does not mean that the model must, in order to do its work, be able to spell out the causal mechanisms that would bring such circumstances into existence. It must be a situation in which our legitimating beliefs (including central moral beliefs) are formed and argument for them is sustained in conditions of absolutely free and unlimited discussion and deliberation in which all parties to the institutions and practices being set up are placed in a position such that they could recognize that they are freely consenting to their establishment under conditions in which the only constraints on their acceptance derive from the force of the better argument or the more careful deliberation. Where we so discourse we have undistorted, nonideological discourse. Moreover, where we so reason and actually succeed in achieving a consensus, we do not have merely a consensus, we have a rational consensus.

In our class-divided, gender-divided, ethnically divided and religiously oriented cultures (with the religious divisions that standardly brings), we do not get such a consensus. But if counterfactually we were to get a consensus under the conditions of undistorted discourse that I have just described—a consensus that is conceivable no matter how unlikely it may be that we will actually obtain it—then in such a circumstance we would have conditions in place for rational discourses based on undistorted discourse and we would have, if we so discoursed, nonideological discourses. A critical theory of society articulates a model of discourse that if followed would take us beyond the distortions of ideology and give us a certain kind of objectivity.[17] In appealing to a theory of society, WRE should appeal to a critical theory because critical theory would adumbrate a conception of a theory of society that could help provide the corrections needed for the not infrequent ethnocentrism of partial reflective equilibria.

There is, as we have noted, also the problem of incommensurability, where incommensurability is not construed as untranslatability (something we have seen Davidson lays to rest) but as there obtaining essentially contested standards of appraisal where there can be no objectively justified resolution as to which standards are the more adequate. There are those who will say that the history of ethics, like the history of philosophy and of culture more generally, is a series of contingencies or accidents of the rise and fall of various, often incommensurable, language games and forms of life. Philosophers stubbornly retain a nostalgia for the Absolute, but that, after all, like a return to pure laissez faire, is just nostalgia because no such Archimedean point is available to us. There are no ahistorical standards of rationality or objectivity providing us with ahistorical reasons for acting; reasons that can be seen to be good independently of time, place, and circumstance.

What should be challenged, Peter Winch, Thomas Kuhn, Jacques Derrida, and Richard Rorty to the contrary notwithstanding, is whether there really are such incommensurable abysses, whether we really suffer from a conceptual imprisonment caught up, as it is claimed we are, in various incommensurable hermeneutical circles.[18] Much in both our intellectual and political culture sees us as being ineluctably creatures of incommensurable perspectives. There are rival points of view concerning the truth or falsity, the warrantability or unwarrantability of scientific theories or moral conceptions, the propriety of political arrangements or the aesthetic qualities of works of art. But on examination we find that we have incommensurabilities incapable of being brought under a set of rules or procedures that will tell us how rational agreement can be achieved or how we could reasonably settle disputes. We are not infrequently given to understand that we are just stuck with incommensurabilities.

We are not, however, so stuck. And WRE, rather than sanctifying or rationalizing our alleged stuckedness, can be generalized in such a way that we may free ourselves from "conceptual imprisonment." When faced with an incommensurability claim, the claimants on either side of the putative abyss should bracket the contested claim for a time and, as in the initial stages of WRE, try to isolate between themselves (that is, between the contestants) whatever assumptions and procedures they both take to be noncontroversial in that context.[19] Where some common ground is found, as is virtually certain if the search is more than perfunctory, further deliberations between them should start from a point of view where only these shared assumptions and procedures are taken for granted in the deliberation or dispute. The strategy again is to work outward from a consensus—what predictably will be a widening consensus—toward the contested areas. With such a consensus firmly in mind and perspicuously arranged, we again make an onslaught on the disputed area working carefully with lines of inference from the area concerning which there is consensus. There can, of course, be no a priori guarantees that we will find such a background consensus or be able, reasoning carefully from that consensus, to resolve the issues or at least narrow them. But that there are no such guarantees should not be worrisome if we have good empirical reasons to believe such consensus is achievable. And we do have this. Even if we only have the initial consensus, we can know that strong incommensurability theses are mistaken. We are not caught in radically different conceptual universes, points of view, or forms of life between which there are, and indeed can be, no bridges to provide the point of entry through which we could make a rational and objective resolution of what sets us at odds. We do not have to be rationalists to not believe in a postmodernist alienation of reason.[20]

10

Wide Reflective Equilibrium and the
Transformation of Philosophy

I

To the dismay of some, to the delight of others, and to the
annoyance of still others, there has been, even in the Anglo-
American-Scandinavian cultural ambience, a breakup of consensus
about what philosophy is. Two recent anthologies, *After Philosophy*
and *Post-Analytic Philosophy*, tell a good bit of the story.[1] Faced
with this breakup, I am neither dismayed, delighted, nor annoyed.
Instead, I am rather cautiously optimistic, thinking it a hopeful sign,
a chance, where our ways of doing things have become moribund, to
take a radically different turning. In Part 1 I argued that in some
distinct ways philosophy, if it has not actually come to an end,
should have.[2] Philosophy, after its once proud cultural role, now
lives, and rightly so, a marginalized existence. But I have also
argued in the previous chapters of Part 2 that there can and should
be a radical transformation in which philosophy as a distinct kind of
critical theory, integrally linked to the human sciences, can, Richard
Rorty and Jacques Derrida to the contrary notwithstanding, again
come to play an important role in our cultural life.

Dieter Misgeld, stressing particularly what I have said in this
connection about moral philosophy, has subjected this view to a

sympathetic critique.[3] In probing that critique, I want both to clarify and amplify my own views. My aim here is not so much to refute or counter Misgeld. That confrontational style has its rather severe limitations; point-counterpoint in such circumstances can quickly become a bore (particularly to the reader). My aim, rather, is to further develop in the light of Misgeld's criticisms my conception of wide reflective equilibrium and to exhibit its strategic role in the transformation of philosophy. I shall conclude in Section IV with a response to a different Derridian reaction to proceeding as I have.

II

Misgeld seems at least to agree with me that a transformation of philosophy, and thus of moral philosophy, is in order, that this transformation should be in the direction of a critical theory of society, and that it should involve a reconciliation of the neopragmatist critique of foundationalism with critical theory, and that an adequate critical theory will, among other things, be a form of social critique addressing real and often large-scale social problems. Moreover, it will, as well, provide guidance for philosophers as to their role as reflective critics of culture and of contemporary ideologies. He differs from me about the details of how this critical work is to be done, how the underlying conceptions are to be construed, and he believes that the reconciliation between neopragmatism and critical theory should be different than the one I entertain.[4] He also, though he only asserts this, believes my method of wide reflective equilibrium will not do the work I set for it. It is, he believes, a fifth wheel in my machinery, a wheel that turns no machinery.

I shall in response argue here that the method of wide reflective equilibrium provides the theoretical cement that is needed both in my account and, in effect, in Misgeld's alternative account of critical theory at the juncture of normative critique with both theory and practice. In this domain it helps tie critical theory to the world, to provide a coherent account of the unity of theory and practice, and to afford, where normative critique is at issue, a test of a whole range of the claims of emancipatory social theory. Precisely such a methodology will show us that both the ordinary norms of the life-world and critical reflective norms are essential in communicative rationalization. Wide reflective equilibrium exhibits how they are related and what their respective legitimate spheres are. Without such a conception, critical theory is in danger of becoming a free-floating metanarrative—a loose cannon—that will turn into just another grand theory devoid of critical thrust or the analogue of an empirical test in the moral domain.[5]

I shall now tie this in with the specifics of Misgeld's critique. Critical theory, Misgeld tells us, is incompatible with the claim that we can know how, through practicing the method of wide reflective equilibrium, to secure an ever-widening range of consensus in moral and political judgments. But where exactly, or even inexactly, are the elements of incompatibility? Why should critical theory reject wide reflective equilibrium? My argument is that it should not.

Misgeld tells us that wide reflective equilibrium does not do justice to the embeddedness of our present judgments about society in our life-world. But that is false, for wide reflective equilibrium, with its coherence pattern of justification, requires that we start and return, again and again, to our actual considered judgments: To the practical, firmly embedded specific norms of our life-world. And where there is—as there frequently is—in our social life the rhetorical and ideological manipulation of ethical questions there is the self-correcting requirement, given wide reflective equilibrium, of squaring these moral convictions with more general moral principles, with at least certain closely scrutinized positions of some moral theories, with our best factual knowledge, with the best validated background psychological and social theories available to us, and with similarly warranted theories of nature. If there is some reason to expect manipulation, initial moral convictions must run at least some of that gauntlet to be rightly regarded as legitimate. Where some of the moral convictions we start with are subject to rhetorical or ideological manipulation, a determined application of that procedure will correct that. We repair and sometimes even extensively rebuild the ship at sea. *Pace* Misgeld, wide reflective equilibrium gives us very good ways of detecting the rhetorical manipulation of ethical questions or the suppressing of ethical questions, and it affords us a procedure for criticizing those very practices and for engaging in the critique of ideology. This makes it an ally of critical theory and not something, as Misgeld believes, incompatible with it. No grounds at all have been provided for saying that wide reflective equilibrium should not become a key methodological tool of critical theory.

I did (*pace* Rorty), particularly in Chapter 8, stress a pragmatism with method, and I did, in the broad way that the pragmatists construed scientific method, stress its importance for critical theory. I do not, any more than Habermas, want critical theory to be just another metanarrative, another "grand theory" without empirical constraints.[6] I do indeed want a holistic theory but not an undisciplined, uncontrolled speculative theory above anything so vulgar as empirical tests. (To say this, of course, is not to say anything about *decisive* disconfirmation.) But if such a critical theory is our aim, then the use of scientific method must be a part of critical theory. But to have, if you will, these "positivist" concerns is no reason at all to construe scientific method so narrowly that scientific knowledge is all taken to be a form of technological knowledge ruling out of its domain communicative and reflective knowledge. The pragmatists never construed scientific method and scientific knowledge so narrowly and in such a scientistic way; there is no reason why they should identify reason with instrumental reason and be incapable of making a critique of instrumental rationality. With their stress on the continuum of means and ends, they had a very different picture of rationality than that of Hobbes or Hume or in our time of Bertrand Russell or David Gauthier. Some contemporary pragmatists, e.g., Hook and Nagel, are political conservatives, though they (like Rorty) see themselves as social democrats; this self-conception is not linked to their pragmatist methodology, however, but is rooted in their historical experiences (the purge trials, World War II, the cold war, and the like). As Habermas, though not Horkheimer and Adorno, recognizes, nothing in pragmatism justifies tying it, as the latter two did, to U. S. business values or to a conception of knowledge that is incapable of resisting the functional subordination of knowledge to the demands of new forms (scientistically rationalized) of political power and social regulation. Scientific knowledge and communicative and reflective knowledge should not be taken as mutually exclusive, and there is no good reason for a critical theory to do so.

Critical theory, as both Misgeld I construe it, is a large-scale narrative of modernity, though it is clear from my articulation that this is not all it is. However, in the transformation of philosophy I envisage (and I think Misgeld, following Habermas, envisages), this narrative will not be a metanarrative. It will not be just another speculative philosophy of history without empirical constraints. It will indeed be "a grand theory" but still an empirical theory. If it is not falsifiable, it is at least infirmable on empirical grounds. It is not, that is, a theory that holds no matter how the world turns. It is not a theory that will always be accepted no matter what its evidential support. This would be true both for any particular critical theory that might be constructed and for the very idea of constructing a theory of such scope and import.

It is important to get a systematic social theory that has as a part of its central core a set of warrantedly assertable truth claims. (If Misgeld's characterization is correct, Habermas has produced just such a theory.) Critical theory so construed is distinct from political philosophies as we have come to know them and from moral theories such as we find them in the tradition of moral philosophy. It is a theory with an emancipatory thrust, and with that emancipatory thrust there is a normative critique and a set of moral and other evaluative comments on social institutions. Assessments are made of social institutions, both current institutions and those viewed as possible (historically feasible). It tries to give an adequate account of what society is actually like and of what a good society, what truly human society, given historically feasible possibilities, would look like. But still, in such a critical theory of society, prominence is given to sociology over ethical theory and political philosophy. That is to say, even in normative critique, prominence is given to the empirical-cum-theoretical over any attempt to moralize the world, including moralizing the world through abstract moral argument. Traditional moral philosophers—normative ethicists as they like to call themselves—have typically deceived themselves into thinking they have accomplished more than they have. This is particularly true in the generally dreary domain of applied ethics.

We need a theory—and this is what Misgeld takes Habermas's critical theory to be doing—that, in trying to carry out the Enlightenment project of modernity, advocates a certain attitude toward the future of modernity. We should, by being willing to think hypothetically, indeed counterfactually, direct our thinking to a certain range of possible social choices, given our past history. We need a comprehensive social theory to articulate perspicuously this range and to determine what would be the morally desirable set of social choices within this range.

In my schematization of a critical theory I have a niche for moral theory and practical reasoning, though hardly, as I have been at pains to stress, an independent niche. And in creating this niche I have also shown how we can get a grip on our practical moral problems—problems over which in social life there are often enough sharp conflicts giving rise to all manner of ideological responses. Misgeld, however, is mistaken in thinking I am arguing that, ignoring politics, we can work out these problems in good Popperian fashion by analyzing our moral beliefs one by one. Nothing in my account gives to understand that. Indeed, in Chapter 7 there is an explicit disavowal of that. For we must see ethics and politics as inextricably intertwined; we must come to see that serious social moral problems pervasively tend also to be political problems, and we must come to seek the resolution of our historically determinate moral problems against the background of theories of social change and of possible epochal social development. Certain kinds of work relations, to take an example, seem very wrong indeed, but the moral criticisms we would make of them cannot reasonably be independent of what work relations are possible in an industrial world and what they are and can be in turn cannot be answered independently of whether socialism and, if so, what kind of socialism, is on our historical agenda. We need to display the possibilities—genuine causal possibilities—here and try to make some reasonable judgment about which of them are the most desirable.

It is in doing the latter that the method of wide reflective equilibrium is particularly important. Suppose (to oversimplify) that one of the possibilities is so to organize work that we have small, worker-controlled and -owned firms often competing with each other, and another is to have large state-owned and hierarchically controlled factories run by the state (i.e., by a bureaucracy of state managers) but where the wages are high, the workplace clean and safe, the hours reasonable, and workers have minimal responsibility but considerable security. Which, where these are our only feasible alternatives, is the more desirable future to try to make our own? In trying to reach a conclusion we would try to trace out the probable life consequences of the various choices. We would need to make specific moral judgments about various work situations here and relate them to the more general values of our society, such as the comparative value we would attach in conditions of moderate scarcity to security, autonomy, happiness, creativity, and the like. Taking all these and other elements together, we would try (if we would use WRE) to get the most coherent package of considered judgments and policy recommendations that we would on reflection be prepared to accept. At the start we may very well be inclined to think (like Isaiah Berlin) that the disparity in the weight people give to these disparate values is just too great for anything remotely like this to be achievable. But where there is a resolute and intelligent effort to apply something like the method of wide reflective equilibrium, it is not so evident that we could not attain something approaching an informed and reflective consensus. At the very least it is not the case that reason dictates such pessimism even if it is the safest bet. Again, it is well to keep in mind Gramsci's slogan about the pessimism of the intellect and the optimism of the will, though it is important that it not be an optimism that flies in the face of reason. In our use of the method of wide reflective equilibrium, we should, following Habermas, seek as an ideal—though often or perhaps always only as an heuristic ideal—to carry out the deliberations under conditions of undistorted discourse where the ideals of discursive freedom and argumentational fairness obtained. To the extent that our deliberations about what is right or wrong, just or unjust, in seeking to attain a reflective equilibrium, are carried out under conditions approximating those of undistorted discourse, we can be more confident of their adequacy. That such an idealization can in fortunate circumstances have something like an approximation does not seem so wildly utopian.

We have here with the use of wide reflective equilibrium a coherentist model of justification. A further desideratum is to get a consensus about when we are in such a state. The hope is, against postmodernist skepticism, to gain not only a consensus but a *rational* consensus. If we can approximate Habermasian conditions of undistorted discourse, and if we have a consensus in moral belief rooted in a mutually recognized and accepted wide reflective equilibrium, then we have a rational consensus. I say that under such a circumstance we would have a rational consensus because our beliefs under such circumstances would not be ideologically distorted and would cohere together in the widest possible equilibrium. In this equilibrium our specific, reflective, considered judgments would match our moral principles, which in turn would best match and would also be rationalized by a moral theory that resulted from a comparison of the range of moral theories historically available or constructible by careful thought, where each theory (to facilitate the comparison) was in turn cast in the same role. It would also be the case, where we had for a time attained reflective equilibrium, that both the considered judgments and the theories would match with what we know about the world, the best available human sciences and social theories, the best account we have of the role of morality in society, and our best natural science knowledge, including the cosmological claims that in that circumstance could most reasonably be made. (The latter are important where religious issues are likely to enter into our moral deliberations.)

The overarching aim is to get the best possible fit of all these diverse elements which are themselves the best-warranted elements in their respective domains. Taking such elements together, we seek to forge a coherent package. When we have such coherence, we have for a time attained wide reflective equilibrium, though, as our knowledge and understanding increases, we will get other and more adequate wide reflective equilibria. No critical theory can in its substantive claims be a once-and-for-all thing, eternally fixed like a Cartesian philosophy, yet we can hope (perhaps utopianly) for a development analogous to that in natural science. If a consensus rooted in such a wide reflective equilibrium is not a rational consensus, what, then, would a rational consensus look like? It seems to me, though I am unsure how to further argue for it, that such a consensus is just what we would take a rational consensus in such domains to be. (This indeed may be an implicit but nonstipulative definition of what counts as "a rational consensus" in such contexts.)

III

Misgeld both thinks that such a theory is too utopian and doubts that such a theory could have an emancipatory thrust. I certainly do not mean to suggest that it could replace class struggle or revolutionary action, though in certain circumstances (say, if Sweden or Iceland were the world) it *might* be able to replace the latter and in any circumstance it could give us a clearer sense of what the revolutionary activity is to achieve.

In maintaining that my schemata for a critical theory misses the pragmatist and neopragmatist (e.g., Rorty) stress on solving the particular normative problems of human beings, Misgeld overlooks the role of particular considered judgments in wide reflective equilibrium. In attaining such a wide equilibrium, we must include (vitally include) particular considered judgments, given by our sense of justice and right, operating in determinate contexts where particular moral problems arise. (Here my remarks in the previous chapter about *Sittlichkeit* are vital.) These judgments are in turn rationalized in the way the method of wide reflective equilibrium specifies. This rationalization involves a shuttling back and forth between theories, principles, and concrete moral judgments with a mutual correction between them until we have, considering them together, the best fit. This is a method for coming to grips with determinate problems of human beings that could be utilized in social disputes and by people doing applied ethics, and it answers to the interests of the pragmatists in a more determinate way than they were able to specify themselves. Moreover (*pace* Misgeld), wide reflective equilibrium provides a way of coherently appealing both to the general and the theoretical and, as well, to the particular and "the practical" in the attempt to provide a theory of social recon- struction. Indeed, the way I have schematized the idea of a critical theory, it builds a pragmatic awareness of the limits of theory into the very design of the theory. And this in turn fits nicely with Habermas's argument in *The Theory of Communicative Action* that the social scientist does not have a privileged position in social assessment, for he, like everyone else, must rely on a potential for critical reasoning that participants in the society, with their different forms of discourse (theoretical, practical, and aesthetic), already possess, though typically not in a highly articulate form. As Misgeld himself puts it, Habermas's "communicative model of social action attributes to people acting and speaking in the society 'just as rich an interpretive competence as the observer himself'."[7] With this nonprivileging of the observer's perspective, there is no suppression, as there is in scientistic modes of thought, of commonsense conceptions of what is good and bad, right and wrong, or fair and unfair, though this is not to suggest that these commonsense conceptions cannot or should not be criticized or that we cannot come to have more adequate moral beliefs. And it is not to deny Gramsci's insight that ideology is pervasive here, though it is to deny that it is all-pervasive—utterly ubiquitous—and uncorrectable because we are lost (perhaps conceptually imprisoned) in the sea of ideology. (If everything must be ideology then nothing is. There must be a nonvacuous contrast between what is ideological and what is not for the term "ideological" to have a determinate meaning.) This also gives us a basis, and wide reflective equilibrium provides a rationale for it, of noneclectically integrating ethnomethodological, phenomenological, and hermeneutical conceptions of social action into a critical theory of society.

Misgeld sides with a Rortyan neopragmatism in rejecting the idea that a critical theory of society can, as I maintain, provide a method that will be an important aid for solving the problems specific to modern societies and history.[8] For Misgeld it could only be a background view, a theoretical narrative, perspicuously displaying how various key social problems are related and how they belong to the history of modernity. It cannot give us a rigorous explanation of the emergence of these problems or a rigorous normative resolution of them. All it can do with its narrative structure is to depict—at best perspicuously display in a loose association—clusters of difficulties and survival problems that afflict modern societies and indicate various sociologically feasible resolutions. Reflecting on these problems taken together and interlocked can help us reflect on how our history is to be understood. It can, Misgeld tells us, only be taken as a narrative that can lead us to look beyond piecemeal and ad hoc solutions to discrete problems by deepening our sense of how all these problems are linked in the history of societies.

I agree that critical theory should do all those things. I further agree that the picture of modernity in all its facets given by Habermas and Wellmer is of considerable value indeed and in the ways Misgeld indicates.[9] But what I do not see is why critical theory must limit itself to such narrative articulation. Why can it not also engage in causal explanation, as we find Weber and Marx sometimes doing, and in moral critique, as we find Dewey, Rawls, Mill, and

Marx sometimes doing? These elements of a critical theory along with the setting out of narratives should be seen as complimentary and not as rivals. A comprehensive critical theory, as I schematized it, will contain all three elements melded into an integrated whole. Moreover, to the extent that critical theory is successful in utilizing and integrating these elements, the charge that it is just another grandiose metanarrative will be deflected.

Surely, standing where we do now, we would want a comprehensive critical theory to be critically relevant to the fundamental social questions of the day. But that does not at all mean that we could just churn out the specific answers from the theory. To look for anything like a mechanical decision-making is silly. More generally, the routine churning out of such specific answers is no more reasonable or necessary on the theory's own account than that we be able to simply churn out answers to engineering problems or applied physics problems from theoretical physics. But in a way analogous to the way theoretical physics is keenly relevant to those practical domains, so the hope is that a comprehensive critical theory of society would be relevant to the live social problems that bedevil us. It would be a very impoverished critical theory indeed that could not (again *pace* Misgeld) take a position on the advisability in certain types of circumstances, e.g., in South Africa at present, of a purely reformist road as against a road that had revolution as its end, or vice-versa.[10] Misgeld would so hobble or limit (to use a more neutral word) critical theory that such choices would not be in its purview, but he has given us no good reasons for sticking with such a defeatist limitation any more than he has for saying that critical theory can only articulate a narrative and cannot engage in causal explanation or normative critique. Again, a critical theory that uses wide reflective equilibrium will have what in moral domains is the equivalent of practical social experimentation, keeping close, as Misgeld would have it, to daily detail. It will not be removed from daily life in the way Misgeld alleges critical theory to be. Misgeld neglects the possibilities for a coherent unity of theory and practice (something Habermas, like Marx, repeatedly sought) in a properly articulated critical theory. Indeed, I would be skeptical that critical theory could actually be *critical* if it had not attained something approximating that unity.[11] *Perhaps*, as Misgeld believes, this is too utopian. Since critical theory is self-consciously critical about its own program, including the potential for its own success, it is hard to see how this familiar criticism has much force. What would be true, and on the theory's own telling, is that if nothing like this is approximated in the next two to three decades, and if these were decades of peace and continued material advance on a global scale, then critical theory would have been shown to be a bad research program, or at least we would have good reason to be extensively skeptical about its potential.

IV

In closing I turn to a different type of reaction to such a use of wide reflective equilibrium as a methodological core of a comprehensive critical theory. There are the Derridian conceptions of dissemination and deconstruction directed against theory construction and hermeneutics. I seek in a good Quinean way to set out beliefs, including our moral beliefs, into a coherent web. Deconstruction and dissemination seek to disrupt, to break our confidence and complacency by getting us to see, as David Hoy well puts it, our traditions, our forms of life, our webs of belief, "not as a harmonious, progressive whole, a cozy web of beliefs, but as a tissue of fabrications, a patchwork of remnants."[12] Indeed, Gadamer, Winch, and Heidegger are right in believing that we have come to be who and what we are through our own historical tradition—how else could we be socialized?—but that does not justify our accepting its *authority*. Hermeneuticists such as Gadamer are mistaken (logocentric is Derrida's phrase) in assuming "that texts or the 'call of Being' have an authoritative say to which we must listen respectfully."[13]

I think we should respond with both a yes and no here. We have to say no in the sense that unless we have an initiation into a culture or tradition we will have, except perhaps in some very rudimentary sense, no understanding at all. For establishing for a culture what is intelligible and for the norms with which we must start, there can be no avoiding such an initiation, such a participant's understanding.[14] Traditional norms are inescapable and cannot but have an *initial* authority. It is also reasonable to see if we can put our various moral beliefs (some given in tradition), or at least a considerable cluster of them widely felt to be particularly important, into a coherent package. There is no a priori reason why we should fail or that, even if we are careful, we must fail. That is the no to the deconstructionist claim.

However, there is a yes to be said here as well. Among our moral beliefs some are surely likely to be little better than superstitions. Others become effectively "ours" through domination, manipulation, or because we have cosmological conceptions that are not only outmoded but without rational warrant. In certain contexts, and indeed particularly in our contexts with our class divisions, with the depth and pervasiveness of ideological indoctrination and mystification through the culture industry, it is important ot come to recognize that some of our moral beliefs (perhaps more than we ever expected) are fabrications, a patchwork of remnants. We should be wary indeed of getting these beliefs into some reflective equilibrium, and in seeking equilibria, we should also beware of too quick a closure. Faced with the initial situation in which we are enculturated into a tradition, we then, even as our web of belief is stamped in and developed, come to have, perhaps due to our big brains, something of the capacity to question or at least in various ways to react against our enculturation.[15] Still, we need to have first been enculturated into some tradition to even be able to so react. For the human animal, tradition is the first word. That notwithstanding, dissemination (the Derridian notion) is surely important here; sometimes we do not want—or at least should not want—a cozy web of belief; we need, instead, to shake up our beliefs or even to through and through undermine certain of them and sometimes the ones to be undermined are anything but peripheral beliefs. But we cannot do this to all our beliefs holus-bolus. For if we rejected them all, we could not even iconoclastically react to our fabrications, to our remnants, to recognize them as fabrications or remnants that we might react against or reject as inappropriate to our lives. At any given time, some norms from our traditional cluster must stand fast at least initially. If that were not so, we would not even be able to be iconoclasts or to transvaluate values.

In a particular circumstance, however, we might be utterly baffled as to which moral beliefs are to be undermined, which are to be stood by, which modified, and the like. We might not even begin to know enough in a particular situation to know how to get our beliefs into something even approximating reflective equilibrium.

All we might have is a rather inchoate feeling that something is rotten in the state of Denmark. I think we should both be wary of that feeling and respect it. It could be an irrational reaction, but it might also be an inarticulate moral sensitivity that we should respect. It is rationalism gone wild to think we should just generally set aside such gut feelings. They may answer to something very important in us for which later we may come to find a more rationalized voice. To reject those feelings, always, or even usually, to set them aside or bracket them, particularly when they are dwelt on or persist in a cool hour, is a questionable philosophical conservatism with possible overly rigid consequences in the political domain. It is possibly an irrational fear of what *may* be the irrational. Such caution, such distrust of the sentiments, is—or so it seems to me—*not* an attitude that furthers human emancipation. We should not so monolithically and routinely set aside as irrational what we morally feel through and through, even when we cannot at some given time, or perhaps ever, adequately rationalize it. Sometimes in the roughness of our social world we can do little more, sticking with our inchoately moral sense, than resist the forces that oppress us and dominate us. Sometimes, that is, we can only fight back with whatever resources we have against the forces that oppress us and sometimes, where our alienation is very deep, the task is to come to see *that* we are oppressed and something of how we are oppressed. Foucault has been of immeasurable help in this.

The task of the unmasker, say a Foucault or a Chomsky, is sometimes just to show the moral agent (Moore's plain person) that in so resisting there is nothing unreasonable in her behavior. And, of course, the moral philosopher or social theorist, in one of her roles, is also a moral agent (after all, she is not a blithe spirit). Yet without reneging on her determination to resist and to trust her inchoate moral feeling, the moral agent, who is also a moral theorist and a moral critic, should do her utmost to find a rationale for those feelings—a rationale that would withstand reflective scrutiny—and, failing that, try to see if there is a "dark side" to those feelings that, if brought to light, would make them (or some of them) problematical, perhaps even so problematical that they would be good candidates for extinction. In such scrutinizing, wide reflective equilibrium is indispensable. It is what we must do to gain a reflective and critical morality.

11

In Defense of Wide Reflective Equilibrium

I

The account I have argued for in the last two chapters is a defense of morality without philosophical foundations. Indeed, it is a view designed to set aside many of the considerations that have exercised philosophers since the rise of moral philosophy as we now understand it. It seems to me that traditional moral philosophy rests on a mistake. That is to say, accounts such as the various varieties of utilitarianism, deontology, contractarianism, rights-based theories, or perfectionism cannot attain the kind of justificatory purchase they seek and need; those, as well as the once fashionable metaethical turns, and the "new subjectivism" of J. L. Mackie and Gilbert Harman are largely pointless. Moral philosophy needs to redefine its role. A start is to develop in the understanding of moral domains as thorough an antifoundationalism and coherentism as Quine, Davidson, and Rorty have developed in what was once called epistemology. (I would take "foundationalist epistemology" to be pleonastic.) In the previous two chapters I have argued for an account of justification in ethics that is a distinctive variant of the appeal to considered judgments in wide reflective equilibrium. And such an account is plainly a coherentist account. I will here seek to show how such an account can reasonably set aside the epistemological and traditionalist considerations it has been tagged with by some of its most acute critics (i.e., Joseph Raz and David Copp). My account, as this book has made evident, is a coherentist model of justification. But the elements that go into *wide* reflective equilibrium, if thought through carefully, burst asunder all autonomous conceptions of moral philosophy, redefining moral philosophy in such a way that it becomes a part of a general conception of critical theory tendering an emancipatory approach to human problems (including moral problems) that remains systematically empirical-cum-theoretical, where moral theory and social theory come to be closely integrated into the human sciences. This shift, if carried through properly, will bring a sea change all around: to moral theory, to social theory, and even to elements of the human sciences. Moral philosophy, if that is still the right name for it, comes to be something radically different than it was for Kant, Mill, Sidgwick, and W. D. Ross.

Having developed this programmatic account,[1] I want to turn to the more negative and defensive task of rebutting some perceptive criticisms of wide reflective equilibrium that, if sound, would undermine it as a moral methodology and, in the process, do serious damage to critical theory. To succinctly fix my account, I shall first briefly characterize the way I want to construe wide reflective equilibrium. Then I will turn to an examination of Raz's and Copp's criticisms. I hope the result will not only be a successful rebuttal of those criticisms but will also afford a more adequate understanding of this method and its underlying rationale.

II

What I call *wide* reflective equilibrium was, as I previously noted, first developed in another context by Goodman and Quine. John Rawls then took it up as a central method in moral theory.[2] It was subsequently developed by Jane English, Daniels, and myself as a moral methodology and was in turn given a more general application by Putnam and Rorty.[3]

Someone who is committed to wide reflective equilibrium is committed to a holistic, antifoundationalist account of morality. There is, on such an account, no conception of basic or fundamental moral beliefs or principles that will provide an unchallengeable basis for moral beliefs. WRE sets aside any such quest for certainty, any such effort to discover or even construct moral foundations for moral beliefs in accordance with which we could provide a framework to assess extant moralities or judge the rationality of taking the moral point of view. For WRE there can be no such ahistorical, perfectly general, Archimedean point. Indeed, the very idea of seeking an Archimedean point will be seen to be a mistake.

Using a coherentist model, WRE instead starts with our considered judgments given in the traditions that form a part of our culture. (The equilibrium we seek is clearly a social equilibrium.) It does not, with talk of desires, wants, preferences, or even considered preferences try to "get behind" what are in this life-world our most firmly fixed considered judgments or convictions given to us in our traditions.[4] It does not try to show how these considered judgments, one by one, match with or answer to or "really are" something more fundamental.

WRE seeks first to set out perspicuously what for a time are our most firmly fixed considered judgments, winnowing out those convictions we would only have when we were fatigued, emotionally excited, drunk, caught up with an ideology, misinformed about the facts, and the like. Proceeding from such a cluster of considered convictions—that is, firmly held, winnowed, moral beliefs—WRE then seeks to match them with more general moral principles (which may themselves be more abstract considered judgments) that also explain, rationalize (show they have an underlying rationale), and in this distinctive way justify these considered judgments.

However, WRE goes beyond that, for if it were to limit itself to such a rationalizing of considered convictions, it would, as some of its careless critics have maintained, be a form of intuitionism: the matching of more specific moral judgments with more general ones, sometimes rejecting particular considered judgments that are not in accordance with the more abstract principles and sometimes modifying or even abandoning those abstract principles (say, the principle of utility or perfectionist principles) that failed to match with a whole cluster of firmly held, more specific considered judgments.[5] The point in a rational reconstruction of our considered judgments is to get them into a coherent and consistent package. But this narrow or partially reflective equilibrium would never give us a *critical* morality.

WRE seeks to get beyond this narrow reflective equilibrium to a wide reflective equilibrium that not only gets specific considered convictions in equilibrium with abstract moral principles but also unifies both into a consistent whole with moral and social theories and with other scientific theories about human nature. In rationalizing and, in some instances, criticizing specific considered judgments we appeal to abstract moral principles as well as to whole moral theories, empirical-cum-theoretical theories about the function(s) of morality in society, social structure, the basis of solidarity in society; theories of social stratification, class, and gender; theories about ideology, human nature, and the like. The goal is to get our considered convictions, jettisoning some along the way, into a coherent fit with general moral principles, background social theories, and the like. We seek a consistent and coherent equilibrium to which we would on reflection assent.

There are no moral foundations here, no underlying foundationalist moral epistemologies, no principles à la Bentham, Kant, or Sidgwick, that just must be accepted as self-evident intuitions or basic beliefs on which everything else rests. Nothing in WRE is basic or foundational. Instead, we weave and unweave the web of our beliefs until for a time, though only for a time, we have the most consistent and coherent tapestry that best squares with everything we believe we know and to what on reflection we are most firmly committed.[6] There are some fixed points we *may* always in fact retain anywhere, anytime, but they are still, logically speaking, provisional fixed points that are not, in theory at least, beyond question if they turn out not to fit in with the web of our beliefs and reflective commitments, commitments that will not be extinguished when we take them to heart under conditions of undistorted discourse.[7]

III

Joseph Raz, in "The Claims of Reflective Equilibrium," carefully queries WRE. He wants to know how WRE leads to the endorsement of reliable beliefs.[8] What is there, he asks, about the process of shuttling back and forth between the various beliefs, views, and convictions that gives these views their soundness? What, if anything, is there to it more than saying that our views, to be correct, must be informed and consistent (309)?

It is plain enough, Raz continues, that WRE can clarify the implications of views we already hold (310). But it would seem at least that it cannot have more force than the views from which WRE is derived. We have moral convictions at the start of engaging in the moral deliberation characterized as WRE; we will have moral convictions, which may or may not be identical with those initial convictions, at the end of such deliberations. Raz asks why we should have any greater confidence in the moral convictions we have at the finish than we have at the start (309).

Raz thinks, most strangely it seems to me, that WRE gives us no reason for greater confidence. But, for starters, he characterizes reflective equilibrium in a most inadequate way, setting up a straw man. "Suppose," to quote Raz, "I reach reflective equilibrium but that you know that my deliberations were greatly influenced by a large number of clearly false factual assumptions, or were arrived at by a series of logical howlers such as affirming the consequent, or were based on accepting a demonstrably false epistemological theory" (309). But if I (for example) so reasoned, then, whatever I thought, my views would not in fact be in WRE. We start from the moral convictions extant in our traditions, but we must, in reasoning in accordance with WRE, get them to square with out best available canons of correct reasoning. In the above case I have plainly failed to do that, so I have not got my views into WRE, or indeed into anything like a good approximation of it, though I may very well be under the illusion that I have. But I have no privileged access here.

However, let us go back to Raz's query. Why believe that correctly pursuing WRE "leads to the endorsement of reliable views" (310)? Indeed, Raz acknowledges, there is value in WRE, for "it is likely to make people better aware of the implications of views which they already hold. Our firm beliefs may well help us decide cases about which we are hesitant, engaging in the process of reflective equilibrium may well help us see how" (311). Though this is clearly valuable, it does not carry us very far; as Raz continues,

> the undoubted value of seeing clearly the implications of our own views on many occasions cannot, however, blind us to the fact that these implications cannot have more force than the views from which they derive. The method of reflective equilibrium cannot be *the* method of

moral theory unless it can provide us with grounds for confidence in our
views, and not only with an understanding of their implications regarding
which we were in doubt. (311)

Why, he reiterates, have confidence in the considered
judgments that remain after we have carefully reasoned in accordance with WRE? Why endorse these as reliable views? I am
thoroughly baffled here by Raz, and fear I may be missing something. It seems to me the answer is obvious. I need—or so it seems
to me—simply respond that we take such considered judgments to be
reliable and do so with confidence because they are based on the
most coherent package we can get of everything we can reasonably
be expected to know or reliably believe, and this includes making
careful comparisons with all the reasonably available alternatives.
But this seems so blindingly obvious that it is difficult to believe that
Raz could have overlooked it.

Perhaps Raz might resist by saying that ab initio we have no
reasons for taking our initial considered judgments to be reliable and
given that, and given the truistic principle garbage in, garbage out,
we have no good reason to take the considered judgments that
result from WRE to be reliable. But whether that is so depends on
what is done to the garbage in the process. We all know that some
remarkable things have been done in processing garbage. It is not
always the case that garbage in, garbage out. In WRE, to drop the
metaphor, some considerable constraints and critical inspection are
put on our initial considered judgments such that what remains after
that process should lose a lot of whatever waywardness and arbitrariness the initial judgments may have had. Moreover, and as a
distinct point, there is no reason not to believe that the considered
judgments we start with—or at least some of them—have a certain
initial credibilty. Some are the most firmly entrenched considered
judgments we have. As such they are part of the core convictions
of our culture; they have a long and complicated tradition to
support them. (This is also true, though to a lesser extent, of the
other, less firmly entrenched considered judgments. Remember they
are all *our* considered judgments, our *Sittlichkeit*, and in this important way hardly arbitrary.) One does not have to be a conservative
to believe they have some initial credibility. If the most deeply
entrenched moral judgments here would not have *initial* credibility,
what moral judgments would? And if it is replied that *none* do or

could, then it can be reasonably asked: How else are we to make a start or find a footing in ethics? Considered judgments are to ethics what evidence is to science. But again the analogy holds: There is no simple determining of the truth of any complex scientific theory from the evidence. A similar thing needs to be said of the justification of an ethical theory from considered judgments.

I have moved from consensus rooted in tradition to a claim to some initial justification for our considered judgments. But Raz resists that as well (311-12). I argue, as does Daniels, that *if* WRE leads to a stable consensus, perhaps sustaining something of an initial consensus, and, more importantly, producing an extended and perhaps (in part) different consensus, then we have good reason to believe that our resulting considered moral judgments have a reasonable objectivity.[9] Raz, like Copp, takes that to be confusing justifying a conclusion of a given person or persons in a culture at a given time and place with justifying a conclusion. After all, Raz comments, some people or even whole groups of people may "be very gullible and happy to accept rather silly premises" (312). That last remark is surely true of many individuals, but it is far less plausible (to put it minimally) when applied to a whole tradition, including, most plainly, our complex Western one—with its long history and its tradition of critical inquiry. Moreover, as Rawls stresses, justification, unlike proof, is a pragmatic notion.[10] We have no tolerably clear understanding of what it would be like simply to justify a conclusion, period, as distinct from justifying it to some person or group (including—*pace* Rorty—the very wide group of humankind).

Raz goes on to argue that even an extensive agreement rooted in WRE would not count as justification unless it secured agreement "based on moral truth" (312). But the very notion of "moral truth," if we go beyond a Ramsey-like conception of truth (simple disquotational theory), is problematic. One of the advantages of pursuing moral philosophy in the way Rawls, Daniels, and I do is that it is so structured that it can remain utterly neutral on that thorny metaethical issue and a number of related issues, e.g., the fact/value issue. Whether or not moral utterances can in any interesting sense be said to be true or false, they can be shown to be justified by WRE just as certain imperatives could by the same method, be shown to be justified even though, plainly, no question of their truth or falsity could even arise.

Raz further argues that WRE cannot guide our choice between conflicting moral views. It "cannot offer guidance in choosing between conflicting views held concurrently or diachronically" (318). It cannot account for why a "morality is normative and binding. Morality provides reasons for certain actions and beliefs which do not directly and exclusively depend on the fact that we already know that these are reasons for such actions and beliefs" (325). Again it seems to me that Raz is mistaken. Our initial considered judgments capture the element of sentiment here, though they are not "pure sentiments" (if indeed there ever is such a thing). Reflective equilibrium in a distinctive way cashes in the structure of critical rationalization, giving us an appraisal that in important, though not in all, respects is independent of our initial considered judgments. These considered judgments give us some of our reasons for our actions, WRE providing us with ways and grounds for critically assessing those actions and their associated beliefs. Thus (*pace* Raz) WRE can guide choices between conflicting moral views, moralities, and moral theories both synchronically and diachronically.

Raz could respond that this presupposes that there is something good about coherence and that we should strive for coherence. That is indeed true. But coherence theories are common enough and in their general features unproblematic enough in our lives and practices. We do not want our views and convictions to be just an incoherent jumble; and we seek to show how they fit together, have a point and a rationale. In showing that point and rationale, we reveal something of their justification, as we do in showing how they hang together in a consistent and coherent pattern.[11] This, I should repeat, is part of what it is to show they are rational and justified. This needs no special justification by WRE but can simply be accepted as an unproblematic background belief. This merely brings out what justification comes to in such domains (323).

Raz also argues that if WRE is to be justified, it rests on "a second- (or third-) order disposition that some of us share. This is a disposition to approve of moral views held as a result of engaging in the method of reflective equilibrium" (326). He goes on to add that this "disposition is itself 'subjective'. Some people who have moral capacities may not share it" (326). I am not entirely confident that the appeal of WRE must rest on that, but, letting that go for the nonce, even if it does, Raz himself in effect signals that something is fishy by putting "subjective" in scare quotes. Why should this disposition to approve be said to be subjective? Is it simply because some who have moral capacities do not share it? But it is arguable (to put it minimally) that in not sharing it they are being less reasonable than they otherwise could be. The person who has this disposition and acts on it reveals in her very behavior that she is a more reasonable and more reflective person—indeed more reflective in her actions—and less given to arbitrariness than the one who does not so act. This shows that one disposition is better justified than the other and that the differences here are not subjective. If, alternatively, it is said to be subjective simply because it is a disposition to approve—*any* disposition to approve at all—then we are engaging in arbitrary verbal stipulation simply taking, in an arbitrary deviation from a linguistic regularity, "subjective disposition to approve" as a redundancy(326).[12]

Raz believes that starting with our pre-WRE considered judgments and stressing coherence and survivability gives us no grounds at all for taking any moral belief to be justified. We need instead to establish the truth of moral realism where we can show that some moral propositions reveal the existence of a moral reality beyond our mere moral capacities and reflective and informed approvals and disapprovals. Such talk is problematic indeed, and it is not clear that we understand what we are talking about when we so speak (327-29). But Raz does think if moral beliefs are to be shown to be justified, we must, how matter how problematic it is, establish the truth of moral realism. Raz is aware that WRE is attractive, for if successful it would provide an account of how moral beliefs can be justified without taking sides on arcane epistemological and semantical issues. He tries to show, however, that its claims, attractive as they are, will not stand up to critical inspection. I, in turn, have tried to rebut his criticisms, seeking to make viable or at least plausible the claim that the rest position should be the attractive and simplifying view, i.e., WRE, and thus making it the case that the burden of proof is to show why we should not remain content with that critically commonsensest rest position. We often should not be content with common sense or even take as unproblematic what in some cases is said to be common sense, but philosophers perhaps more than anyone else need always (or almost always) give us good reasons for departing from common sense.

IV

Raz remarks (*pace* Copp) that an advantage of WRE is that "it combines conservativism with reform. It builds on our existing views and yet allows us to revise any number of them" (329). Copp argues, by contrast, that WRE is a conservative view, and a mistaken conservative view at that.[13] By a "conservative view" in that context, Copp means (in effect engaging in a rather arbitrary *persuasive* definition) a moral view that gives "a privileged place in moral theory to our moral convictions or to those we would have under specified hypothetical circumstances" (141). If we use our considered judgments as a standard for assessing the correctness of moral principles, a morality, or a theory of moral justification, we in effect commit ourselves, Copp would have it, to conservativism in moral philosophy. However, it is very crucial to give this a careful reading, for Copp's label is very misleading. Copp takes it that what he calls "moral conservativism" makes "a common assumption that a theory may be undermined if it can be shown to imply that some of our considered judgments are not justified" (141). But this sense of "conservativism" is not correctly attributable to WRE either as I formulate it or as Rawls, Daniels, or English formulate it. We not only allow but expect that *some* of our considered judgments will not be justified. Indeed, one of the tasks of WRE is to help us sort out which considered judgments are justified and which are not. The firm expectation is that they will not all be justified. So right at the start Copp is off the mark.[14] What is the case on our accounts is that if an abstract moral principle, set of moral principles, or theory of moral justification is massively incompatible with the bulk of reflective considered judgments, then those principles or the parts of the moral theory that are so incompatible with the bulk of our considered judgments would have to be either rejected outright or modified until they were so compatible with those judgments. (Here there is an analogy with what Donald Davidson says more generally about all our beliefs.)

To the demand to quantify or make more precise the term "massive" so that we can say exactly when the extent of incompatibility with our considered judgments is sufficient to require such a rejection, it should be replied that moral theory cannot reasonably provide such precision. Instead, we must rely on the good judgment of reflective moral agents. But being without an algorithm here is not worrisome, for there are plenty of clear cases when a set of principles or a theory is so massively incompatible with the bulk of our considered judgments that it would be unreasonable to hold those principles or accept that theory, just as it would be unreasonable to hold a scientific theory that was massively incompatible with the empirical evidence in its domain. (That we cannot say at what exact point loss of hair constitutes baldness does not at all mean that being bald is not a useful concept. Similar things should be acknowledged in the above domains.)

This is hardly "conservativism" in any accepted or even recognizable sense of that term but, if by stipulation we call this "conservativism," then long live conservatism. We have to criticially inspect the remark "that conflict between theory and our convictions provides us with a justification for rejecting the theory" (140). It fails to take into consideration the following: (a) A conflict between *some* of our considered judgments may not justify the rejection of a theory, but (b) a conflict between very many of our deeply embedded considered judgments would require a rejection of the theory. Suppose, to be absurdly extreme in order to illustrate the point, we had a normative ethical theory that offered as its supreme moral principle "As much pain as is tolerable for as many people as possible is to be caused." There we have a clear case of a principle so massively conflicting with our considered judgments that this conflict gives us a firm ground for rejecting it. Moreover, there is no good reason to believe the latter reading of Copp's sentence, i.e., (b) is either mistaken—that is, that there is anything untoward about making such a claim—or expressive of conservativism, even a "conservative coherentism." And when we recall that the considered judgments in question are those that we—that is, we more or less modernized Westerners—would have in ideal circumstances, the attribution of conservativism is even more bizarre.

Copp, like Raz, draws a distinction between theories of objective justification and personal justification that leaves out of account an alternative conception of an objective justification that is arguably more appropriate to the domain of morality than the ones Copp and Raz offer. When this is noted, another of Copp's worries about a philosophical foundation for morality withers away or at least becomes very problematic. For Copp, we only have an objective justification in ethics when we have a "theory as to when a morality or moral judgments *themselves* may be justified, not an account of the circumstance under which a person is justified in his moral views" (143). The latter is *personal* justification, but we need the former to attain objectivity. And that, Copp would have it, we cannot attain if we use an appeal to considered judgments. But this forgets that there are other alternatives and forgets Thomas Nagel's point that objectivity is a very complex concept with different readings in different domains.[15] Copp simply stipulates a reading of "objectivity" that may turn out to be a Holmes-less Watson in moral domains. The demand for an objectivity that requires that "our moral views are justified themselves" is very problematical. It is not clear that we have anything like that or that we even could come to have or know in any tolerably clear sense what it would be like to have *such* objectivity. What we have here is on a par with moral realism. But there is, by contrast, available to us a whole range of rather more applicable conceptions of objectivity linked with forms of intersubjectivity and conceptions of reasonability. Suppose, to take just one of them, we say that a morality or a set of moral views is justified ("objectively justified" if that isn't pleonastic) when, at a given time in a cool hour, among reasonable people properly informed, these people achieve a reflective consensus on what is to be done and on what moral views to hold. "Reflective consensus" here would mean what they would assent to under ideal conditions when they were dispassionately turning things over and taking them to heart, and "properly informed" would be cashed in in terms of the constraints on WRE or an ideal observer theory. Similarly, "reasonable people" here can be plausibly taken to be people who are not parti pris, who are open to argument and the appeal to evidence, who attend to the causes of their coming to have the considered judgments they have and to the consequences of acting on them, who are willing to reconsider and are concerned with consistency and coherence.

I do not see why this does not give us a reasonable and workable sense of "objectivity'" in moral domains completely in the complete absence of any account of how moral views could be justified *in themselves* (whatever, if anything, that means) or of any commitment to something as obscure as moral realism. But this mundane sense of "objectivity" is an utterly nonmetaphysical conception of objectivity compatible with reflective common sense ("critical commonsensism," to use Peirce's phrase) and with an appeal to our considered judgments.

Related to Copp's persuasive definition of "objectivity" is his view that systematizing theories cannot be justificatory theories (143-44). But why should not the systematizing theories of a WRE sort be regarded as justificatory theories, too? Their scope leaves room for that. We not only systematize moral beliefs in getting our views into WRE, we systematize and compare different sets of moral beliefs and different sets of moral theories with many other things we know or think we know, including conceptions of the social role of morality; the structure of society; accounts of human nature, the mundane, nonmoral facts in the case; the way ideology functions; and the like. This kind of systematizing gives us plenty of lebensraum for the evaluation of competing moralities and moral theories and for criticizing moral judgments. There is no good reason not to regard such systematizing theories as justificatory theories. They are explanatory and interpretative as well, but they are also justificatory. (If some explanations and interpretations are shown to be correct, justification almost comes along with it.) Moreover, there is no reason to believe that in specifying ideal circumstances here we cannot specify a nonvacuous contrast between when these ideal circumstances would obtain and when they would not (145-66).

Copp views WRE, erroneously I believe, as a conservativism, and, as we have noted, he thinks conservativism is mistaken. "At root," he tells us, "conservativism relies on taking our confidence in certain moral judgments to be an index of justification" (149). Normative ethical theories and theories of moral judgments operating under that dispensation—and WRE, of course, encourages that—allow competing normative ethical theories to be "defeated or undermined by *marshalling* counterexamples supported by considered judgements" (147). What Copp calls the conservative theories stand intact when they square with our considered judgments. (Though,

as we have seen, matters are not that simple.)   This, Copp maintains, is a bad thing.   It is important to see *why* this is supposed to
be so and *if* it really is so.

   It is, of course, only "the beliefs in which we would have full
and non-temporary *confidence*" that we call considered judgments
and that "play an essential role in conservative theories of justification" (147).   What, according to Copp, is so wrong with these
theories is that they "beg the question against skepticism" (147).
Why does he say this?   WRE is committed to the belief that "a
theory of moral justification is not tenable if it implies that *no* moral
judgment is justified" (147).   But moral skepticism is just such a
theory, so, Copp argues, WRE begs the question with moral
skepticism.

   We have, in effect, a situation similar to some common
responses to G. E. Moore's critique of epistemological skepticism, a
situation I discussed at length in Chapter 5.[16]   However, we can say
correctly enough both that WRE begs the question with ethical
skepticism and ethical skepticism begs the question with WRE.   So
we need to ask in such a circumstance which, if either, position is
the better to hold.   We are in the familiar situation of trying to
ascertain where the burden of proof lies.   But the burden of proof
here—or so it seems to me—plainly lies with the moral skeptic.   Her
account implies that no moral judgment—*no moral judgment at all*,
not even the most carefully considered judgment—is ever justified.
But this is subject to a reductio, for this implies that we are not
justified in saying that it is wrong to torture little children just for
the fun of it.   But it is plainly more reasonable to believe that that
moral judgment is justified than to believe the general claim—in any
event obscure enough—that no moral judgment is justified.   Faced
with a choice between assenting to moral skepticism and assenting
to the proposition that there is nothing wrong with torturing little
children just for the fun of it, it is plainly more reasonable to refuse
to assent to moral skepticism.   What a reasonable person, not
trapped by philosophy, would do is conclude that somehow it is
more reasonable to assume that there must have been a mistake in
the chain of reasoning leading to moral skepticism than to believe
that the plain person's firm considered judgment is unjustified that
it is wrong (to understate it) to torture little children just for the
fun of it.   It is comparable to the claim that in the domain of

factual belief to believe that there is at least one tree in Ontario is more reasonable than to believe any skeptical epistemological theory that maintains that no factual belief is ever justified.[17]

When questions are begged, a burden of proof issue arises, and *totalizing* skeptical positions are the positions that need to be argued for here. (Indeed, if we take them at face value, it is very difficult, perhaps impossible, to take them seriously.)[18] The plain person's sense of reasonability—a flat-footed staring down of skepticism—must be the position to be dislodged. (Here G. E. Moore on common sense is valuable indeed. Epistemology should, after him, have been different, if existent at all. That it was not says something about the malaise of philosophy.)[19] Perhaps the proper response to moral skepticism is to deflate it, again, as is so often the case in philosophy, taking the fly out of the bottle.[20] Ridicule may be more in order than argument against the totalizing skepticism that Copp thinks it is our philosphical task to refute.

Copp might respond that by so arguing I am implicitly departing from the coherentism of WRE and accepting some kind of commonsense foundationalism because I am implicitly treating some moral judgments deeply embedded in our culture as basic (152). I do not take them to be self-evident or synthetic a priori truths or somehow accurate indicators or representations of a moral reality, as if we understood what any of that talk came to. But, still, do I not take them as somehow basic? Well, I do think that we have "no option (if we want to do moral theory at all) but to begin with the set of moral convictions we find initially credible and to try to construct a moral theory on that basis" (148). Copp does not object to that but only objects when we move from there to the claim that *justification* requires reference to considered judgments (148-49).

I, by contrast, do indeed believe we must both start with these considered judgments and use them in justification as well. But, that notwithstanding, none of them are taken in WRE to be basic in a *foundationalist* sense. Even my paradigm considered judgment, i.e., it is wrong to torture innocent children for the fun of it, could (as any other judgment) *in principle* be shown to be unjustified if it were shown to be incompatible with a host of equally firm considered judgments and other beliefs we think, and with good reason, are grounded in our knowledge of the world. In such an eventuality, we should first, of course, consider whether we had reasoned improperly in concluding that there was such an incompatibility, but if we reasoned together and came to the firm and carefully weighed conclusion that we had not, then even this considered conviction would have to be abandoned.[21] But that is a mere theoretical possibility—a Cartesian methodological doubt, not a real doubt—and there is no actual reason to think that a number of firmly held considered judgments (what I have called moral and evaluative truisms) are even the least bit shaky. We can see here how we can, as we can in the factual case, preserve consistently both a fallibilism and a critical commonsensism in a good Peircean manner. Any considered judgment whatsoever could at some time be up for grabs, but not all of them together. (For some doubts about things being quite this easy see note 21 to this chapter.)

There may indeed be suspicious formative factors that go into certain of our considered judgments skewing them ideologically. Indeed, I believe that is almost certainly so. Some of them may be little more than class biases or religious or antireligious biases. Such considered judgments, however, would be winnowed out by the resolute application of WRE. But we cannot block out all or even most such considered judgments in reasoning about what to do, though, as I have just said, any of our considered judgments taken seriatim could be challenged, though certain of them, no matter how cross-cultural and developmental we get, would most probably never in fact be challenged.

Certain idealized considered judgments (taken together) are in some way *a* standard of justification in moral deliberation but in no way *the* standard, and they have no pride of place over other matters in weaving and unweaving our web of belief until we get a consistent and coherent set of beliefs with which on reflection we would stick. Considered judgments, that is to say, do not have pride of place here any more than do moral principles, moral theories, background factual beliefs, theories about the function of morality, and the like. Nothing has pride of place. Nothing is basic in terms of which everything else must be justified. Considered judgments are an indispensable element in fixing moral belief in a reflective way, but they are not the only or the prime element, thus functioning as *the* or a central standard for warranted moral belief (155). An appeal to considered judgments is, however, in the way I have indicated, an essential element of such a standard in WRE. They are part of the standard it gives us. We could not drop references to them in WRE. *If* that is the mark of a conservative coherentism, then a conservative coherentism it is. But again we should keep in mind that that reflects an arbitrary *persuasive* definition of "conservatism."

No single considered judgment, no matter how fervently and reflectively held, could undermine the coherent package of moral beliefs that makes up an essential part of WRE. That the considered judgment does not fit, if that is so, is a good reason for rejecting it *or* for believing that we have not yet got our beliefs in wide reflective equilibrium. No considered judgment has such strategic or justificatory power. Indeed, given a commitment to the thoroughgoing coherentism of WRE, it could not *remain* a *considered* judgment where we could not, at least after some considerable effort, show how it could fit into what was a wide reflective equilibrium, though we must also consider the possibility, perhaps even the likelihood, if it is a deeply embedded considered judgment and it remains recalcitrant to our *purported* WRE, that we have not yet actually attained WRE (156-57). Again, we do not and cannot have a mechanical decisionmaking procedure here. Raz is right (*pace* Copp) in stressing how judgment is unavoidable in moral reasoning. It should be added, however, that this does not gainsay what I have just said: That there is the logical possibility that we might get such a conflict does not give us any reason at all to think we actually will get one.

But a psychological sense of confidence in such an unruly moral belief or set of such unruly moral beliefs is not sufficient to justify them when they do not cohere with an extensive, coherent package of beliefs of a diverse sort (of the kind that would go into WRE). Indeed, for a reasonable person reasoning in accordance with WRE, it is very likely that this initial psychological sense of confidence would be extinguished when this reasoning was carried through. But whether it would or not, this confidence is not sufficient to justify the belief *in such a circumstance*.

What Copp, like Raz, fundamentally wants is some account, other than a coherentist one, of the initial credibility of our considered judgments (160). For *initial* credibility, I would respond, it is enough that they are judgments we on reflection have a firm confidence in when we have a reasonable knowledge of the facts and are being impartial and reasonable. (Recall how "reasonable" was specified above.) Such considered judgments are the best candidates, as I argued in responding to Raz, for *initial* credibility that we can have. Such considerations are sufficient to give considered judgments *some* initial plausibility and thus *some* initial justification. And, moving from there, the closer we come to getting them into WRE, the stronger their justification will become. (Remember something can be more or less well justified.) Copp tells us that what he calls a "conservative coherentism would...be implausible because it would take our considered judgments in ideal circumstances to be a standard of justification *ab initio*, while admitting that they need to be justified" (165). Copp's contention here, however, is mistaken for it is not that they have *no* prior justification. They have *some* and so provide a starting point, a preliminary standard (if you will), though by no means all that we can reasonably ask for by way of a standard or standards. To further bolster them—to get a more adequate cluster of standards, a fuller justification—we turn to what we can get from resolutely and intelligently pursuing WRE. But without that they still have, if they are so held, some initial plausibility. Justification, unlike validity, is not an all-or-nothing affair.[22]

Notes

Chapter 1

1. Richard Rorty, *Philosophy and the Mirror of Nature* (Princeton, NJ: Princeton University Press, 1979), *The Consequences of Pragmatism* (Minneapolis, MN: University of Minnesota Press, 1982), and *Contingency, Irony, and Solidary* (Cambridge: Cambridge University Press, 1989).

2. Rorty, *Philosophy and the Mirror of Nature.*

3. Rorty, *The Consequences of Pragmatism*, xv.

4. *Ibid.*

5. *Ibid.*

6. *Ibid.*

7. *Ibid.*, 211-30.

8. Alasdair MacIntyre, "The Claims of Philosophy," *London Review of Books* 2, no. 11 (June 1980), 16-17.

9. Rorty, *The Consequences of Pragmatism*, 211-30.

10. Rorty sees the logical positivists as a reactionary movement (philosophically speaking). Where they were foundationalists and concerned with the autonomy of philosophy to that extent that is indeed so. But their challenge to the Tradition was frontal and vital in their attempt to eliminate metaphysics. That they sometimes unwittingly took a few metaphysical turns themselves is unfortunate. But they did much to eliminate metaphysics in any interesting sense. Rorty in effect recognizes this when he remarks: "the positivists were absolutely right in thinking it imperative to extirpate metaphysics when 'metaphysics' means the attempt to give knowledge of what science cannot know." Rorty, *Philosophy and the Mirror of Nature*, 384.

11. Alvin Goldman, *Epistemology and Cognition* (Cambridge, MA: Harvard University Press, 1986).

12. Systematic analytical philosophers not infrequently have as their ideal of what good theory should look like mathematics and physics. Philosophy should be exact philosophy and exact philosophy should look as much like this as possible. For me by contrast philosophy should be more in a narrative tradition and should be closely linked with the human sciences. The very conception of "exact philosophy" should be suspect. It may be rigor misplaced and not a servant of truth or warranted assertability. This, of course, is not to condone obscurantism. But it is not the case that the choice in philosophy is between the logicians and the lotus-eaters.

13. Richard Rorty, "Pragmatism, Davidson and Truth" in Ernest Lapore, ed., *Truth and Interpretation* (Oxford: Basil Blackwell, 1986), 333-55. But see Donald Davidson, "The Structure and Content of Truth," *Journal of Philosophy* LXXXVII, no. 6 (June 1990), 279-328.

14. I discuss Rawls's methodology particularly in relation to his work subsequent to *A Theory of Justice* in my "John Rawls's New Methodology," *McGill Law Journal* 35, no. 3 (May 1990), 573-601 and in "Rawls Revising Himself: A Political Conception of Justice," *Archiv für Rechts und Sozialphilosophie* (forthcoming).

15. Kai Nielsen, "Emancipatory Social Science and Social Critique" in Daniel Callahan and Bruce Jennings, eds., *Ethics, the Social Sciences and Policy Analyses* (New York: Plenum Press, 1973), 113-57.

Chapter 2

1. I have tried to same something about that in my first chapter, and I return to it in Chapters 3 and 4.

2. Alasdair MacIntyre: "Philosophy and its History," *Analyse & Kritik*, Jahrgang 4, (October 1982), 102-104; "The Claims of Philosophy," *London Review of Books* 2, no. 11 (June 1980), 16-17; Jonathan Bennett, "Wisdom and Analytical Philosophy," *Analyse & Kritik*, Jahrgang 4 (October 1982), 98-101. I discuss a key argument developed in MacIntyre's "Claims of Philosophy" in the present chapter. I discuss his "Philosophy and Its History" in Chapter 3.

3. MacIntyre, "The Claims of Philosophy," 16-17.

4. Bernard Williams, "Auto-da-Fe," *The New York Review of Books* XXX, no. 7 (April 1983), 33-37.

5. Quentin Skinner, "The End of Philosophy," *The New York Review of Books* XXIII, no. 4 (March 19, 1981), 46-48.

6. Richard Rorty, *The Consequences of Pragmatism* (Minneapolis, MN: University of Minneapolis Press, 1982).

7. MacIntyre, "The Claims of Philosophy," 16-17.

8. This theme is developed in much greater detail by MacIntyre in his "Philosophy and Its History."

9. MacIntyre, "The Claims of Philosophy," 15-16.

10. Skinner, "The End of Philosophy."

11. *Ibid.*, 48.

12. *Ibid.*

13. *Ibid.*

14. Richard Rorty, *The Consequences of Pragmatism*, 222. This is not quite true of all analytic philosophers. Ian Hacking and J. Kim, for example, agree with Rorty in believing that the Kantian project of assessing cultural norms is impossible to carry out while still believing that realism can be defended against Rorty's critique. I try to refute this quite different claim in Chapter 4.

15. *Ibid.*

16. *Ibid.*

17. *Ibid.*

18. *Ibid.*, 123.

19. *Ibid.*

20. *Ibid.*, 219.

21. *Ibid.*, 220-21.

22. *Ibid.*, 60-71.

23. *Ibid.*, 220.

24. *Ibid.* Even here there is less a unity of style than Rorty maintains. Rorty also sees them as being politically united as liberals. *Ibid.*, 229. Rorty's own commitment to a conservative form of liberalism comes out in his "Pragmatism Without Method" in *Sidney Hook: Philosophy of Democracy and Humanism*, Paul Kurtz, ed. (Buffalo, NY: Prometheus Books, 1983), 259-73. For an acute analysis and critique of the underlying political and ideological assumptions in Rorty, see Joe McCarney, "Edifying Discourses," *Radical Philosophy*, no. 32 (Autumn 1982), 4-7. I should hasten to add, however, that much more needs to be said about this. I would argue that while Rorty is surely a conservative liberal, his remarks about being a social democrat to the contrary notwithstanding, one might, without any inconsistency, accept his critique of philosophy and still be a Marxist or anarchist. Rorty, however, sees himself as defending a form of conservative liberalism that is in reality by now a traditionalist conservativism. But there is no internal relation between his metaphilosophy

and his politics. People on the Left can also be profoundly skeptical about Archimedean points in philosophy.

25. Rorty, *The Consequences of Pragmatism*, 221.

26. *Ibid.*

27. *Ibid.*

28. *Ibid.*, 222.

29. Jonathan Bennett, "Wisdom and Analytical Philosophy," 98.

30. *Ibid.*

31. Max Weber, *From Max Weber: Essays in Sociology,* H. H. Gerth and C. Wright, trs. (New York: Oxford University Press, 1958), 77-156.

32. Bennett, "Wisdom and Analytical Philosophy," 98.

33. *Ibid.*

Chapter 3

1. Richard Rorty, *The Consequences of Pragmatism* (Minneapolis, MN: University of Minnesota Press, 1982), 106.

2. Alasdair MacIntyre, "Philosophy and Its History," *Analyse & Kritik* I, no. 1 (October 1982), 101-15.

3. *Ibid.*, 111.

4. *Ibid.*, 109. The paper referred to is "Philosophy in America," reprinted in *The Consequences of Pragmatism*, 211-30.

5. *Ibid.*

6. Ian Hacking, "Is the End in Sight for Epistemology?" *Journal of Philosophy* LXXVII, no. 10 (October 1980).

7. Actually I think MacIntyre's claims should be questions, though I shall not pursue it here. What I am most in sympathy with is his claim that Rorty's account is too fixed on philosophy as a distinct discipline with an internal history. Rorty, as Isaac Levi and Bernard Williams have both differently argued, does not find an adequate place for science in his account. It is far too much seen as just one language game among others. See Isaac Levi, "Escape from Boredom: Edification According to Rorty," *Canadian Journal of Philosophy* XI, no. 4 (December 1981), 589-601, and Bernard Williams, "Auto-da-Fé," *New York Review of Books* XXX, no. 7 (18 April 1983), 33-37. I discuss this in Chapter 8.

8. Rorty, *The Consequences of Pragmatism*, 46.

9. MacIntyre, "Philosophy and Its History," 104.

10. *Ibid.*

11. *Ibid.*, 105.

12. *Ibid.*

13. Rorty, *The Consequences of Pragmatism*, 211-30.

14. MacIntyre, "Philosophy and Its History," 105.

15. *Ibid.*, 105-06.

16. *Ibid.*, 111-12.

17. *Ibid.*, 108.

18. *Ibid.*, 110.

19. *Ibid.*

20. Rorty, *The Consequences of Pragmatism*, xv.

Chapter 4

1. Jaegwon Kim, "Rorty on the Possibility of Philosophy," *Journal of Philosophy* LXXVII, no. 10 (October 1980), 588-97. All reference to Kim's article will be given in the text.

2. Ian Hacking, "Is the End in Sight for Epistemology?" *Journal of Philosophy* LXXVII, no. 10 (October 1980), 579-88.

3. Alasdair MacIntyre, "Philosophy, the 'Other' Disciplines, and Their Histories," *Soundings* LXV, no. 2 (Summer 1982), 127-45.

4. Richard Rorty, *Philosophy and the Mirror of Nature* (Princeton, NJ: Princeton University Press, 1979), 311.

5. *Ibid.*, 317.

6. *Ibid.*, 317-22.

7. Richard Rorty, *The Consequences of Pragmatism* (Minneapolis, MN: University of Minnesota Press, 1982), 142.

8. I refer to his remarks at the symposium held in Boston on December 30, 1980 at the Eastern Division of the American Philosophical Association.

9. John Rawls, *A Theory of Justice* (Cambridge, MA: Harvard University Press, 1971), 51-52.

10. John Cooper, in correspondence with me, has argued that.

11. Rorty, *Philosophy and the Mirror of Nature*, 45.

12. Charles Taylor, "Minerva Through the Looking-Glass," *Times Literary Supplement* (December 26, 1980), 1466-67.

13. Hacking, "Is the End in Sight for Epistemology?"; Kim, "Rorty on the Possibility of Philosophy"; Isaac Levi, "Escape from Boredom: Edification According to Rorty," *Canadian Journal of Philosophy* XI, no. 4 (December 1981), 589-601; Alvin Goldman, review of *Philosophy and the Mirror of Nature*, *The Philosophical Review* XC, no. 3 (July 1981), 424-29; Robert Schwartz, review of *Philosophy and the Mirror of Nature*, *Journal of Philosophy* LXXX, no. 1 (January 1983), 51-67; and Bruce Hunter, critical notice of *Philosophy and the Mirror of Nature*, *Canadian Journal of Philosophy* XII, no. 3 (September 1982), 621-45. It is Hacking (p. 586) who makes the qualification "at least for now." This response seems incredible to me, as if some day the situation might be better.

14. See the reviews of Rorty's *Philosophy and the Mirror of Nature* by Goldman and Hunter.

15. See the reviews of Rorty's *Philosophy and the Mirror of Nature* by Hacking and Levi.

16. Hacking, review of Rorty's *Philosophy and the Mirror of Nature*, 586.

17. *Ibid.*, 585.

18. *Ibid.*, 586.

19. Goldman, review of Rorty's *Philosophy and the Mirror of Nature*, 427.

20. Taylor, "Minerva Through the Looking-Glass."

Chapter 5

1. Alvin Goldman: *Epistemology and Cognition* (Cambridge, MA: Harvard University Press, 1986); Review of *Philosophy and the Mirror of Nature* by Richard Rorty, *The Philosophical Review* XC (July 1981), 424-29; "A Causal Theory of Knowing," *Journal of Philosophy* 64 (1967), 255-372; "Discrimination and Perceptual Knowledge," *Journal of Philosophy* 73 (1976), 771-91; and "What Is Justified Belief?" in *Justification and Knowledge*, George Pappas, ed. (Dordrecht: Reidel, 1979). See also Bruce Fried's useful critical notice of *Epistemology and Cognition* in *Canadian Journal of Philosophy* 18, no. 1 (March 1988), 125-

45. Future page references to *Epistemology and Cognition* will be given in the text. All other references will be given in the endnotes.

2. Goldman, review Rorty, 424-29.

3. Rudolf Carnap, "Truth and Confirmation" in *Readings in Philosophical Analysis*, Herbert Feigl and Wilfrid Sellars, eds. (New York: Appleton-Century Crofts, 1949), 119-27.

4. Richard Rorty: *Philosophy and the Mirror of Nature* (Princeton, NJ: Princeton University Press, 1979); *The Consequences of Pragmatism* (Minneapolis, MN: University of Minnesota Press, 1982). Kai Nielsen: "How to Be Skeptical about Philosophy," *Philosophy* 61, no. 235 (January 1986), 83-94; and "Rorty and the Self-Image of Philosophy," *International Studies in Philosophy* XVIII, no. 1 (1986), 19-28.

5. Sidney Hook has trenchantly criticized claims about there being something that can rightly be called a distinctively philosophical knowledge in his *Quest for Being* (New York: St. Martin's Press, 1960), 209-28. See in this context Rorty's important, though I think in ways importantly mistaken, "Pragmatism Without Method" in *Sidney Hook: Philosopher of Democracy and Humanism*, Paul Kurtz, ed. (Buffalo, NY: Prometheus Books, 1983), 259-74. The pragmatists powerfully undermine claims to "First Philosophy" or philosophy as a foundational discipline in a way that Goldman does not take sufficiently to heart. (So frequently in philosophy there is a lapse in historical memory even when it is our recent history.)

6. Goldman, review of Rorty, 428.

7. *Ibid.*, 426.

8. Nelson Goodman, *Ways of Worldmaking* (Indianapolis, IN: Hackett, 1978); Hilary Putnam, "Why Reason Can't be Naturalized" in *After Philosophy*, Kenneth Baynes et al., eds. (Cambridge, MA: MIT Press, 1987), 222-44; Hilary Putnam, *The Many Faces of Realism* (La Salle, IL: Open Court, 1987); Charles Taylor, "Overcoming Epistemology" in *After Philosophy*, 464-88; and see as well the books of Rorty's cited in note 4.

9. Goldman, review of Rorty, 428.

10. *Ibid.*, 427-28.

11. *Ibid.*, 427.

12. *Ibid.*

13. *Ibid.*

14. *Ibid.*

15. Charles Taylor, *Philosophy and the Human Science* (Cambridge: Cambridge University Press, 1985), 1-57.

16. Goldman, review of Rorty, 427. Rorty in both *Philosophy and the Mirror of Nature* and *The Consequences of Pragmatism* has hammered that point home, a point most contemporary epistemologists with their myoptic vision ignore.

17. Charles Taylor, *Philosophy and the Human Science*.

18. Goldman, review of Rorty, 427.

19. Rorty brings out in a very compelling way how attractive that view is. If he is right we have with it gotten rid of a lot more philosophical rubble. Richard Rorty, "Pragmatism, Davidson and Truth" in *Truth and Interpretation*, Ernest Lapore, ed. (Oxford: Basil Blackwell, 1986), 333-355. Hartrey Field, however, while showing the power of disquotational theories (as well as their variety) with exhaustive sophistication and pertinacity of argument, also shows that things, after all, are not quite that straightforward (the old philosophical lesson). Hartrey Field, "The Deflationary Conception of Truth" in *Fact, Science and Morality*, Graham Macdonald and Crispin Wright, eds. (Oxford: Basil Blackwell, 1986), 55-118. Anyone interested in truth and the issues of realism and antirealism and the drive to get beyond what may be, as Rorty and Fine believe, a sterile debate should carefully study and take to heart these two essays. It is also interesting to reflect where, if at all, Field's essay might force revisions on Rorty's subtle common sense and give, if it does, the Tradition another inning.

20. The articles by Rorty and Field cited in the previous note would seem, at least, to give the lie to that. It should also be noted that what is taken to be essential for realism is a conception of truth which Donald Davidson argues is deeply mistaken. This conception of

truth along with metaphysical realism is roundly rejected by Davidson, who has often been taken to be a realist. Yet Davidson, as firmly as Rorty, also rejects epistemological theories of truth and antirealism, though, unlike Rorty, he does not take a deflationary attitude toward Philosophy. Donald Davidson, "The Structure and Content of Truth," *Journal of Philosophy* LXXXVII, no. 6 (June 1990), 279-328.

21. Rorty, "Pragmatism, Davidson and Truth" and Putnam, *The Many Faces of Realism* and his "On Truth" in *How Many Questions?* Leigh S. Cauman et al., eds. (Indianapolis, IN: Hackett, 1983), 35-56.

22. Putnam, *Reason, Truth and History* (New York: Cambridge University Press, 1981), 52-53.

23. G. E. Moore, *Philosophical Papers* (London: Allen and Unwin, 1959), 32-59, 127-50, 227-51. Of Moore's many commentators, Arthur E. Murphy has best brought out the *general import* of Moore's work here. See Arthur E. Murphy, "Moore's 'Defense of Common Sense'" in *The Philosophy of G. E. Moore*, P. A. Schilpp, ed. (New York: Tudor Publishing, 1942), 301-17.

24. Donald Davidson, *Inquiries into Truth and Interpretation* (Oxford: Clarendon Press, 1984), 183-241, and his "Coherence Theory of Truth and Knowledge" and "Empirical Content" both in *Truth and Interpretation*, Lepore, ed., 307-32.

25. C. B. Martin, in an intricate and fascinating article "The New Cartesianism," *Pacific Philosophical Quarterly* 65 (1984), 236-58, argues against a cluster of striking claims of Donald Davidson's. To wit, his claims that all our beliefs cannot be false together, that if we understand what belief is we will come to appreciate that most of our beliefs are true, that among our beliefs those most securely held and which cohere best with the main body of our beliefs are the most apt to be true and that it is impossible that anyone could be mostly wrong about how things are. "Massive error," Davidson tells us, "about the world is simply unintelligible, for to suppose it intelligible is to suppose there could be an interpreter (the omniscient one) who correctly interpreted someone else as being massively mistaken, and this we have shown to be impossible" (quoted from Martin, p. 244). This cluster of, on their face, puzzling beliefs, along with Davidson's defense of them, Martin calls "the New Cartesianism." This "Cartesianism," like the old one, suffers, Martin believes, from a priorism and begs the question with the skeptic. The skeptic is neither refuted nor do we have a proof that his concerns can be legitimately set aside. (If these things do not come to the same thing.) Everything here rests, Martin would have it, on the power of Davidson's a priori argument to show that the majority of our beliefs *must* be true. But, while Davidson systematically and strategically calls to our attention, as Martin recognizes, a number of natural and reasonable enough assumptions, which should, if we reflect on them, give us very reasonable grounds for believing that many, perhaps most, of our commonplace beliefs are true, Davidson gives us no sound *a priori proof* or *demonstration* that they *must* be so and *so* he does not, with his "transcendental arguments," refute global skepticism or even properly set it aside. Martin also believes (though paradoxically enough he wants us to take skepticism seriously)—perhaps reflecting little more than a loyalty to the Tradition—that we can justifiably fairly peremptorily (as Locke does) set skepticism aside, though he thinks we should do so in Locke's manner. (He gives Locke's grounds in three magnificent quotations from Locke given on pp. 239-40 of Martin's text.) Such a Lockean critique of skepticism relies, in considerable measure, on pointing out the folly of expecting demonstration here. It adverts to that and then goes on to show, demonstration or no demonstration, how deeply unreasonable global skepticism is. Locke shows, as G. E. Moore reshowed, that global skepticism is a silly view that no reasonable person could hold if he thought at all clearly about what he was saying. But, as Martin remarks, this is very different than trying in some grand a priori way to rule skepticism out (256). Davidson, on Martin's reading, in typical philosophical fashion (the rationalist in us dies hard), tries that and predictably fails. ("The heart of rationalism," as Fredrich Waismann said somewhere, "is irrational.") Davidson, the logic-driven philosopher that he is, does give arguments that not infrequently sound like a priori transcendental arguments for the

claim that our beliefs massively *must* be true. Martin rightly skeptically queries that. (Indeed we ought to know ahead of time that it can't work, just as we know ahead of time, *pace* Malcolm, that no ontological argument can work.) However, that Davidson should be so understood, given his thorough naturalism, holism, and Quinean rejection of the analytic/synthetic distinction, is extremely doubtful. But I am not in the body of my text even remotely concerned with Davidson's exegesis. That is why I refer to a Davidsonian argument, though Ian Hacking (not an uninformed or naive interpreter) did take something close to what I have given as being Davidson's argument. Be that as it may, I am concerned to present a recognizably Davidsonian argument that does make some plain and uncontroversial enough empirical assumptions (assumptions which are plainly true) and then argues that, if they are accepted, then we can defend the claim that our and others' beliefs are massively true. If we do communicate and communicate across cultures then it must be the case that most of our beliefs are true. That, that is, must be true for such communication to be possible. But (to cite the true empirical truism) such communication does occur, though, of course, not always perfectly or even typically perfectly, and thus, if the Davidsonian argument is correct, it must be the case that most beliefs are true. The skeptic can deny that we do communicate or that we have reasonable grounds for believing that we communicate, but that, as Martin recognizes himself, is a silly view. It is more reasonable to believe the skeptic's argument has gone wrong somewhere than to believe that there is no communication across cultures and that field linguists and anthropologists always fail in constructing translation manuals. (That some ethnomethodologists may not see what is plain to see only shows that some anthropologists are also prey to bad metaphysics. I have left space for the philosophical underlaborer task of cleaning the Augean stable.) My Davidsonian argument in the text is more Locke-like and Moore-like than Cartesian, but this reveals something that Martin should like, namely, that Locke, Moore, and Davidson (or certain of their views) triangulate against skepticism. But we should also say something that Martin should not like so well, namely, that here all metaphysics drops out. Martin remarks profoundly and rightly: "The final ontic confusion is the failure to see that however much one may be ignorant or mistaken about the nature of the real world and one's place in it, there is no other place to be" (231). But this is not itself a deep ontological insight or discovery but good Wittgensteinian therapy or Moorean common sense (or both) to be used in the context of breaking the spell of, to be pleonastic, a bad metaphysical picture rooted most firmly in Cartesianism and Kantianism. Martin should ask, what he asks of Davidson's claims, is it plausible to ask for a grand or otherwise a priori demonstration of that claim? It is plainly true but unclear (to put it minimally) how we would demonstrate it.

26. Norman Geras, *Marx and Human Nature: A Refutation of a Legend* (London: New Left Books, 1983).

27. See the references to Moore and Murphy in note 23.

28. Steven Lukes, "Some Problems about Rationality" in *Rationality*, Bryan R. Wilson, ed. (Oxford: Basil Blackwell, 1970), 144-213 and "On the Social Determination of Truth" in *Modes of Thought*, Robin Horton and Ruth Finnegan, eds. (London: Faber and Faber, 1973), 230-48. Martin Hollis, "The Limits of Irrationality" and "Reason and Ritual" both in *Rationality*, 214-20 and 221-39 respectively and his "Witchcraft and Winchcraft," *Philosophy of the Social Sciences* 2 (1973), 89-103. Kai Nielsen, "Rationality and Relativism," *Philosophy of the Social Sciences* 4 (1974) and Kai Nielsen, "Rationality and Universality," *The Monist* 59, no. 3 (July 1976), 441-54.

29. Davidson, *Inquiries into Truth and Interpretation*, 183-98.

30. Ian Hacking, "On the Frontier," *New York Review of Books* XXXI, no. 20 (December 20, 1984), 54-8. For a perspicuous depiction of the varieties of objectivity, see Thomas Nagel, "The Limits of Objectivity," *The Tanner Lectures* Volume 1 (Salt Lake City, Utah: University of Utah Press, 1980), 77-139. The work of John Rawls and Norman Daniels extensively operates with this conception of objectivity. How we are not, all the same, trapped

in an ethnocentrism here is brilliantly portrayed by Charles Taylor in *Philosophy and the Human Sciences*, 116-33.

31. Rorty, "Pragmatism, Davidson and Truth," 333-55.

32. Ian Hacking, *Why Does Language Matter to Philosophy?* (Cambridge: Cambridge University Press, 1975), 148.

33. *Ibid.*, 154. This may not even be true of considerable parts of our own language. Considerations forced on us by considerations derived from intuitionism in mathematics and logic *may* make it the case that the logic of our own language does not have the uniform structure attributed to it by Davidson.

34. *Ibid.*, 156. Davidson, "The Structure and Content of Truth," 290-326.

35. Hacking, "Wittgenstein the Psychologist," *New York Review of Books* XXIX (April 1, 1982), 42-44 and his "Styles of Scientific Reasoning" in *Post-Analytic Philosophy*, John Rajchman and Cornell West, eds. (New York: Columbia University Press, 1985), 145-64.

36. Of course, if Davidson is proceeding purely a priori, as Martin thinks he is, then it is a metaphysical enterprise and, as Martin shows, a vulnerable one. But a Davidsonian account need not take such a high a priori road as it has not in my (possibly) scaled down formulation of it. But it is *thereby* also not metaphysical. Rorty remarks, significantly I think, "...the positivists were absolutely right in thinking it imperative to extirpate metaphysics, when 'metaphysics' means the attempt to give knowledge of what science cannot know" *(Philosophy and the Mirror of Nature*, 384). (And this, note, from an opponent of scientism and from someone who regards logical positivisms as, philosophically speaking, a reactionary movement.) Metaphysics (when it has a determinate sense that links it with the Tradition) wants to give us a priori knowledge of "ultimate reality" or the underlying structure of the world or the basic "categories of being." But there is no such knowledge to be had and probably the very conception of gaining such knowledge is incoherent. The sad thing is that so very late in the day there are still philosophers around who want to be ontologically serious and do what, if it can be done at all, can only be done by science. Philosophers ought to either close up shop or turn to other things. (I have suggested some other things in the articles referred to in the next note.)

37. I have tried to say something of how this should go in my "Philosophy as Critical Theory," *Proceedings and Addresses of the American Philosophical Association*, Supplementary Volume 61, no. 1 (September 1987), 89-108, my "Can There be Progress in Philosophy?" *Metaphilosophy* 18, no. 1 (January 1987), 1-30 and my "Scientism, Pragmatism, and the Fate of Philosophy," *Inquiry* 29, no. 3 (September 1986), 277-304. Moreover, even Davidson's conceptual investigations are empirically grounded as is evident from his "Structure and Content of Truth." Putnam tries to undermine Davidson's argument about conceptual relativism. But his intriguing cases would only show, even if the arguments generated around them are sound, something like Hacking suggests, namely, that there might be some localized relativism, not that there would be the ubiquitous conceptual relativism of the scheme and content dichotomy. Hilary Putnam, "Truth and Convention: On Davidson's Refutation of Conceptual Relativism" in *Relativism: Interpretation and Confrontation*, Michael Krausz, ed. (Notre Dame, IN: University of Notre Dame Press, 1989), 173-89.

Chapter 6

1. Richard Rorty, *The Consequences of Pragmatism* (Minneapolis, MN: University of Minnesota Press, 1982), xiv-xv.

2. Michael Williams, "The Elimination of Metaphysics" in *Fact, Science and Morality*. Graham MacDonald and Crispin Wright, eds. (Oxford: Basil Blackwell, 1986), 21-23.

3. This comes out principally in the selection from his notes bearing on culture made by Georg von Wright and published as *Culture and Value* (Oxford: Basil Blackwell, 1980).

4. Georg von Wright, "Wittgenstein on Certainty" in *Problems in the Theory of Knowledge*. Georg von Wright, ed. (The Hague: Martinus Nijhoff, 1972), 47-60.

5. Christopher Norris, "Philosophy as *Not* Just a 'Kind of Writing': Derrida and the Claim of Reason" in *Redrawing the Lines*. R.W. Dasenbrock, ed. (Minneapolis, MN: University of Minnesota Press, 1988), 189-203 and Richard Rorty, "Two Meanings of 'Logocentrism': A Reply to Norris" in *Redrawing the Lines*. R.W. Dasenbrock, ed. (Minneapolis, MN: University of Minnesota Press, 1988), 204-16.

6. Georg von Wright, "Wittgenstein on Certainty" in *Problems in the Theory of Knowledge*, 26 and 51.

7. Ludwig Wittgenstein, *On Certainty* (Oxford: Basil Blackwell, 1969), 28; Peter Winch, *Trying To Make Sense* (Oxford: Basil Blackwell, 1987), 28 and 31.

8. Wittgenstein, *On Certainty*, 22, 24, 33, 52, 59, 65, 73, 79, 89. For all his criticism of Moore for his claiming to know where there is no possibility of either knowing or not knowing, there is a fundamental sense in which he thinks Moore was right and there is no room for philosophical doubting or the philosophical skeptic. "There are," Wittgenstein remarks, "however, certain types of cases in which I rightly say I cannot be making a mistake, and Moore has given a few examples of such cases" (89).

9. Wittgenstein, *On Certainty*, 24 and 33. Norman Malcolm, "Wittgenstein's 'Scepticism' in *On Certainty*," *Inquiry* 31, no. 3 (September 1988), 65-67.

10. See Wittgenstein himself here, *On Certainty*, 28 (#209) and 34 (#262).

11. Colin Lyas, "The Groundlessness of Religious Belief" in *Reason and Religion*. Stuart C. Brown, ed. (Ithaca, NY: Cornell University Press, 1977), 158-80.

12. *Ibid.*, 172-79.

13. Wittgenstein, *On Certainty*, 79.

14. *Ibid.*, 15 and 87.

15. *Ibid.*, 51.

16. Von Wright, "Wittgenstein on Certainty," 55. But how could it be an "accepted truth" and still not be something that we could correctly be said to know? An "unknowable truth" is a weird kind of notion.

17. Wittgenstein, *On Certainty*, 51.

18. But, as John Hunter and Stanley Cavell claim, it may for Wittgenstein be more biological than cultural. Wittgenstein remarks of the certainty rooted in forms of life that he wants "to conceive it as something that lies beyond being justified or unjustified; as it were, as something animal." Wittgenstein, *On Certainty*, 47; John Hunter, *Essays After Wittgenstein* (Toronto, Ontario: University of Toronto Press, 1973); and Stanley Cavell, *This New Yet Unapproachable America: Lectures after Emerson after Wittgenstein* (Albuquerque, NM: Living Batch Press, 1989), 29-75.

19. Note in the last sentence the implicit reference to "in the beginning was the deed." Wittgenstein, *On Certainty*, 15.

20. *Ibid.*, 17.

21. *Ibid.*

22. *Ibid.*, 31.

23. *Ibid.*, 33.

24. *Ibid.*, 65-67.

25. Von Wright, "Wittgenstein on Certainty," 58.

26. Wittgenstein, *On Certainty*, #162.

27. *Ibid.*, #205.

28. Von Wright, "Wittgenstein on Certainty," 52; Wittgenstein, *On Certainty*, #155.

29. Wittgenstein, *On Certainty*, #92 and #608-612.

30. *Ibid.*, #471.

31. *Ibid.*

32. *Ibid.*, #144.

33. *Ibid.*, #140.
34. *Ibid.*, #145.
35. *Ibid.*, #225.
36. *Ibid.*, #161.
37. *Ibid.*, 27 and 32-33.
38. *Ibid.*, #54, 155 and 194.
39. *Ibid.*, #234.
40. Norman Malcolm, "Wittgenstein's 'Scepticism' in *On Certainty*," *Inquiry* 31, no. 3 (September 1988). Wittgenstein, *On Certainty*, #516.
41. Wittgenstein, *On Certainty*, #516.
42. Malcolm, "Wittgenstein's 'Scepticism' in *On Certainty*."
43. *Ibid.*, 284.
44. *Ibid.*, 286.
45. *Ibid.*
46. See Wittgenstein on the value and necessity of translating into the concrete. Ludwig Wittgenstein, *Culture and Value* (Oxford: Basil Blackwell, 1980), 6-7.
47. Norman Malcolm, *Nothing Is Hidden: Wittgenstein's Criticism of His Early Thought* (Oxford: Basil Blackwell, 1986), 275.
48. Peter Winch, "True or False?" *Inquiry* 31, no. 3 (September 1988), 273-75.
49. Wittgenstein, *Culture and Value*, 14.
50. Cavell, *This New Yet Unapproachable America*, 20-75.
51. *Ibid.*, 19.
52. Von Wright, "Wittgenstein in Relation to His Times" in *Wittgenstein and His Times*. Brian McGuinness, ed. (Oxford: Basil Blackwell, 1982), 109.
53. Wittgenstein, *On Certainty*, 6.
54. *Ibid.*, 79.
55. *Ibid.*, 8.
56. *Ibid.*, 9.
57. *Ibid.*, 63.
58. *Ibid.*, 64.
59. *Ibid.*, 60.
60. Von Wright, "Wittgenstein in Relation to His Times," 116.
61. For his distrust of science itself and not just scientism see Wittgenstein, *On Certainty*, 56. This is a late entry from 1947.
62. *Ibid.*, 3, 4, 17, 32, 33, 43-6, 53, 64, 72-3, 82, 95, and 96.
63. I have tried to carry forward those kinds of arguments in various ways in my *Contemporary Critiques of Religion* (New York: Herder and Herder, 1971), *Skepticism* (New York: St. Martin's Press, 1973), *An Introduction to the Philosophy of Religion* (London: Macmillan Press, 1982), *Philosophy and Atheism* (Buffalo, NY: Prometheus Press, 1985) and *God, Scepticism and Modernity* (Ottawa, Ontario: University of Ottawa Press, 1989).
64. Wittgenstein, *On Certainty*, 42.
65. *Ibid.*, 7 and 42.
66. *Ibid.*, 46.
67. *Ibid.*, 46 (emphasis in original).
68. *Ibid.*
69. Cavell, *This New Yet Unapproachable America*, 31.
70. *Ibid.*, 31.
71. *Ibid.* and Peter Winch, "True or False?" *Inquiry* 31, no. 3 (September 1988), 85-92.

Chapter 7

1. Richard Rorty, *Philosophy and the Mirror of Nature* (Princeton, NJ: Princeton University Press, 1979); Richard Rorty, *The Consequences of Pragmatism* (Minneapolis, MN: University of Minnesota Press, 1982); Richard Rorty, "Pragmatism without Method" in *Sidney Hook: Philosopher of Democracy and Humanism*, Paul Kurtz, ed. (Buffalo, NY: Prometheus Books, 1983). My arguments to show that Rorty's dissolution of traditional philosophy is essentially on the mark here occur in Part 1 of this volume.

2. Rorty shows the importance he attributes to historical considerations in his "The Historiography of Philosophy: Four Genres" in *Philosophy in History*, Richard Rorty et al., eds. (Cambridge: Cambridge University Press, 1984), 49-75.

3. Alvin Goldman, review of *Philosophy and the Mirror of Nature* in *The Philosophical Review* XC, no. 3 (July 1981), 424-29 and Bruce Hunter, critical notice of *Philosophy and the Mirror of Nature* in *Canadian Journal of Philosophy* XII, no 3 (September 1983), 621-45 show how a kind of eviscerated and uninteresting "foundationalism" might survive Rorty's critique. Robert Schwartz, I believe, shows a far better grasp of the significance of Rorty's work here and what Rorty has and has not accomplished. Robert Schwartz, review of *Philosophy and the Mirror of Nature* in *Journal of Philosophy* LXXX, no. 1 (January 1983), 51-67.

4. Ian Hacking, "Is the End in Sight for Epistemology?" and Jaegwon Kim, "Rorty in the Possibility of Philosophy" both in *Journal of Philosophy* LXXVII, no. 10 (October 1980). See my response in Chapter 4.

5. I do not like the sexist ring of "the problems of men," but that phrase, coming from a time when we were even less sensitive about sexist language than we are now, is so much identified with a programmatic claim of Dewey's—a claim that is not at all sexist—that I cannot forbear using it. That Dewey most certainly does not appear to have been a sexist makes me somewhat, but only somewhat, less uneasy about using a phrase with a sexist ring.

6. John Dewey, *Reconstruction in Philosophy* (Boston, MA: Beacon Press, 1957); John Dewey, *The Quest for Certainty* (New York: Putnam, 1960); John Dewey, *Problems of Men* (New York: Philosophical Library, 1946), 3-20, 169-79, 211-353; John Dewey, "The Need for a Recovery in Philosophy" in *Creative Intelligence* by John Dewey et al., eds. (New York: Holt, 1917).

7. Richard Rorty, "Postmodernist Bourgeois Liberalism," *Journal of Philosophy* LXXX, no. 10 (October 1983), 583-89 and Richard Rorty, "Habermas and Lyotard on Postmodernity" in *Habermas and Modernity*, Richard J. Bernstein, ed. (Cambridge, MA: MIT Press, 1985), 161-75.

8. This is actually a conception which Rorty takes from Wilfrid Sellars.

9. Tom Bottomore clearly brings out the differences between Habermas's account and the Frankfurt school account it is heir to. Tom Bottomore, *The Frankfurt School* (London: Tavistock, 1984).

10. See the references to Rorty cited in note 7 and his "Pragmatism Without Method" cited in the first note.

11. Here Habermas's response to Rorty is vital. See Jürgen Habermas, "Questions and Counterquestions" in *Habermas and Modernity*, 192-98.

12. Rorty, *The Consequences of Pragmatism*, 191-208.

13. *Ibid.* and his "Postmodernist Bourgeois Liberalism," 583-89.

14. Rorty, "Habermas and Lyotard on Postmodernity" in *Habermas and Modernity*, 169-71.

15. Habermas, "Questions and Counterquestions" in *Habermas and Modernity*, 192-95.

16. This is Habermas's characterization of Lyotard's term of art, not Lyotard's own. Rorty adds the following elements to this characterization: Metanarratives are "narratives which describe or predict the activities of such entities as the noumenal self or the Absolute Spirit or the Proletariat. These metanarratives are stories which purport to justify loyalty to,

or breaks with, certain contemporary communities, but which are neither historical narratives about what these other communities have done in the past nor scenarios about what they might do in the future." Rorty's "Postmodernist Bourgeois Liberalism," 585.

17. Habermas, "Questions and Counterquestions," 196.

18. *Ibid.*

19. *Ibid.* A key critical question is whether there are any such unavoidable processes.

20. *Ibid.*

21. *Ibid.*, 193.

22. *Ibid.*

23. *Ibid.*, 194.

24. *Ibid.*, 195.

25. *Ibid.*

26. *Ibid.*, 196.

27. *Ibid.*, 197.

28. Richard Rorty, "A Reply to Six Critics," *Analyse & Kritik* 6, no. 1 (June 1984), 78-98, and Richard Rorty, "Postmodernist Bourgeois Liberalism."

29. See here Noam Chomsky, *Radical Priorities*, 2nd revised edition (Montreal: Black Rose Books, 1984), 233-66 and Noam Chomsky, *Towards a New Cold War* (New York: Pantheon Books, 1979), 60-114.

30. Rorty, *The Consequences of Pragmatism*, 211-30.

31. I have criticized them along those lines in my *Equality and Liberty* (Totowa, NJ: Rowman and Allenheld, 1985), 45-99; "Against Ethical Rationalism" in *Gewirth's Ethical Rationalism*, Edward Regis Jr., ed. (Chicago: The University of Chicago Press, 1984), 59-83; and "Critique of Pure Virtue" in *Virtue and Medicine*, E. Shelp, ed. (Dordrecht, Netherlands: D. Reidel, 1984), 133-50. See, as well, my *Why Be Moral?* (Buffalo, NY: Prometheus Press, 1989), 207-68.

32. John Rawls, "Kantian Constructivism in Moral Theory," *Journal of Philosophy* LXXVII, no. 9 (September 1980), 515-72.

33. John Dewey, *Experience and Nature* (New York: Dover, 1958), 418. Donald Davidson, "The Structure and Content of Truth," *The Journal of Philosophy* LXXXCII, no. 6 (June 1990), 279.

34. Rorty, "A Reply to Six Critics," 78.

35. See references to Rorty in note 7.

36. Rorty, "Habermas and Lyotard on Postmodernity," 165.

37. Rorty, "Postmodernist Bourgeois Liberalism," 585, 587.

38. *Ibid.*, 585.

39. *Ibid.*

40. Rorty, "Habermas and Lyotard on Postmodernity," 165-66.

41. *Ibid.*, 166.

42. Rorty, "Postmodernity Bourgeois Liberalism," 583.

43. *Ibid.*, 584.

44. *Ibid.*

45. *Ibid.*

46. Kai Nielsen, "Reason and Sentiment: Skeptical Remarks about Reason and the Foundations of Morality" in *Rationality Today*, Theodore F. Geraets, ed. (Ottawa: University of Ottawa Press, 1979), 249-79, and Alan Gilbert, "Equality and Social Theory in Rawls's 'Theory of Justice'," *The Occasional Review* (Autumn 1978), 95-117.

47. Rorty, "Postmodernist Bourgeois Liberalism," 585.

48. *Ibid.*

49. *Ibid.*, 589.

50. *Ibid.*, 585.

51. Peter Winch, "Language Belief and Relativism" in *Contemporary British Philosophy*, H. D. Lewis, ed. (London: Allen & Unwin, 1976), 322-37.

52. Rorty, "Postmodernist Bourgeois Liberalism," 583.

53. *Ibid.*, 584.

54. Habermas, "Questions and Counterquestions," 198.

55. Sometimes "foundationalism" is used in such a broad way that any argued claim that there are objective warranted beliefs counts as "foundationalism." But that is wildly to stretch the meaning of that term so as to include accounts as foundationalist that are not philosophical as well as Quinean, Davidsonian, or Deweyan coherentist accounts as foundationalist. But that, surely, is to eviscerate its claim.

56. Chomsky, *Language and Responsibility*, Chapters 1 and 2.

57. I owe this point to Hilliard Aronovitch.

Chapter 8

1. This is very clear in his interview "From Philosophy to Postphilosophy," *Radical Philosophy* 32 (Autumn 1982). See also in the same journal issue the discussion of Rorty's views by Joe McCarney, "Edifying Discourses."

2. Richard Bernstein, "Philosophy in the Conversation of Mankind," *Review of Metaphysics* XXXIII, no. 4 (1980), 760.

3. *Ibid.*, 763.

4. He makes it clear in his revealing "A Reply to Six Critics," *Analyse & Kritik* 6, no. 1 (1984), 84-86, that that is not what he intends, though he freely admits that he put some of these things badly in the last part of *Philosophy and the Mirror of Nature*.

5. See Rorty's remarks about this in his "A Reply to Six Critics," 78-98.

6. Bernstein, "Philosophy in the Conversation of Mankind," 763.

7. *Ibid.*, 765.

8. Rorty, *Philosophy and the Mirror of Nature* (Princeton, NJ: Princeton University Press, 1979), 372.

9. *Ibid.*, 392.

10. Rorty makes plain his own dissatisfaction with some of the things he said in *Philosophy and the Mirror of Nature* in his "A Reply to Six Critics," and he also indicates some of the lines on which he would set it straight (78-98). Some of those lines are further developed in his *Consequences of Pragmatism* (Minneapolis, MN: University of Minnesota Press, 1982), xxiii-xvii, 160-90, 211-30, and in his "Pragmatism without Method" in *Sidney Hook: Philosopher of Democracy and Humanism*, Paul Kurtz, ed. (Buffalo, NY: Prometheus Books, 1983), 259-83.

11. Bernstein, "Philosophy in the Conversation of Mankind."

12. *Ibid.*, 767.

13. *Ibid.*

14. *Ibid.*

15. John Dewey, *Reconstruction in Philosophy* (Boston, MA: Beacon Press, 1957); *The Quest for Certainty* (New York: Putnam, 1960); *Problems of Men* (New York: Philosophical Library, 1946), 3-20, 169-79, 211-353; *Essays in Experimental Logic* (New York: Dover, 1953), Chapters I, XII, XIII and XIV; and "The Need for a Recovery in Philosophy" in *Creative Intelligence*, John Dewey et al., eds. (New York: Holt, 1971), 3-69.

16. Bernstein, "Philosophy in the Conversation of Mankind," 771.

17. *Ibid.* 771. Bernstein takes this to be something Rorty would deny, but it is clear enough by the time he got around to writing "A Reply to Six Critics" and "Pragmatism without Method" (articles Bernstein did not have available to him) that Rorty would affirm just that.

18. *Ibid.*

19. See my "Considered Judgments Again," *Human Studies* 5 (1982), 109-118, and my *Equality and Liberty: A Defense of Radical Egalitarianism* (Totowa, NJ: Rowman and Allenheld,

1985), 13-41. See references there to Rawls and Daniels in note 18, p. 39 and, for a parallel notion, see Rorty's "Pragmatism Without Method," 264. See also the three chapters that follow.

20. Isaac Levi, "Escape from Boredom: Edification According to Rorty," *Canadian Journal of Philosophy* XI, no. 4 (1981), 589-602.

21. *Ibid.*, 591.

22. *Ibid.* See also Rorty's "A Reply to Six Critics," 96-97. It is also important to recognize that this search for some measure of truth or what can at a given time be warrantedly asserted is distinct from what may be a will-o'-the-wisp, namely a search for a *philosophical* theory of truth.

23. Bernard Williams's critique here is to the point. See "Auto-da-Fé," *New York Review of Books* XXX, no. 7 (August 28, 1983), 33-36.

24. Rorty, *Philosophy and the Mirror of Nature*, 316. See also his "Reply to Six Critics" and "Pragmatism Without Method."

25. Levi, "Escape from Boredom: Edification According to Rorty," 591.

26. *Ibid.*

27. *Ibid.*

28. David Armstrong, "Continuity and Change in Philosophy," *Quadrant* XVII, nos. 5-6 (September-December, 1973), 19-23.

29. Noam Chomsky powerfully captures this ideological function in his *Towards a New Cold War* (New York: Pantheon, 1979), 60-114 and his *Radical Priorities*, 2nd revised edition (Montreal: Black Rose Books, 1984), 297-302.

30. Levi, "Escape from Boredom: Edification According to Rorty," 591.

31. Andrew Levine in effect does that often brilliantly in his *Arguing for Socialism* (London: Routledge & Kegan Paul, 1984).

32. Levi, "Escape from Boredom: Edification According to Rorty," 591.

33. *Ibid.*

34. *Ibid.*

35. *Ibid.*

36. *Ibid.*

37. *Ibid.*

38. *Ibid.*

39. *Ibid.*, 596.

40. John Dewey, *Logic: The Theory of Inquiry* (New York: Holt, 1938), 79.

41. For very crucial remarks about truth see Rorty's remarks about Davidson in the concluding pages of his "A Reply to Six Critics," 96-7. See also his "Pragmatism, Davidson, and Truth" in *Truth and Interpretation* (a festschrift for Davidson), E. Lepore, ed. (Minneapolis, MN: University of Minnesota Press, 1985), 333-55.

42. Levi, "Escape from Boredom: Edification According to Rorty," 598.

43. *Ibid.*

44. *Ibid.*

45. *Ibid.*

46. *Ibid.*, 600.

47. Bernard Williams, in a probing essay on Rorty ("Auto-da-Fé"), considers in a perceptive manner whether Rorty has appreciated the pivotal role of science in the conversations of mankind or the distinctive type of conversation that it does make: how it aims to talk about the world and not just about talk about the world. Unlike the pragmatists, Williams believes that we should attend to the aim of science and not—or so he believes—try to isolate something called scientific method. Pragmatists, I should add, sought to talk about the aim as well as the method, and indeed believed there would be little understanding of the one without an understanding of the other. But Williams's point, like Popper's, is that there is little to understand in trying to understand scientific method. It is the aim of science we should get clear about. I think that what *in general* we would say about that would be as

platitudinous as what in general we would say about scientific method. But, as I argue in the text, the assertion of platitudes sometimes has a point.

48. Rorty, "A Reply to Six Critics," 78-98, and "Pragmatism Without Method."

49. Rorty, "A Reply to Six Critics," 79-80.

50. *Ibid.*, 86.

51. Rorty brings this out in the following splendid passage in "Pragmatism Without Method." It should also be noted how much this is like Rawls's conception of wide reflective equilibrium. Rorty writes:

But experience does not show this, any more than it shows the opposite. Having general epistemic principles is no more intrinsically good or bad than having moral principles—the large genus of which epistemic ones are a species. The whole point of Dewey's experimentalism in moral theory is that you need to keep running back and forth between principles and the results of applying principles. You need to reformulate the principles to fit the cases, and to develop a sense for when to forget about principles and just rely on know-how. The new fuzzies in philosophy of science tell us that the apparatus of "the logic of confirmation" got in the way of understanding how science had been operating. This is a plausible, though not a self-evident, claim. As such, it resembles the claim Dewey made in *Human Nature and Conduct* (a book that has been ably defended by Hook against those who found it fuzzy). Dewey there urged that the traditional attempt to describe moral problems in terms of clashes between Kantian and utilitarian principles was getting in the way of an understanding of moral deliberation. His central argument was that the use of new means changes ends, that you only know what you want after you've seen the results of your attempts to get what you once thought you wanted. Analogously, post-positivist philosophy of science has been saying that we only know what counts as being "scientific" in a given area, what counts as a good reason for theory-change, by immersing ourselves in the details of the problematic situation. On this view, the wielder of an ahistorical scientific method—a method for judging "validity" rather than mere "strength"—is on a par with the ideal wielder of practical syllogisms, the person who knows in advance what results he or she desires and has no need to adjust his or her ends. Such idealizations may sometimes be heuristically useful, but we have no special duty to construct them. (264)

52. Rorty, "A Reply to Six Critics," 78.

53. See the reference in note 48.

54. The things of Nagel's that are particularly relevant here are his *Logic without Metaphysics* (Glencoe, IL: Free Press, 1956), 3-18, 39-102, 143-89; *Sovereign Reason* (Glencoe, IL: Free Press, 1954), 50-57, 101-40, 266-308; and *Teleology Revisited* (New York: Columbia University Press, 1979), 64-94, 7-28.

55. Rorty, "Pragmatism Without Method," 260.

56. *Ibid.*, 260-61.

57. Nagel, *Teleology Revisited*, 29-48.

58. Rorty, "Pragmatism Without Method," 262.

59. *Ibid.*, 262-63.

60. *Ibid.*, 263.

61. *Ibid.*

62. *Ibid.*, 264.

63. Rorty, "A Reply to Six Critics," 96-97.

64. In his "Postmodernist Bourgeois Individualism," *Journal of Philosophy* LXXX, no. 10 (October 1983), 583-84, given to the Eastern Division of the American Philosophical Association, it sounded at times as if he were doing just that. This was particularly evident when he was pressed in the discussion by Joshua Cohen to say something about the

substantive implications in such domains of his views about what it would be like for philosophers to say what should be done in any problematic situation.

65. Martin Hollis, *Invitation to Philosophy* (Oxford: Basil Blackwell, 1985), 41-47. He nicely schematizes the routine in a diagram on p. 44.

66. *Ibid.*, 6.

67. *Ibid.*, 8.

68. Williams, "Auto-da-Fé," 34.

69. *Ibid.*

70. *Ibid.*

71. *Ibid.*

72. *Ibid.* Williams quoting Rorty.

73. *Ibid.*, 36.

74. *Ibid.*

75. This is well shown in the programmatic essays in *Philosophy in History*, Richard Rorty et al., eds. (Cambridge: Cambridge University Press, 1984), 17-124.

Chapter 9

1. There are a variety of crisscrosses here. There can be contractarian theories that are utilitarian; projectivist or noncognitivist theories both of which can be construed as ontological theses about values or as theses about the logical status of moral utterances or as epistemological theses about whether, and if so in what way, some moral reactions can be knowledge claims. But a noncognitivist or projectivist might also be a utilitarian, a perfectionist, a deontologist, or a contractarian. We have, in fine, a considerable range of combinations and permutations here.

2. John Rawls: *A Theory of Justice* (Cambridge: Harvard University Press, 1971), 19-21, 48-51, 577-87; "The Independence of Moral Theory," *Proceedings and Addresses of the American Philosophical Association* XLVII (1974/75), 7-10. Norman Daniels: "Wide Reflective Equilibrium and Theory Acceptance in Ethics," *Journal of Philosophy* 76 (1979); "Moral Theory and Plasticity of Persons," *The Monist* 62 (July 1979): "Some Methods of Ethics and Linguistics," *Philosophical Studies* 37 (1980); "Reflective Equilibrium and Archimedean Points," *Canadian Journal of Philosophy* 10 (March 1980); "Two Approaches to Theory Acceptance in Ethics" in *Morality, Reason, and Truth* David Copp and David Zimmerman, eds. (Totowa, NJ: Rowman and Allanheld, 1985); "An Argument about the Relativity of Justice," *Revue Internationale de Philosophie* (1989). Jane English, "Ethics and Science," *Proceedings of the XVI Congress of Philosophy*. Kai Nielsen: "On Needing a Moral Theory: Rationality, Considered Judgments and the Grounding of Morality," *Metaphilosophy* 13 (April 1982); "Considered Judgments Again," *Human Studies* 5 (April-June 1982); and *Equality and Liberty* (Totowa, NJ: Rowman and Allanheld, 1985), Chapter 2.

3. John Rawls, "Justice as Fairness: Political not Metaphysical," *Philosophy and Public Affairs* 14, no. 3 (Summer 1985), and "The Independence of Moral Theory." See also Kai Nielsen, "Rawls and the Socratic Ideal," *Analyse & Kritik* (1991, forthcoming).

4. John Rawls, "The Independence of Moral Theory" and "A Well-Ordered Society" in *Philosophy, Politics, and Society*, fifth series, Peter Laslett and James Fishkin, eds. (New Haven: Yale University Press, 1979), 6-20.

5. G. A. Cohen, "Reconsidering Historical Materialism" in *Marxism, Nomos* XXVI, J. R. Pennock and John W. Chapman, eds. (New York: New York University Press, 1983), and Isaiah Berlin, *Vico and Herder* (London: Hogarth Press, 1976), 145-216.

6. John Rawls, *A Theory of Justice*, 580-81.

7. *Ibid.*

8. Charles Taylor, *Philosophy and the Human Sciences* (Cambridge: Cambridge University Press, 1985), 155. Given the slaughter and degradation of humans by humans so characteristic of the twentieth century from Hitlerism and Stalinism, to South Africa, to the actions of the U. S. government in sustaining what it regards as it own sphere of influence either on its own or through its proxies, it is hard to believe that there really are out there the beliefs of which Taylor speaks. It is very difficult to refrain, when we consider all the killing, from irony or just plain sarcasm concerning Taylor's claims. What can be said is that while the people portrayed in Icelandic sagas could hack away at each other with a clear conscience, we need complicated rationalizations to butcher and torture each other. Without these rationalizations there is a widespread horror and revulsion at the killing and the infliction of suffering. So there is a tortured way in which we really do believe that needless suffering is to be avoided.

9. J. L. Mackie: *Contemporary Linguistic Philosophy: Its Strength and Its Weakness* (Dunedin, New Zealand: University of Otago Press, 1956); *Ethics: Inventing Right and Wrong* (Harmondsworth, England: Penguin Books, 1977); and *Hume's Moral Theory* (London: Routledge & Kegan Paul, 1980). For a discussion of Mackie's views, projectivism more generally, and the rejection of objective prescriptivity, see the essays in Ted Honderich, ed. *Morality and Objectivity* (London: Routledge & Kegan Paul, 1985).

10. Rawls, *A Theory of Justice*, 21, 579.

11. See the references in note 2 and most particularly Daniels's "Reflective Equilibrium and Archimedean Points."

12. Michel Foucault, "Human Nature: Justice Versus Power" in *Reflexive Water*, Fons Elders, ed. (London: Souvenir Press, 1974), 168. This is a debate with Noam Chomsky.

13. Bernard Williams, *Ethics and the Limits of Philosophy* (Cambridge, MA: Harvard University Press, 1985), 74, 120, 151-53, 171-73, 198.

14. It would have to be what has been called "grand theory." See *The Return of Grand Theory in the Human Sciences* Quentin Skinner, ed. (London: Cambridge University Press, 1985). To be valuable, however, it would have to have the constraints Frederick Crews notes in his "The House of Grand Theory," *New York Review of Books* XXXIII, no. 9 (May 29, 1986), 36-43.

15. Crews, "The House of Grand Theory," rightly stresses the need for such contraints but wrongly claims that Marxist or Freudian theories must be retrograde in this respect, functioning more like religious *Weltanschauungen* than scientific theories. Richard Miller shows how Marxist accounts can be genuine social science, meeting the constraints Crews requires, without the positivist fetters that Crews takes to be hobbling. See Richard Miller, *Analyzing Marx* (Princeton, NJ: Princeton University Press, 1984). See also Rodger Beehler's critical notice of Miller's book in the *Canadian Journal of Philosophy* (1987).

16. Perhaps the most crucial thing to see here is his exchange with Rorty. See Richard Rorty, "Habermas and Lyotard on Postmodernity," and Jürgen Habermas, "Questions and Counter Questions" both in Richard J. Bernstein, ed. *Habermas and Modernity* (Cambridge, MA: MIT Press, 1985). But see as well Habermas's "The Genealogical Writing of History: On Some Aporias in Foucault's Theory of Power," *Canadian Journal of Political and Social Theory* X, nos. 1-2 (1986), 1-9, and his "Modernity Versus Postmodernity," *New German Critique*, no. 22 (Winter 1981), 3-14. For Habermas's most comprehensive account here see his *Philosophical Discourse of Modernity* (Cambridge: Cambridge University Press, 1987). See also Kai Nielsen, "Cultural Identity and Self-Definition," *Human Studies* (1987).

17. For a sense of the complexity of the concept of objectivity see Thomas Nagel, "The Limits of Objectivity" in *The Tanner Lectures on Human Values*, Vol. 1, Sterling McMurrin, ed. (Salt Lake City: University of Utah Press, 1980), 77-139. See also Bernard Williams's *Ethics and the Limits of Philosophy* and two discussions of his book, one by H. L. A. Hart, *New York Times Review of Books* XXXIII, no. 12 (July 17, 1986), 49-52, and the other by Thomas Nagel, *Journal of Philosophy* LXXXIII, no. 6 (June 1986), 351-59.

18. See Chapters 7 and 8. See also Isaac Levi, "Escape from Boredom: Edification According to Rorty," *Canadian Journal of Philosophy* XI, no. 4 (December 1981), 589-602.

19. See, for more detail, Chapter 8, and Levi, "Escape from Boredom: Edification According to Rorty."

20. The present chapter is a revision of an essay translated into French by J. Couture to appear in J. Couture, ed. *Ethique et Rationale*.

Chapter 10

1. Kenneth Baynes et al., *After Philosophy: End or Transformation?* (Cambridge, MA: MIT Press, 1986), and John Rajchman et al., *Post-Analytic Philosophy* (New York: Columbia University Press, 1985).

2. Misgeld was responding to earlier versions of work now incorporated into two previous chapters of this book. The earlier versions he was responding to were Kai Nielsen: "Challenging Analytic Philosophy," *Free Inquiry* 4, no. 4 (Fall 1984); "Rorty and the Self-Image of Philosophy," *International Studies in Philosophy* 18 (1986), 19-28; "How to be Skeptical about Philosophy," *Philosophy* 61, no. 235 (January 1986), 83-93; "Scientism, Pragmatism and the Fate of Philosophy," *Inquiry* 29, no. 3 (September 1986), 277-304; "Can There be Progress in Philosophy?" *Metaphilosophy* (January 1987); and "Searching for an Emancipatory Perspective: Wide Reflective Equilibrium and the Hermeneutical Circle" in *Anti-Foundationalism and Practical Reasoning*, Evan Simpson, ed. (Edmonton, Alberta: Academic Press, 1987).

3. Dieter Misgeld, "The Limits of a Theory of Practice: How Pragmatic Can a Critical Theory of Society Be?" in *Anti-Foundationalism and Practical Reasoning*, 165-81.

4. My views here, views Misgeld examines, come out most fully in Chapter 8.

5. Frederick Crews, "The House of Grand Theory," *New York Review of Books* XXXIII, no. 9 (May 29, 1986), 36-43.

6. I make this particularly evident in Chapters 7 and 9.

7. Dieter Misgeld, "Modernity and Social Science," *Philosophy and Social Criticism* (1987), 11. See also his review essay on Habermas's *Theorie des Kommunikativen Handelns, Canadian Journal of Sociology* 8, no. 4 (Fall 1983), 433-52.

8. Richard Rorty, "Pragmatism Without Method" in *Sidney Hook: Philosopher of Democracy and Humanism* Paul Kurtz, ed. (Buffalo, NY: Prometheus Books, 1983), 259-73. My response to this is in "Scientism, Pragmatism and the Fate of Philosophy."

9. Albrecht Wellmer, "Reason, Utopia and the *Dialectic of Enlightenment*" in *Habermas and Modernity*, Richard Bernstein, ed. (Cambridge, MA: MIT Press, 1985), 35-66.

10. I attempted to do that in my "South Africa: The Choice Between Reform and Revolution," *Philosophical Forum* (1987).

11. On arguments about how critical the extant Habermasian critical theory actually is, see Nancy Fraser, "What's Critical about Critical Theory?" *New German Critique*, no. 35 (Spring-Summer 1985), 87-131, and Joe McCarney, "How Critical Is Critical Theory?" *Radical Philosophy* (1986).

12. David Hoy, "Jacques Derrida" in *The Return of Grand Theory in the Human Sciences* Quentin Skinner, ed. (Cambridge: Cambridge University Press, 1985), 61. See also David Hoy, *The Critical Circle* (Berkeley, CA: University of California Press, 1982).

13. Hoy, "Jacques Derrida," 61.

14. Kai Nielsen, "Sociological Knowledge: Winch, Marxism and *Verstehen* Revisted," *Philosophy and Phenomenological Research* XLII, no. 4 (June 1982), 465-91. See also my "Rationality and Relativism," *Philosophy of the Social Sciences* 4, no. 4 (December 1974), 313-32 and my "Rationality and Universality," *Monist* 59, no. 3 (July 1976), 441-55.

15. This is something that both Charles Saunders Peirce and John Dewey fixed into our philosophical consciousness.

Chapter 11

1. For earlier versions see Kai Nielsen: "On Needing a Moral Theory: Rationality, Considered Judgments and the Grounding of Morality," *Metaphilosophy* 13 (April 1982); "Considered Judgments Again," *Human Studies* 5 (April-June 1982); *Equality and Liberty* (Totowa, NJ: Rowman and Allanheld, 1985), Chapter 2; "Searching for an Emancipatory Perspective: Wide Reflective Equilibrium and the Hemeneutical Circle" in *Antifoundationalism and Practical Reasoning*, Evan Simpson, ed. (Edmonton, AB: Academic Printing and Publishing, 1987); "Reflective Equilibrium and the Transformation of Philosophy," *Metaphilosophy* 1988; "Philosophy as Critical Theory," *Proceedings and Addresses of the American Philosophical Association* supplement to 61, no. 1 (September 1987), 89-108; "On Sticking with Considered Judgments in Wide Reflective Equilibrium," *Philosophia* 13, nos. 3-4 (1985), 316-21. See also Marsha Hanen, "Justification as Coherence" in *Law, Morality and Rights*, M. A. Stewart, ed. (Dordrecht, The Netherlands: D. Reidel, 1983), 67-92.

2. John Rawls, *A Theory of Justice* (Cambridge, MA: Harvard University Press, 1971), 19-21, 48-51, and 577-87; John Rawls, "The Independence of Moral Theory," *Proceedings and Addresses of the American Philosophical Association* 47 (1974/75), 7-10.

3. Jane English, "Ethics and Science," *Proceedings of the XVI Congress of Philosophy*. Norman Daniels: "Wide Reflective Equilibrium and Theory Acceptance in Ethics," *Journal of Philosophy* 76 (1979); "Moral Theory and Plasticity of Persons," *Monist* 62 (July 1979); "Some Methods of Ethics and Linguistics," *Philosophical Studies* 37 (1980); "Two Approaches to Theory Acceptance in Ethics" in *Morality, Reason and Truth*, David Copp and David Zimmerman, eds. (Totowa, NJ: Rowman and Allanheld, 1985). Hilary Putnam, *Realism and Reason* (Cambridge: Cambridge University Press, 1983), 229-47. Richard Rorty, "The Priority of Democracy to Philosophy" in *The Virginia Statute of Religious Freedom*, Meryl Patterson and Robert Vaughan, eds. (Cambridge, MA: Harvard University Press, 1987).

4. Kai Nielsen, "Searching for an Emancipatory Perspective: Wide Reflective Equilibrium and the Hermeneutical Circle," and "Cultural Identity and Self-Definition," *Human Studies* (1987).

5. *Ibid.* and articles by Daniels cited in note 3.

6. Rorty, "The Priority of Democracy to Philosophy."

7. See references to Rawls in note 2 and see, as well, Thomas McCarthy, *The Critical Theory of Jürgen Habermas* (Cambridge, MA: MIT Press, 1978), Chapter 4; Jürgen Habermas, *Theorie des Kommunikativen Handelns* (Frankfurt: Suhrkamp Verlag, 1981); and David Ingram, *Habermas and the Dialectic of Reason* (New Haven, CT: Yale University Press, 1987).

8. Joseph Raz, "The Claims of Reflective Equilibrium," *Inquiry* 25, no. 3 (September, 1982), 307-30. All future references to Raz will be given in the text.

9. See the references in notes 2 and 3.

10. Rawls, *A Theory of Justice*, 580-81.

11. Stuart Hampshire, "A New Philosophy of the Just Society," *New York Review of Books* 3, no. 3 (February 24, 1972), 34-39.

12. J. N. Findlay, *Language, Mind and Value* (London: Allen and Unwin, 1963), 165-81 and W. D. Falk, *Ought, Reasons and Morality* (Ithaca, NY: Cornell University Press, 1986), 248-60.

13. David Copp, "Considered Judgments and Moral Justification: Conservatism and Moral Theory" in *Morality, Reason and Truth*, 141-68. Future references to Copp are in the text.

14. Copp has in conversation objected that this too much relies on his preliminary formulations. Indeed there I *start* at his beginning, but I do not see that he ever *retracts* that initial mistake.

15. Thomas Nagel, "The Limits of Objectivity" in *The Tanner Lectures on Human Values* Vol. 1 (Salt Lake City, UT: University of Utah Press, 1980), 77-139.

16. C. J. Ducasse, "Moore's Refutation of Idealism" in *The Philosophy of G. E. Moore*, P. A. Schilpp, ed. (New York: Tudor Publishing, 1952), 225-51, and Roderick Chisholm, "Philosophers and Ordinary Language," *Philosophical Review* LX (1951), 317-28.

17. Kai Nielsen, "On Refusing to Play the Sceptics Game," *Dialogue* (1973). See also Chapters 5 and 6.

18. John Wisdom, *Philosophy and Psycho-Analysis* (Oxford: Basil Blackwell, 1953).

19. A. E. Murphy, "Moore's 'Defence of Common Sense'" in *The Philosophy of G. E. Moore*, 301-17.

20. Richard Rorty, *The Consequences of Pragmatism* (Minneapolis, MN: University of Minnesota Press, 1982), 160-90.

21. I feel uneasy about this argument. It is good pragmatist fallibilism, but that notwithstanding it seems to me entirely too rationalistic. Considerations enter in the moral domain similar to considerations in the "factual domain" I discussed in Chapter 6 when discussing Wittgenstein's framework beliefs in the *Vor Wissen*. "People have heads" and "Fire burns" are not analytic or synthetic a priori yet they are not up for falsification or disconfirmation either. (Talk of "verifiability in principle" is pretty opaque here.) If we doubted such truisms we could not be confident of anything else including our logical or mathematical beliefs or our alleged grounds for doubting these truisms. If they are doubtful, anything else is equally doubtful. Someone who doubted them would plainly be mad. It seems at least in a parallel manner in moral domains as if any chain of argument that led us to reject that moral belief—that moral truism (and truisms like it)—would be something we would have very good reasons not to trust. Such a moral belief for a moral agent seems at least to be a belief that stands fast come what may. Yet the fallibilist line of reasoning argued above in the text seems thoroughly reasonable, and there are some disanalogies between the factual domain and the moral domain here. There is (for example) the amoralist. His actions, though thoroughly unprincipled, might not in all circumstances be unintelligent, let alone unintelligible. We would call him mad, but there may be plain ways in which he need not be irrational. Moreover, and distinctly, it is in general dangerous to make claims to substantive moral propositions that are to hold fast come what may. This can lead to Anscombean dogmatism with baleful consequences. (Indeed it not only can, it has.) Yet in this particular instance is it not the right way to go? Generally, as is plain in the text, I favor a fallibilist strategy and attitudes. Yet in instances such as this one, I am inclined to take a Wittgensteinian turn and in effect, and paradoxically, be a fallibilist about fallibilism. But I do not like paradoxes and generally do not trust how philosophers typically play around with them. I distrust the transcendental arguments they not infrequently give rise to. (It is too easy a way, for example, of disposing of skepticism or relativism.) The philosophical situation here seems to me far from satisfactory. But I am not confident that I have up my sleeve a good way of rectifying it. Here I do not know how to put together the genuine insights of Dewey and Wittgenstein. *Perhaps* this shows something about the unreality of philosophy. However, it should be noted that either way of going (the fallibilist way or the Wittgensteinian way) will not help Copp and will be, as well, uncongenial to his way of reasoning. It should also be noted that what I remark in this note about a Wittgensteinian turn does not give another inning to the foundationalist. Chapter 6 should have made that plain enough. For a following out of the narrative of the amoralist, see my *Why Be Moral?* (Buffalo, NY: Prometheus Books, 1989). *Perhaps* attending to the amoralist will give us the resolution I seek. The person who would deny the Moorean truisms (Wittgenstein's *Vor Wissen*) is through and through mad. The amoralist, by contrast, may only be *morally* mad. He could (*pace* Plato) be morally mad while still being *clearheadedly* unprincipled, carefully calculating,

astutely manipulative, and thoroughly uncaring. Such behavior is, alas, intelligible. Not believing Wittgenstein's *Vor Wissen* is not.

22. Rawls, *A Theory of Justice*, 579-81.

Index

Acts/action, 97−98, 100, 101, 102−103, 173, 182, 225, 226. *See also* Philosophy, theory vs. practice
Adams, Henry, 5
Adorno, Theodor, 61, 121, 220
After Philosophy (Baynes et al), 217
After Virtue (MacIntyre), 193
Ambrose, Alice, 126
Amoralism, 268(n21)
Analytical philosophy, 3, 7−8, 17, 22, 24−25, 31, 34, 41, 115, 120, 146, 147, 157, 163−164, 212
  common preoccupations, 36−37
  death of, 128, 135, 141, 143, 144
  as Kantian, 54
  scientific, 50
Analytic-synthetic distinction, 28, 30, 96, 174, 255(n25)
Antirealism, 64, 69, 71, 72, 75, 80, 112, 253−254(nn 19, 20). *See also* Realism
Apel, Karl-Otto, 163
Arendt, Hannah, 121
Aristotle, 210
Armstrong, David, 115
Arnold, Matthew, 92, 93, 113, 116
Art, 51, 52, 69, 175
Atheism, 59, 118. *See also* Religion
Augustine, Saint, 210
Austin, J. L., 152
Ayer, A. J., 37, 64, 90, 92, 118, 119, 146

Barth, Karl, 42
Belief(s), 37, 47, 58, 84, 86, 87, 88−89, 104, 168, 182, 240, 254−255(n25)
  background, 95−96. *See also* Commonsense
  -forming, 62−63, 68
  framework, 96, 100, 102, 105, 106, 110, 112. *See also* Preknowledge; World-picture
  hinge. *See* Belief(s), framework
  legitimating, 213, 214. *See also* Ideology
  moral, 228−230, 234, 239. *See also* Wide reflective equilibrium, and

considered judgments
and scientific method, 176, 181. *See also* Science, scientific method
ungrounded, 95−96, 101, 106
Benjamin, Walter, 121
Bennett, Jonathan, 15−16, 23−25
Bergmann, Gustav, 127
Bergson, Henri, 143
Berlin, Isaiah, 223
Bernstein, Richard, 163, 165−166, 176, 183
Blanshard, Brand, 143
Bohm, David, 48
Bohr, Niels, 48
Bourgeoisie, 150
Brandt, Richard, 197
Burden of proof issues, 244, 245

Cantor, Georg, 48
Carnap, Rudolf, 37, 41, 50, 61, 90, 92, 118, 127, 144, 147
Cartesianism, 3, 31, 39, 40, 42, 61, 67, 93, 105, 157, 181, 224, 254−255(n25). *See also* Descartes, Rene
Causality, 63, 64, 77
Cavell, Stanley, 22, 114, 115, 121, 257(n18)
Certainty, 61, 208
  primitive, 111, 112, 122, 257(n18). *See also* Propositions, objectively certain
  psychological feeling of, 109
  quest for, 42, 51, 57, 59, 61, 205, 233
  See also Foundationalism, modest
Chomsky, Noam, 52, 53, 140, 160, 171, 230
"Claims of Reflective Equilibrium, The" (Raz), 234−240
Coercion, 213
Cognitive psychology, 53, 62
Cohen, Joshua, 50, 160
Coherence/coherentism, 88, 89, 93, 113, 155, 170, 174, 199, 200, 203, 204, 205, 206, 223, 224, 231, 238, 241, 245, 247, 248, 261(n55)
Commonsense, 91, 110, 111, 174, 180,

and *Sittlichkeit*, 198–199, 207, 236
theories, 231
truisms of, 201, 206, 246, 268(n21)
See also Ethics; Wide reflective
equilibrium
Morgenbesser, Sidney, 191

Nagel, Ernest, 181, 182, 185, 191, 220
Nagel, Thomas, 242
Narratives, 192–193, 195, 220–221,
226. *See also* Metanarratives
Naturalism, 50, 63, 129
Naturalistic fallacy, 63
Natural rights, 151
Naude, Bayers, 153
Neopositivism, 31
Neopragmatism, 7, 130, 156, 197, 218,
226. *See also* Rorty, Richard, and
pragmatism
Neurath, Otto, 90, 92, 115, 118
Nielsen, Kai, 151
Nietzsche, Friedrich, 29, 164
Nihilism, 113, 114, 147, 175, 177, 202
Noncognitivism, ethical, 50
Normative issues. *See* Norms
Norms, 5–6, 12, 64, 130, 132, 133, 137,
148, 174, 175, 196, 198--199,
218–219, 228, 229, 250(n14)
Nozick, Robert, 5, 197

Objectivism, 207
Objectivity, 30, 40, 87, 130, 167, 177,
215, 237, 242, 243
On Certainty (Wittgenstein), 10, 93,
98–99, 113, 114, 121
On Democracy (Cohen and Rogers), 160
Ontology, 57, 58, 59

Paradox, 43–44, 95, 268(n21)
Pareto, Vilfredo, 159
Peace, 116
Peirce, Charles Sanders, 58, 176, 181,
191, 205, 243, 246
Perception, 77, 94, 187
Persuasion, 103–104, 135, 167, 177,
178, 247
Philosophical Investigations
(Wittgenstein), 10, 91, 114, 121
Philosophy
analytic. *See* Analytical philosophy
applied, 19–21
and argumentative ability, 21–23, 33,
144

and articulation of concepts, 20–21
as conversation, 47, 164, 168
as critical theory, 11, 127. *See also*
Critical theory
and culture, 4, 23, 24, 32, 36, 42, 52,
125, 192. *See also*
Foundationalism; Wittgenstein,
philosophy of culture
after demise of Tradition, 175–176.
See also Critical theory; Philosophy,
post-Philosophical; Tradition
dual role, 175
edifying, 164
and explanatory adequacy, 18
First. *See* First Philosophy
as foundationalist, 91–92, 125–126,
163, 164, 180, 253(n5). *See also*
Foundationalism
of history, 138, 221
history of, 27, 29, 30, 31–32,
126–127, 166, 193, 215
institutional impediments to, 32–33
and intellectual thoroughness, 23–24
linguistic, 58. *See also* Language(s)
of logic, 3. *See also* Logic
origin of philosophical problems,
16–17
and other disciplines, 28, 33, 34–35,
36, 41, 158
overseer role of, 36, 49, 52, 125,
140–141, 191. *See also*
Foundationalism; Philosophy, as
foundationalist
perennial, 37, 127, 141, 146, 157. *See
also* Tradition
philosophy vs. Philosophy, 5, 210.
See also Philosophy, untechnical
conception of
political, 221
post-Philosophical, 191–192. *See
also* Philosophy, after demise of
Tradition
principal task of, 51
and science, 40–42, 52, 54, 58,
62–63, 164–165. *See also* Science,
philosophy of
self-image of, 4, 15–25, 39, 43, 51,
125, 145
and self understanding, 25
as social criticism, 127, 174, 180, 192.
See also Critical theory; Problems
of men
sociological approach to, 34–35